# IFIP Advances in Information and Communication Technology 725

## IFIP Advances in Information and Communication Technology

The IFIP AICT series publishes state-of-the-art results in the sciences and technologies of information and communication. The scope of the series includes: foundations of computer science; software theory and practice; education; computer applications in technology; communication systems; systems modeling and optimization; information systems; ICT and society; computer systems technology; security and protection in information processing systems; artificial intelligence; and human-computer interaction.

Edited volumes and proceedings of refereed international conferences in computer science and interdisciplinary fields are featured. These results often precede journal publication and represent the most current research.

The principal aim of the IFIP AICT series is to encourage education and the dissemination and exchange of information about all aspects of computing.

More information about this series at https://link.springer.com/bookseries/6102

Jason Staggs · Sujeet Shenoi
Editors

# Critical Infrastructure Protection XVIII

18th IFIP WG 11.10 International Conference, ICCIP 2024
Arlington, VA, USA, March 18–19, 2024
Proceedings

Springer

*Editors*
Jason Staggs
University of Tulsa
Tulsa, OK, USA

Sujeet Shenoi
University of Tulsa
Tulsa, OK, USA

ISSN 1868-4238 ISSN 1868-422X (electronic)
IFIP Advances in Information and Communication Technology
ISBN 978-3-031-81887-5 ISBN 978-3-031-81888-2 (eBook)
https://doi.org/10.1007/978-3-031-81888-2



This Springer imprint is published by the registered company Springer Nature Switzerland AG
The registered company address is: Gewerbestrasse 11, 6330 Cham, Switzerland

# Preface

The cyber infrastructure – comprising computers, embedded devices, networks and software systems – is vital to operations in every sector: chemicals, commercial facilities, communications, critical manufacturing, dams, defense industrial base, emergency services, energy, financial services, food and agriculture, government facilities, healthcare and public health, information technology, nuclear reactors, materials and waste, transportation systems, and water and wastewater systems. Global business and industry, governments, indeed society itself, cannot function if major components of the critical infrastructure are degraded, disabled or destroyed.

This book, *Critical Infrastructure Protection XVIII*, is the eighteenth volume in the annual series produced by IFIP Working Group 11.10 on Critical Infrastructure Protection, an active international community of scientists, engineers, practitioners and policy makers dedicated to advancing research, development and implementation efforts related to critical infrastructure protection. The book presents original research results and innovative applications in the area of critical infrastructure protection. Also, it highlights the importance of weaving together science, technology and policy to craft sophisticated, yet practical, solutions that will help secure information, computer and network assets in the various critical infrastructure sectors.

This volume contains nine selected papers from the Eighteenth Annual IFIP Working Group 11.10 International Conference on Critical Infrastructure Protection, which was held at SRI International in Arlington, Virginia, USA on March 18–19, 2024. A total of 18 full-length papers were submitted for presentation at the conference. The papers were refereed in a single-blind manner by members of the conference program committee and other individuals, all of them internationally-recognized experts in critical infrastructure protection, with each submission receiving three reviews on average. The nine accepted papers were rewritten by the authors after the conference to accommodate the suggestions provided by the referees and by the conference attendees. The nine post-conference manuscripts were subsequently revised by the editors to produce the final chapters published in this volume.

The chapters are organized into four thematic sections: (i) Infrastructure Security; (ii) Advanced Manufacturing Security; (iii) Industrial Control System Security; and (iv) Infrastructure Modeling. The coverage of topics showcases the richness and vitality of the discipline, and offers promising avenues for future research in critical infrastructure protection.

This book is the result of the combined efforts of several individuals and organizations. In particular, we thank Laura Tinnel for her tireless work on behalf of IFIP Working Group11.10. We also thank the National Science Foundation, U.S. Department of Homeland Security, National Security Agency and SRI International for their support of IFIP Working Group11.10 and its activities.

Finally, we wish to note that all opinions, findings, conclusions and recommendations in the chapters of this book are those of the authors and do not necessarily reflect the views of their employers or funding agencies.

November 2024

Jason Staggs
Sujeet Shenoi

# Organization

## General Chair

| | |
|---|---|
| Laura Tinnel | SRI International, USA |

## Program Chairs

| | |
|---|---|
| Jason Staggs | University of Tulsa, USA |
| Sujeet Shenoi | University of Tulsa, USA |

## Program Committee

| | |
|---|---|
| Irfan Ahmed | Virginia Commonwealth University, USA |
| Stefan Axelsson | Stockholm University, Sweden |
| Raymond Chan | Singapore Institute of Technology, Singapore |
| Kam-Pui Chow | University of Hong Kong, China |
| Chiara Foglietta | Università Roma Tre, Italy |
| Richard George | Johns Hopkins University Applied Physics Laboratory, USA |
| Janne Hagen | Norwegian Water Resources and Energy Directorate, Norway; and University of Oslo, Norway |
| Michael Haney | University of Idaho, USA |
| Elizabeth Kurkowski | Johns Hopkins University Applied Physics Laboratory, USA |
| Stefano Panzieri | Università Roma Tre, Italy |
| Mason Rice | Oak Ridge National Laboratory, USA |
| Leon Strous | De Nederlandsche Bank, The Netherlands |
| Øyvind Toftegaard | Norwegian University of Science and Technology, Norway; and Norwegian Energy Regulatory Authority, Norway |
| Zachary Tudor | Idaho National Laboratory, USA |

# Contents

**Infrastructure Modeling**

# Contributors

**Mohamed Abomhara** Norwegian University of Science and Technology, Gjøvik, Norway

**Doney Abraham** Norwegian University of Science and Technology, Gjøvik, Norway

**Irfan Ahmed** Virginia Commonwealth University, Richmond, VA, USA

**Silvia Ansaldi** National Institute for Insurance Against Accidents at Work, Rome, Italy

**Mohd Anwar** North Carolina Agricultural and Technical University, Greensboro, NC, USA

**Rima Asmar Awad** Oak Ridge National Laboratory, Oak Ridge, TN, USA

**Gabriela Ciocarlie** University of Texas at San Antonio, San Antonio, TX, USA

**Joel Dawson** Oak Ridge National Laboratory, Oak Ridge, TN, USA; Cybersecurity Manufacturing Innovation Institute, San Antonio, TX, USA

**Zoran Duric** George Mason University, Fairfax, VA, USA

**Kyle Everett** University of Texas at San Antonio, San Antonio, TX, USA

**Yahya Forihat** Virginia Commonwealth University, Richmond, VA, USA

**Nataša Gajić** Norwegian University of Science and Technology, Trondheim, Norway

**Jason Green** North Carolina Agricultural and Technical University, Greensboro, NC, USA

**Simone Guarino** University Campus Bio-Medico of Rome, Rome, Italy

**Chris Hathhorn** Two Six Technologies, Arlington, VA, USA

**Mahdi Hesar** North Carolina Agricultural and Technical University, Greensboro, NC, USA

**Matthew Jablonski** George Mason University, Fairfax, VA, USA

**Jeffrey Kimmell** Oak Ridge National Laboratory, Oak Ridge, TN, USA; Cybersecurity Manufacturing Innovation Institute, San Antonio, TX, USA

**Juan Lopez** Oak Ridge National Laboratory, Oak Ridge, TN, USA

**Vladimir Orlyanchik** Oak Ridge National Laboratory, Oak Ridge, TN, USA; Cybersecurity Manufacturing Innovation Institute, San Antonio, TX, USA

**Ahmad Patooghy** North Carolina Agricultural and Technical University, Greensboro, NC, USA

**John Prevost** University of Texas at San Antonio, San Antonio, TX, USA

**Gordon Robertson** Oak Ridge National Laboratory, Oak Ridge, TN, USA

**Michael Rogers** Tennessee Technological University, Cookeville, TN, USA

**Kyle Saleeby** Georgia Institute of Technology, Atlanta, GA, USA

**Abdolhossein Sarrafzadeh** North Carolina Agricultural and Technical University, Greensboro, NC, USA

**Roberto Setola** University Campus Bio-Medico of Rome, Rome, Italy

**Michael Sprayberry** Oak Ridge National Laboratory, Oak Ridge, TN, USA

**Logan Sturm** Oak Ridge National Laboratory, Oak Ridge, TN, USA;
Cybersecurity Manufacturing Innovation Institute, San Antonio, TX, USA

**Curtis Taylor** Oak Ridge National Laboratory, Oak Ridge, TN, USA;
Cybersecurity Manufacturing Innovation Institute, San Antonio, TX, USA

**Duminda Wijesekera** George Mason University, Fairfax, VA, USA

**Stephen Wolthusen** Norwegian University of Science and Technology, Gjøvik, Norway

**James Wright** Norwegian University of Science and Technology, Gjøvik, Norway

**Sule Yayilgan** Norwegian University of Science and Technology, Gjøvik, Norway

# Infrastructure Security

# Evaluating Cyber Security Risks and Mitigation Strategies for Smart Grids Based on Business Case Scenarios

Doney Abraham(✉), Sule Yayilgan, and Mohamed Abomhara

Norwegian University of Science and Technology, Gjøvik, Norway
doney.abraham@ntnu.no

**Abstract.** The integration of smart grid technologies in energy infrastructures is a significant shift towards efficient, sustainable and reliable electricity management, but it also brings cyber security challenges to the forefront. This study delves into the cyber security vulnerabilities of key smart grid assets such as smart meters, advanced metering infrastructure systems and distributed energy resources such photovoltaic systems, virtual power plants and battery parks. A comprehensive three-step methodology is employed to identify attack vectors, analyze attack tactics and specify the appropriate mitigation strategies. The confidentiality, integrity and availability model and MITRE ATT&CK framework are employed to identify the four main attack vectors and specify the appropriate mitigation strategies based on established security principles. The results highlight the need to implement robust security measures to safeguard smart grid assets and offer strategic guidance for addressing the cyber security challenges. The study enriches the discourse on smart grid security by providing actionable insights for improving energy system reliability and resilience.

**Keywords:** Smart Grids · Business Cases · Cyber Security · Attack Vectors · Risk Identification · Attack Mitigation

## 1 Introduction

Smart grid technology is responsible for a transformative era in energy management that promises efficiency, reliability and sustainability by integrating information and communications technologies in traditional energy infrastructures. However, the nexus of digital and physical systems introduces cyber security challenges that pose significant risks to the integrity and stability of critical energy infrastructures [9,10]. As smart grids proliferate, safeguarding these systems from cyber attacks is essential to ensure secure, uninterrupted energy flows.

The cyber security challenges inherent in smart grids stem from their highly interconnected and decentralized nature that expands their attack surfaces [16]. The threats are vast and varied, from remote intrusions targeting smart meters to sophisticated attacks on advanced metering infrastructure (AMI) systems and


Published by Springer Nature Switzerland AG 2025
J. Staggs and S. Shenoi (Eds.): ICCIP 2024, IFIP AICT 725, pp. 3–21, 2025.
https://doi.org/10.1007/978-3-031-81888-2_1

distributed energy resources (DERs). These threats potentially impact the confidentiality, integrity and availability of critical data as well as the safe and reliable operation of energy systems, underscoring the need for a holistic approach to smart grid cyber security [18].

This chapter assesses the cyber risks associated with critical smart grid assets such as smart meters, advanced metering infrastructure systems, flexible resources in customer premises, automated substations, photovoltaic systems, virtual power plants and battery parks [8,13]. A comprehensive cyber risk assessment methodology involving three steps was employed to identify attack vectors, analyze the attacker tactics and specify mitigations. The assessment has identified four attack vectors that represent significant risks to smart grid assets, illustrating the diverse methods by which attackers may exploit vulnerabilities. Targeted mitigation strategies are proposed to defend against potential attacks. The strategies leverage established security approaches such as the confidentiality, integrity and availability (CIA) model [30] and the MITRE ATT&CK framework [2] to enhance the cyber security postures of smart grid infrastructures.

This study contributes to the broader discourse on smart grid cyber security. It offers actionable insights and recommendations that can guide energy sector stakeholders toward more secure and resilient energy systems. By elucidating the complex cyber security landscape of smart grids and providing a roadmap for navigating the security challenges, the study contributes to the evolution of secure energy systems in the digital era.

## 2 Smart Grid Business Case Scenarios

Business case scenarios are key elements in the evolving landscape of smart grid technologies because they consider the integration of advanced digital solutions with traditional power systems to enhance efficiency and sustainability. This section describes five smart grid business case scenarios identified by Toftegaard et al. [27]. Abraham et al. [1] have simulated the five business cases to explore the consequences of cyber attacks. Each business case scenario captures a unique intersection of technological innovation and operational necessity, helping address the challenges of modernizing electrical grids to accommodate increasing energy demand, integrate renewable energy sources and enhance grid stability.

**Remote Access to Smart Meter Circuit Breakers.** This business case involves the deployment of smart meters that enable utilities and consumers to manage electricity usage and circuit breaker operations remotely. Remote access to smart meter circuit breakers enhances the efficiency of managing smart grids and improves interactions between consumers and the grid. It facilitates enhanced demand response strategies, allowing for precise control over power consumption during peak periods. Also, it optimizes energy usage and improves overall power grid efficiency and reliability by promoting energy savings and preventing overloads.

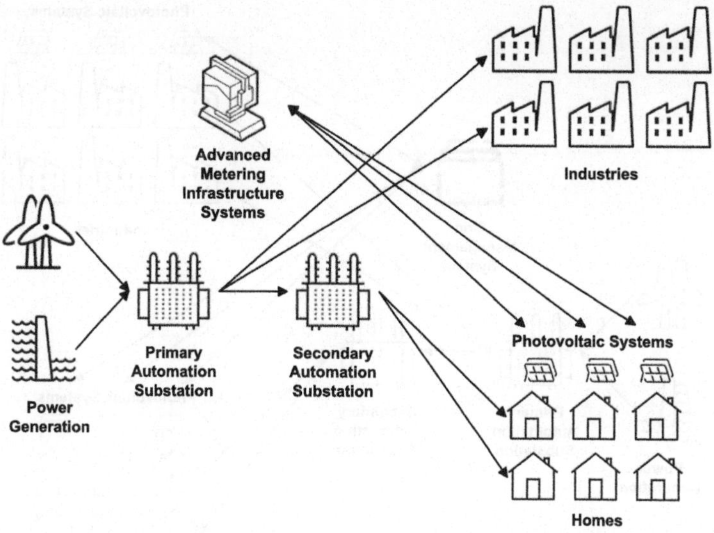


**Fig. 1.** Remote access to smart meter circuit breakers

Figure 1 illustrates the remote access to smart meter circuit breakers business case. However, the functionality elevates cyber security risks because the remote access mechanisms can be leveraged for unauthorized purposes and targeted by cyber attacks. Safeguarding data integrity and securing communications are paramount to preventing malicious control of circuit breakers that could compromise user privacy or cause service disruptions.

**Flexible and Balanced Grid Management.** Flexible and balanced grid management are vital to aggregating renewable energy sources and optimizing energy distribution to maintain grid stability. Sophisticated management systems can dynamically regulate energy generation, consumption and storage. The objective is to balance supply and demand while minimizing the risk of power outages and reducing the reliance on traditional energy sources. Utilities leverage data analytics and real-time monitoring to achieve flexible and balanced grid management, accommodating a growing share of renewable energy resources and ensuring stable, sustainable power supply.

Figure 2 illustrates the flexible and balanced grid management business case. The complex interplay of distributed energy resources introduces cyber security challenges, particularly with regard to safeguarding data and control signals that underpin the dynamic adjustments. Securing the supporting systems from cyber attacks that manipulate energy distribution are vital to preventing grid instability and widespread power outages.

**Substation Automation Circuit Breakers.** This business case involves upgrading substations with intelligent control systems that automate circuit

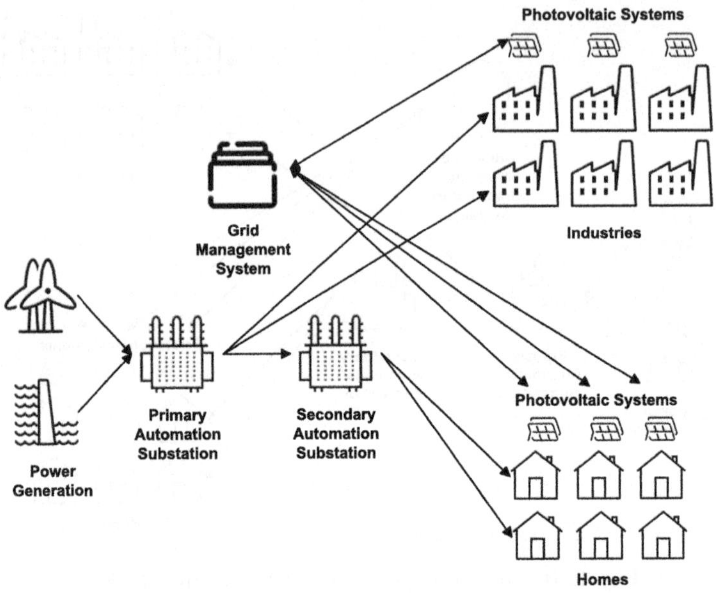


**Fig. 2.** Flexible and balanced grid management

breaker operation. The automation enhances power grid efficiency and reliability by enabling remote monitoring and control, rapid responses to fault conditions and improved voltage control. Substation automation contributes to resilience by ensuring that electrical distribution is reliable and adaptable to changing load conditions.

Figure 3 illustrates the substation automation business case. The reliance on automation and remote control raises significant cyber security concerns. Cyber attacks that target automated circuit breakers could result in uncontrolled power flows and/or isolation of critical loads, endangering grid stability and potentially causing physical infrastructure damage. Cyber security strategies that mitigate these risks are integral to the design and operation of substation automation systems.

**Virtual Power Plants.** Virtual power plants (VPPs) constitute a transformative business case because they aggregate distributed energy resources such as photovoltaic systems (e.g., solar panels), wind turbines and energy storage systems to operate as single power generation entities. Virtual power plants utilize sophisticated software and control systems to dispatch electricity from decentralized sources in response to grid demand, enhancing grid optimization and increasing grid reliability. They also facilitate the shift towards distributed energy systems that effectively integrate and manage renewable energy resources, reduce carbon emissions and foster energy independence.

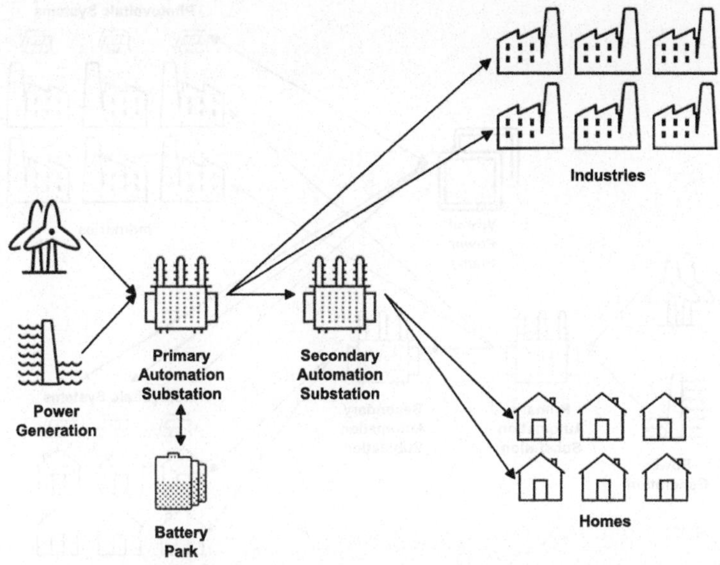


**Fig. 3.** Substation automation circuit breakers

Figure 4 illustrates the virtual power plants business case. The cyber security risks associated with virtual power plants stem from their reliance on communications networks to aggregate and dispatch energy. Cyber attacks could disrupt the operational integrity of virtual power plants and degrade or deny their ability to respond to changing grid demand. Secure communications protocols and continuous monitoring of anomalies are essential to securing virtual power plants from cyber attacks.

**Battery Park Management Systems.** Battery park management systems are designed to operate and manage large-scale energy storage facilities efficiently. The systems play a critical role in stabilizing power grids by storing excess energy during low demand and releasing energy during peak demand. Battery park management systems employ sophisticated software to monitor battery health, optimize charging and discharging cycles, and predict energy storage needs based on grid demand forecasts. These capabilities are crucial to integrating intermittent renewable energy sources, enhancing grid flexibility and ensuring continuous and reliable energy supply.

Figure 5 illustrates the battery park management systems business case. Cyber security challenges to battery park management systems involve protecting energy storage assets from unauthorized access and control. Cyber attacks could result in the inappropriate discharging or charging of batteries, undermining grid stability and reducing the lifespans of energy storage assets. Encrypted communications, regular security assessments and strict access controls are vital to maintaining the integrity and reliability of energy storage operations.

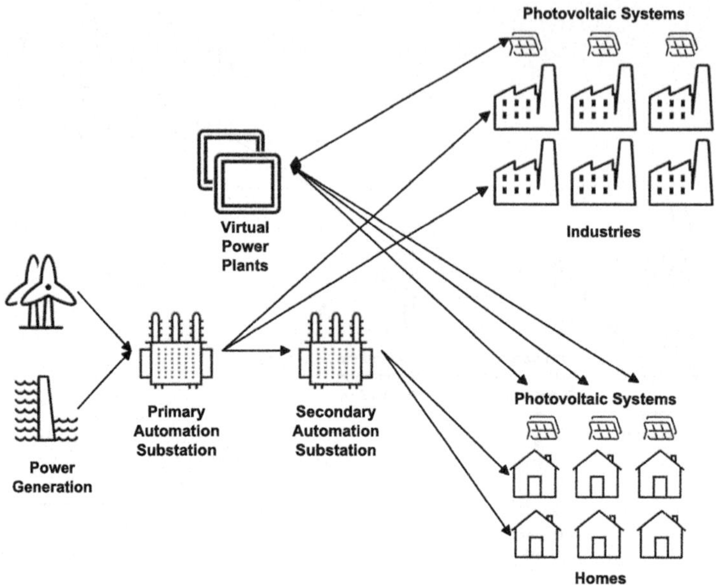


**Fig. 4.** Virtual power plants

## 3 Key Smart Grid Assets

The first step in assessing the risks induced by the integration of smart grid technologies in the energy infrastructure is to identify the key assets, their functionalities and how the assets become cyber attack targets. This section describes the seven key smart grid assets identified in the five business cases discussed in the previous section.

- **Smart Meters:** Smart meters are devices that measure and record electricity usage in real-time, providing consumers with accurate and detailed information about their energy consumption [11]. They are equipped with circuit breakers that can automatically disconnect the power supply in case of faults or overloads, ensuring the safety of electrical systems and preventing damage to appliances in customer premises [22]. Smart meter circuit breakers are designed to monitor parameters such as voltage, current, temperature and leakage, and can be controlled remotely through Internet of Things (IoT) devices [22]. They are also equipped with mechanisms to protect against power surges and other electrical disturbances, ensuring power supply stability and reliability [28]. The incorporation of smart meters with remote circuit breakers in electric power distribution grids is the important first step to building efficient and sustainable smart grids [15].
- **Advanced Metering Infrastructure Systems:** An advanced metering infrastructure comprises smart meters at customer premises and two-way customer-utility communications channels between customers and the utility

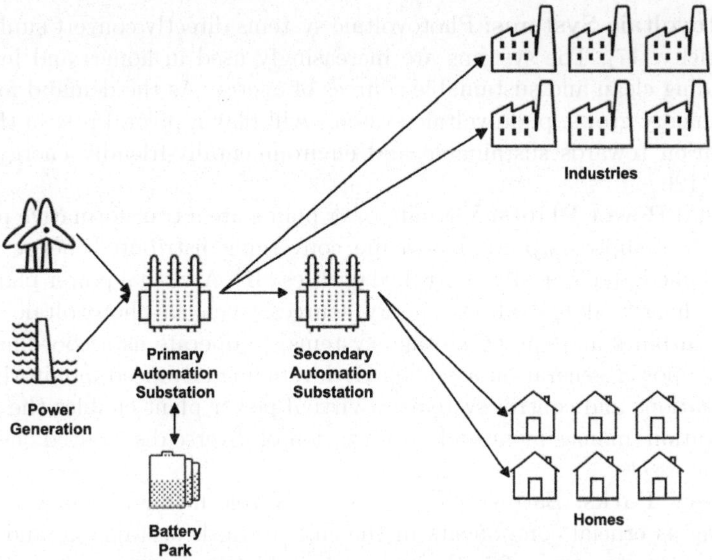


**Fig. 5.** Battery park management systems

employing intermediate data collectors and a head-end (meter data management) system housed at the utility [21]. The infrastructure is designed to collect, store, analyze and report energy usage data in real-time, enabling the utility and customers to monitor and manage energy consumption more efficiently [20,21]. The utility is responsible for managing the advanced metering infrastructure, including monitoring the infrastructure through acquisition reporting, network reporting and billing requirements [4].

- **Flexible Resources at Customer Premises:** Flexible resources encompass diverse appliances and systems that can adjust their energy consumption or production to align with grid conditions and demand response signals. The resources play a pivotal role in optimizing energy usage and enhancing grid stability [24]. Examples of flexible resources include smart appliances such as water heaters, heating systems, heat pumps, air conditioners, electric vehicles and photovoltaic systems. By intelligently managing their operational schedules and/or adjusting power consumption levels, the appliances contribute to an efficient and resilient energy ecosystem. This flexibility allows for improved integration of renewable energy sources, dynamic responses in peak demand periods and a sustainable and responsive energy infrastructure [5].
- **Automated Substations:** Substation automation circuit breakers are an essential component of modern power systems. They are designed to monitor and control circuit breakers at substations for data acquisition, measurement, parameter adjustment and other functions [29]. The circuit breakers are integrated in substation automation systems to provide real-time power usage data and enable real-time monitoring and control [26].

- **Photovoltaic Systems:** Photovoltaic systems directly convert sunlight into electricity [17]. The systems are increasingly used in homes and industries, providing clean and sustainable sources of energy. As the demand for renewable energy grows, photovoltaic systems will play a pivotal role in the global transition towards sustainable and environmentally-friendly energy ecosystems [12].
- **Virtual Power Plants:** Virtual power plants are a transformative paradigm in the contemporary power landscape, converging distributed energy resources into unified, dynamically-controlled entities [31]. A virtual power plant aggregates diverse, decentralized energy sources, such as photovoltaic systems, wind turbines and energy storage systems, to operate as a coordinated and flexible power generation asset [6]. By leveraging advanced monitoring, communications and control systems, a virtual power plant enables the seamless integration, management and optimization of diverse distributed energy generation assets.
- **Battery Parks:** Battery parks play a key role in modern power systems, serving as crucial components in the shift towards sustainable and resilient energy infrastructures [23]. Battery parks, which incorporate advanced energy storage systems, contribute significantly to grid stability and reliability by storing excess energy during periods of low demand and releasing energy during peak demand periods [3]. Battery parks address the intermittency problems of renewable energy sources in modern power systems by serving as buffers to dynamically balance supply and demand. Furthermore, battery parks enhance grid responsiveness to sudden fluctuations and provide rapid responses to frequency regulation, fostering an adaptable and robust energy ecosystem.

## 4 Risk Identification

A three-step methodology is employed to mitigate cyber risks in smart grids [19]. The first step involves the identification of the attack vectors that target smart grid assets based on the business case scenarios. Next, attack tactics are explored and their potential impacts on smart grid assets are described. Finally, comprehensive mitigation plans are developed to maintain security in smart grids.

### 4.1 Attack Vectors

Cyber attacks on industrial control systems are unauthorized intrusions or malicious actions on computerized systems that manage and control critical infrastructure assets, industrial processes or operational technology environments. These attacks manipulate or disrupt the functionality of industrial control system components such as programmable logic controllers, supervisory control and data acquisition systems and human-machine interfaces. Cyber attacks on industrial control systems can result in adverse effects such as equipment malfunction, production downtime, safety hazards, environmental damage and economic losses. Therefore, it is imperative to identify the attack vectors and deploy robust security measures in smart grids. Based on the business case scenarios, smart grids are susceptible to cyber attacks leveraged by four attack vectors.

**Remote Attacks on Smart Meters.** The following attack paths cover the methods that an attacker can use to remotely access and compromise smart meters:

- **Path A1 – Exploiting Firmware or Software Vulnerabilities:** The attacker exploits vulnerabilities in smart meter firmware or software such as buffer overflows or command injections to gain unauthorized access to smart meter configuration settings. The access enables the attacker to execute malicious commands or gain elevated privileges and compromise smart meter functionality.
- **Path A2 – Compromising Communications Networks:** The attacker targets the communications network utilized by smart meters (wireless or smart grid communication network). The attacker intercepts or manipulates communications sent between smart meters and utility systems such as energy consumption readings from smart meters and commands to smart meters.
- **Path A3 – Employing Social Engineering Attacks:** The attacker uses social engineering tactics to impersonate utility personnel or customer service representatives to remotely access smart meters. The attacker deceives customers into providing access to their smart meters or divulging sensitive information.
- **Path A4 – Exploiting Default or Weak Credentials:** The attacker gains unauthorized access to the smart meter configuration settings or controls its operations by exploiting default or weak credentials used by the smart meter configuration interface or remote management system. This involves using default usernames and passwords or conducting brute-force attacks. Through these means, the attacker can bypass authentication mechanisms and gain control of the smart meter, enabling data manipulation or malicious command execution.
- **Path A5 – Gaining Physical Access:** The attacker gains physical access to smart meters by tampering with their hardware or inserting malicious devices. This enables the attacker to intercept, modify and fabricate communications between the smart meter and the central grid management system, potentially compromising the smart grid.

**Attacks Using Advanced Metering Infrastructure.** The following attack paths cover the methods that an attacker can leverage the advanced metering infrastructure to launch attacks:

- **Path B1 – Exploiting Software Vulnerabilities:** The attacker exploits vulnerabilities in advanced metering infrastructure firmware or software such as buffer overflows or command injections. This enables the attacker to gain

unauthorized access to advanced metering infrastructure systems and compromise the smart grid.
- **Path B2 – Compromising Communications Networks:** The attacker targets the communications networks used by advanced metering infrastructure devices (wireless or powerline communications networks). The attacker intercepts or manipulates communications transmitted between advanced metering infrastructure devices and advanced metering infrastructure systems such as energy consumption readings, metering data and smart meter commands.
- **Path B3 – Employing Social Engineering Attacks:** The attacker uses social engineering tactics to impersonate advanced metering infrastructure personnel or customer service representatives to access advanced metering infrastructure systems or networks. The attacker deceives advanced metering infrastructure personnel into providing access to sensitive information or systems, enabling smart grid compromises.
- **Path B4 – Exploiting Default or Weak Credentials:** The attacker gains unauthorized access to advanced metering infrastructure systems via advanced metering infrastructure configuration interfaces or remote management systems using default usernames and passwords or conducting brute force attacks. This enables the attacker to compromise the smart grid.
- **Path B5 – Gaining Physical Access:** The attacker gains physical access to advanced metering infrastructure devices by tampering with their hardware or inserting malicious devices. This enables the attacker to intercept, modify and fabricate communications between advanced metering infrastructure devices, potentially compromising the smart grid.

**Attacks Using Smart Appliances in Customer Premises.** The following attack paths cover the methods that an attacker can use smart appliances in customer premises to launch attacks:

- **Path C1 – Exploiting Software Vulnerabilities:** The attacker exploits vulnerabilities in smart appliance firmware or software such as buffer overflows or command injections. This enables the attacker to gain unauthorized access to the customer premises network or the smart grid.
- **Path C2 – Targeting Home Automation Systems:** The attacker targets the home automation system used to control smart appliances in customer premises, such as smart light bulbs, smart locks and smart security cameras. The attacker exploits vulnerabilities in home automation system firmware or software to gain unauthorized access to the customer premises network or the smart grid.
- **Path C3 – Employing Social Engineering Attacks:** The attacker uses social engineering tactics to impersonate utility personnel or customer service representatives to access the customer premises network or smart grid. The attacker deceives the customer into providing access to sensitive information or systems.

- **Path C4 – Exploiting Default or Weak Credentials:** The attacker gains unauthorized access to a smart appliance configuration interface or remote management system using default usernames and passwords or conducting brute force attacks. This enables the attacker to compromise the smart appliance or remote management system.
- **Path C5 – Gaining Physical Access:** The attacker gains physical access to smart appliances in the customer premises by tampering with their hardware or inserting malicious devices. This enables the attacker to intercept, modify and fabricate communications between smart appliances in the customer premises network.

**Attacks on Battery Park Management Systems.** The following attack paths cover the methods that an attacker can use to attack battery park management systems:

- **Path D1 – Exploiting Software Vulnerabilities:** The attacker exploits vulnerabilities in the battery park management system firmware or software such as buffer overflows or command injections. This enables the attacker to gain unauthorized access to the battery park management system and the connected batteries.
- **Path D2 – Compromising Communications Networks:** The attacker targets the battery park management network (wireless or smart grid network). The attacker intercepts or manipulates data and commands transmitted between the battery park management system and connected batteries to alter energy consumption readings and other battery-related data.
- **Path D3 – Employing Social Engineering Attacks:** The attacker uses social engineering tactics to impersonate utility personnel or customer service representatives to access to the battery park management system or the connected batteries. The attacker deceives battery park personnel into providing access to sensitive information or battery park management systems.
- **Path D4 – Exploiting Default or Weak Credentials:** The attacker gains unauthorized access to the battery park management system using default usernames and passwords or performing brute force attacks on the system configuration interface or remote management system. This enables the attacker to disrupt the operation of the battery storage system and potentially compromise the stability of the smart grid.
- **Path D5 – Gaining Physical Access:** The attacker gains physical access to the battery park management system or connected batteries by tampering with their hardware or inserting malicious devices. This enables the attacker to intercept, modify and fabricate communications between the battery park management system and the connected batteries, potentially compromising the stability of the smart grid.

### 4.2 Risk Impacts

The attack vectors can impact the cyber security protocols in the smart grid. A commonly referenced model for shaping security policies and devising effective cyber security measures is the well-established confidentiality, integrity and availability (CIA) model introduced by Saltzer and Schroeder [25]. The model engages three fundamental concepts:

- **Confidentiality:** Confidentiality focuses on safeguarding sensitive information and ensuring that only authorized entities can access the information. Security mechanisms such as username/password authentication, access control models, policies and encryption techniques are commonly employed to enforce confidentiality.
- **Integrity:** Integrity focuses on maintaining the accuracy, consistency and reliability of information, ensuring that it remains true to its original purpose. Only authorized users are permitted to modify data in authorized ways.
- **Availability:** Availability guarantees authorized access to information and services and prevents unauthorized denial of service. Availability ensures that systems and services remain accessible to authorized users on demand.

The MITRE ATT&CK framework [2] identifies 12 cyber attack tactics that are effective against security measures in industrial control system environments. The cyber attack tactics include: initial access, execution, persistence, privilege escalation, evasion, discovery, lateral movement, collection, command and control, inhibit response function, impair process control and impact. Table 1 shows the MITRE ATT&CK cyber attack tactics, their descriptions and their impacts on confidentiality, integrity and availability.

Table 1 shows that the MITRE ATT&CK industrial control system tactics impact the security measures as follows:

- **Confidentiality:** An attacker employs the initial access, evasion, discovery and collection tactics to gain unauthorized information about the industrial control system environment, which compromises confidentiality.
- **Integrity:** An attacker employs the execution, privilege escalation, lateral movement, command and control, inhibit response function, impair process control and impact tactics in order to manipulate or disrupt system functions, which affects integrity.
- **Availability:** An attacker employs the persistence, command and control, inhibit response function, impair process control and impact tactics to maintain access or cause disruptions.

Since the command and control, inhibit response function, impair process control and impact tactics affect integrity as well as availability, they are the most significant tactics for attacking smart grids. These considerations go beyond the traditional confidentiality, integrity, availability triad, emphasizing safety, environmental impact and holistic security for industrial control systems.

The impacts of the tactics specified in Table 1 are classified as follows [7]:

**Table 1.** Cyber attack tactics and their affected measures

| Tactic | Description | Affected Measures |
|---|---|---|
| Initial Access | Attacker seeks to gain entry into the industrial control system environment | Confidentiality |
| Execution | Attacker seeks to execute code or manipulate system functions, parameters and data in an unauthorized manner | Integrity |
| Persistence | Attacker seeks to maintain a foothold in the industrial control system environment | Availability |
| Privilege Escalation | Attacker seeks to obtain higher-level permissions | Integrity |
| Evasion | Attacker seeks to evade security defenses | Confidentiality |
| Discovery | Attacker seeks information to assess and identify targets | Confidentiality |
| Lateral Movement | Attacker seeks to traverse the industrial control system environment | Integrity |
| Collection | Attacker seeks to gather data and domain knowledge about the industrial control system environment | Confidentiality |
| Command and Control | Attacker seeks to communicate with and control compromised systems, controllers and platforms in the industrial control system environment | Integrity, availability |
| Inhibit Response Function | Attacker seeks to hinder safety, protection, assurance and operator intervention functions from responding to failures or unsafe states | Integrity, availability |
| Impair Process Control | Attacker seeks to manipulate, disable or damage physical control processes | Integrity, availability |
| Impact | Attacker seeks to manipulate, interrupt or destroy systems, data and environment | Integrity, availability |

- **Minor Impacts:** Minor impacts on systems and operations involve disturbances or inconvenience that are manageable and do not significantly disrupt overall functionality. The problems demand minimal effort to rectify and usually entail limited repercussions.
- **Moderate Impacts:** Moderate impacts on systems and operations involve disruptions or performance degradation that affect specific functionalities or processes. Resolving the problems require more effort than problems causing minor impacts. However, the problems are typically manageable and do not present immediate threats to system stability.
- **Major Impacts:** Major impacts on systems and operations involve critical functionalities or processes. Major incidents include significant data loss, system instability and widespread disruptions. Resolving the problems requires urgent attention and considerable resources to mitigate their effects and restore regular operations.
- **Critical Impacts:** Critical impacts involve serious repercussions to systems and operations, including severe degradation or damage to system integrity,

functionality and security. Critical incidents include massive data breaches, significant system downtime and complete system failure, resulting in substantial financial losses, regulatory non-compliance and reputational damage. Resolving the problems requires immediate and comprehensive actions to reduce the negative impacts and prevent further harm.

Table 2 specifies the cyber attack techniques, paths and tactics pertaining to the principal smart grid assets. The table also provides the impact classifications for the key smart grid assets.

Table 2 shows that all the principal smart grid assets are vulnerable to attacks. Smart meters are susceptible to attack paths involving the evasion, command and control, initial access, privilege escalation and impact tactics. Attackers leverage techniques such as exploitation for escalation, commonly used port, connection proxy, spearphishing, exploitation for credential access and damage to property to compromise smart meters, critically impacting the confidentiality, integrity and availability of smart meters.

Advanced metering infrastructure systems are susceptible to attack paths involving the evasion, command and control, initial access, privilege escalation and impact tactics. Attackers employ techniques such as exploitation for escalation, commonly used port, connection proxy, spearphishing, exploitation for credential access and damage to property, critically impacting the confidentiality, integrity and availability of advanced metering infrastructure systems.

Smart appliances in customer premises are susceptible to attack paths involving the evasion, command and control, initial access, privilege escalation and impact tactics. Attackers employ techniques such as exploitation for escalation, manipulation of control, spearphishing, exploitation for credential access and damage to property, critically impacting the confidentiality, integrity and availability of smart appliances in customer premises.

Battery park management systems are vulnerable to attack paths involving the evasion, command and control, initial access, privilege escalation and impact tactics. Attackers utilize techniques such as exploitation for escalation, commonly used port, connection proxy, spearphishing, exploitation for credential access and damage to property, critically impacting the confidentiality, integrity and availability of battery park management systems.

### 4.3 Mitigation Plans

This section outlines the mitigation plans to safeguard confidentiality, integrity and availability (CIA) measures in smart grid. The mitigation strategies are formulated based on fundamental security measures outlined in [14]:

- **Data Confidentiality:** Data confidentiality ensures that sensitive data is accessible only to authorized entities.
- **Data Integrity:** Data integrity ensures that data is correct, consistent and reliable throughout the data lifecycle.
- **Data Availability:** Data availability ensures that data is accessible and usable when needed by authorized entities.

**Table 2.** Cyber attack techniques, paths and tactics for smart grids

| Attack Vector | Attack Path | Tactic | Technique | Impact |
|---|---|---|---|---|
| Smart Meters | A1 | Evasion | Exploitation for escalation (T0820) | Critical |
| | A2 | Command and control | Commonly used port (T0885), Connection proxy (T0884) | Major |
| | A3 | Initial access | Spearphishing (T0865) | Major |
| | A4 | Privilege escalation | Exploitation for credential access (T1212) | Critical |
| | A5 | Impact | Damage to property (T0879) | Critical |
| Advanced Metering Infrastructure Systems | B1 | Evasion | Exploitation for escalation (T0820) | Critical |
| | B2 | Command and control | Commonly used port (T0885), Connection proxy (T0884) | Major |
| | B3 | Initial access | Spearphishing (T0865) | Major |
| | B4 | Privilege escalation | Exploitation for credential access (T1212) | Critical |
| | B5 | Impact | Damage to property (T0879) | Critical |
| Smart Appliances in Customer Premises | C1 | Evasion | Exploitation for escalation (T0820) | Critical |
| | C2 | Command and control | Manipulation of control (T0831) | Major |
| | C3 | Initial access | Spearphishing (T0865) | Major |
| | C4 | Privilege escalation | Exploitation for credential access (T1212) | Critical |
| | C5 | Impact | Damage to property (T0879) | Critical |
| Battery Park Management Systems | D1 | Evasion | Exploitation for escalation (T0820) | Critical |
| | D2 | Command and control | Commonly used port (T0885), Connection proxy (T0884) | Major |
| | D3 | Initial access | Spearphishing (T0865) | Major |
| | D4 | Privilege escalation | Exploitation for credential access (T1212) | Critical |
| | D5 | Impact | Damage to property (T0879) | Critical |

- **Controllability:** Controllability ensures that data and system access and control are maintained and only authorized actions are performed.
- **Transparency:** Transparency ensures the clarity of processes, actions and decisions to authorized entities.
- **Data Breach Communications:** Data breach communications ensure that protocols and procedures are in place for timely and transparent communications with authorized entities during data breaches.

The proposed mitigation plans are strategically aligned with the industrial control system security concepts defined in the MITRE ATT&CK Industrial Control System Mitigations framework. Table 3 shows the mitigation plans for each security measure and the mapping of security measures to MITRE ATT&CK industrial control system mitigations.

Table 3 shows that maintaining data confidentiality requires robust encryption and strict access control policies complemented by spearphishing awareness training. Data integrity is achieved using digital signatures, intrusion detection and regular audits. Data availability is achieved via redundancy, maintenance and backup power sources. Access control measures include role-based permissions and regular access audits. Transparent data management entails clear communications, user-friendly interfaces and responsive customer channels. Data breach communications plans involve clear protocols, defined responsibilities and timely stakeholder communications. These measures collectively maintain the confidentiality, integrity, availability, controllability, transparency and data breach communications effectiveness of smart grid assets.

**Table 3.** Mitigation plans for preserving CIA measures in smart grids

| Security Measure | Mitigation Plans | MITRE Mitigations |
|---|---|---|
| Data Confidentiality | Implement robust encryption mechanisms for transmission between smart meters and utility systems. Enforce strict access control policies to ensure that only authorized personnel can access sensitive information. Train employees to recognize and avoid spearphishing attacks to prevent unauthorized data access. | Access management (M0801), Application layer filtering (M0937), Data backup (M0953), Encrypt sensitive information (M0941), Network segmentation (M0930), User training (M0917). |
| Data Integrity | Employ digital signatures or hash functions to verify the integrity of data transmitted between smart meters and utility systems. Implement systems to monitor unauthorized modifications of metering data. Audit and verify metering data to detect and mitigate integrity breaches. | Data backup (M0953), Code signing (M0945), Network intrusion prevention (M1031), Network segmentation (M0930), Audit (M1047). |
| Data Availability | Implement redundancy and fail-over mechanisms to ensure the availability of smart meters and utility systems. Conduct regular maintenance and updates to prevent downtime due to software vulnerabilities. Establish backup power sources to mitigate disruptions caused by power outages or physical damage. | Data backup (M0953), Safety instrumented systems (M0182), Redundancy of service (M0811), Network segmentation (M0930), Audit (M1047). |
| Controllability | Implement access control mechanisms to limit the actions performed on smart meters and utility systems. Utilize role-based access control to ensure that only authorized personnel have permissions to configure and modify metering parameters. Audit access logs frequently to detect and prevent unauthorized changes. | Access management (M0801), Data backup (M0953), Network segmentation (M0930), User training (M0917). |
| Transparency | Provide clear and transparent communications to customers about collecting and using metering data. Implement user-friendly interfaces to access and manage metering data, enabling customers to review energy consumption and billing data quickly. Establish channels for customers to submit inquiries or complaints regarding data privacy. | Data backup (M0953), Network segmentation (M0930), User training (M0917). |
| Data Breach Communications | Develop and implement a comprehensive data breach plan to notify affected parties. Define the roles and responsibilities of personnel involved in data breach response and communications. Establish timely and transparent communications protocols with customers, regulators and other stakeholders affected by breaches. | Data backup (M0953), Operational information confidentiality (M0809), Human User authentication (M0804), User training (M0917). |

## 5 Conclusions

The comprehensive analysis of cyber risks in smart grid business scenarios has focused on identifying assets, assessing attack vectors, evaluating risk impacts and developing mitigation plans. Key assets in smart grid business case environments are identified along with the various attack paths that target smart grid assets. The analysis reveals that smart grids are susceptible to a range of attacks that critically impact the key security goals of confidentiality, integrity and availability.

The proposed mitigation plans to safeguard smart grid assets from cyber attacks align with the fundamental security measures of confidentiality, integrity, availability, controllability, transparency and data breach communications. The mitigations are also strategically aligned with the industrial control system security concepts defined in the MITRE ATT&CK Industrial Control System Mitigations framework.

Overall, the findings underscore the importance of implementing robust cyber security measures in smart grid environments to mitigate cyber risk. By enhancing the security postures of smart grid assets, stakeholders can safeguard critical assets, mitigate attack impacts and ensure the reliability and resilience of modern energy systems.

Several avenues are available for future research. Further investigation is needed to assess the effectiveness of the proposed mitigation plans in real-world smart grid deployments. This would involve field experiments to evaluate the efficacy of security measures in mitigating cyber threats. It is also important to develop advanced intrusion detection and threat intelligence systems tailored to smart grid environments. These systems could leverage machine learning and anomaly detection techniques to detect and mitigate cyber threats in real time, enhancing the resilience of smart grids. Also of value is the integration of blockchain technology in decentralized smart grid architectures to enhance the security and trustworthiness of smart grid systems. Finally, as cyber threats evolve, continued research is required to stay abreast of emerging threats and vulnerabilities in smart grid systems and adapt security strategies to ensure smart grid reliability and resilience.

## References


1. Abraham, D., Toftegaard, Ø., Jose, B., Gebremedhin, A., Yayilgan, S.: Consequence simulation of prominent smart-grid-enabled business cases. Front. Energy Res. **12**, 1395954 (2024)
2. Alexander, O., Belisle, M., Steele, J.: MITRE ATT&CK for Industrial Control Systems: Design and Philosophy, MITRE Product MP01055863, MITRE, McLean, Virginia (2020)
3. Branco, H., Castro, R., Lopes, A.S.: Battery energy storage systems as a way to integrate renewable energy in small isolated power systems. Energy Sustain. Dev. **43**, 90–99 (2018)

4. Chakraborty, A., Sharma, N.: Advanced metering infrastructure: technology and challenges. In: Proceedings of the IEEE/PES Transmission and Distribution Conference and Exposition (2016)
5. Cochran, J., et al.: Flexibility in 21st Century Power Systems, Technical Paper NREL/TP-6A20-61721, National Renewable Energy Laboratory, Golden, Colorado (2014)
6. Dielmann, K., van der Velden, A.: Virtual power plants – a new perspective for energy generation? In: Proceedings of the Ninth International Scientific and Practical Conference of Students and Post-Graduates Modern Techniques and Technologies, pp. 18–20 (2003)
7. Engert, P., Lansdowne, Z.: Risk Matrix User's Guide, Version 2.2, MITRE Product MP99B0000029, MITRE, Bedford, Massachusetts (1999)
8. Ericsson, G.: Cyber security and power system communications - essential parts of a smart grid infrastructure. Proc. Trans. Power Deliv. **25**(3), 1501–1507 (2010)
9. Fang, X., Misra, S., Xue, G., Yang, D.: Smart grid - the new and improved power grid: a survey. IEEE Commun. Surv. Tut. **14**(4), 944–980 (2012)
10. Gungor, V., Lu, B., Hancke, G.: Opportunities and challenges of wireless sensor networks in smart grid. IEEE Trans. Industr. Electron. **57**(10), 3557–3564 (2010)
11. Hansen, A., Staggs, J., Shenoi, S.: Security analysis of an advanced metering infrastructure. Int. J. Crit. Infrastruct. Prot. **18**, 3–19 (2017)
12. Hernandez-Callejo, L., Gallardo-Saavedra, S., Alonso-Gomez, V.: A review of photovoltaic systems: design, operation and maintenance. Sol. Energy **188**, 426–440 (2019)
13. Karnouskos, S.: Cyber-physical systems in the smart grid. In: Proceedings of the Ninth IEEE International Conference on Industrial Informatics, pp. 20–23 (2011)
14. Khodabakhsh, A., Yayilgan, S., Abomhara, M., Istad, M., Hurzuk, N.: Cyber risk identification for a digital substation. In: Proceedings of the Fifteenth International Conference on Availability, Reliability and Security, no. 109 (2020)
15. King, C., Johnson, L.: Smart meters and systems and method for electrical power reconnection, U.S. Patent No. 9,213,387 (2015)
16. Kumar, P., Lin, Y., Bai, G., Paverd, A., Dong, J., Martin, A.: Smart grid metering networks: a survey on security, privacy and open research issues. IEEE Commun. Surv. Tut. **21**(3), 2886–2927 (2019)
17. Lazaroiu, A., Osman, M., Strejoiu, C., Lazaroiu, G.: A comprehensive overview of photovoltaic technologies and their efficiency for climate neutrality. Sustainability **15**(23), 16297 (2023)
18. Metke, A., Ekl, R.: Security technology for smart grid networks. IEEE Trans. Smart Grid **1**(1), 99–107 (2010)
19. MITRE: Systems Engineering Guide: Collected Wisdom from MITRE's Systems Engineering Experts, Bedford Massachusetts and McLean, Virginia (2014)
20. Mohassel, R., Fung, A., Mohammadi, F., Raahemifar, K.: A survey on advanced metering infrastructure. Int. J. Electr. Power Energy Syst. **63**, 473–484 (2014)
21. NETL Modern Grid Strategy: Powering Our 21st-Century Economy: Advanced Metering Infrastructure, National Energy Technology Laboratory, U.S. Department of Energy Office of Electricity Delivery and Energy Reliability, Washington, DC (2008)
22. Niu, W., Shi, H., Hou, X.: Intelligent circuit breaker. J. Phys: Conf. Ser. **2528**, 012065 (2023)
23. Park, S., et al.: Review of state-of-the-art battery state estimation technologies for battery management systems of stationary energy storage systems. J. Power Electron. **20**, 1526–1540 (2020)

24. Petersen, M., Hansen, L., Molbak, T.: Exploring the value of flexibility: a smart grid discussion. IFAC Proc. Vol. **45**(21), 43–48 (2012)
25. Saltzer, J., Schroeder, M.: The protection of information in computer systems. Proc. IEEE **63**(9), 1278–1308 (1975)
26. Sheng, S., Li, K., Chan, W., Zeng, X., Li, X.: Using substation automation information for electric power load modeling and predictive maintenance of circuit breakers. In: Proceedings of the 3rd IEEE International Conference on Industrial Informatics, pp. 546–551 (2005)
27. Toftegaard, Ø., Abraham, D., Shenoi, S., Hämmerli, B.: Smart-grid-enabled business cases and the consequences of cyber attacks. In: Staggs, J., Shenoi, S. (eds.) Critical Infrastructure Protection XVII: 17th IFIP WG 11.10 International Conference, ICCIP 2023, Arlington, VA, USA, March 13–14, 2023, Revised Selected Papers, pp. 17–39. Springer, Cham (2024). https://doi.org/10.1007/978-3-031-49585-4_2
28. Vlasov, A., Filin, S., Krivoshein, A.: Universal smart circuit breaker concept. In: Proceedings of the International Conference on Industrial Engineering, Applications and Manufacturing (2019)
29. Xu, J., et al.: Research on substation comprehensive information automation system based on smart grid. IOP Conf. Ser. Earth Environ. Sci. **558**, 052059 (2020)
30. Yee, C., Zolkipli, M.: Review of confidentiality, integrity and availability in information security. J. ICT Educ. **8**(2), 34–42 (2021)
31. Zhang, J.: The concept, project and current status of virtual power plants: a review. J. Phys: Conf. Ser. **2152**, 01259 (2022)

# On the Security of Electronic Voting Systems

Jason Green(✉), Abdolhossein Sarrafzadeh, Ahmad Patooghy, Mahdi Hesar, and Mohd Anwar

North Carolina Agricultural and Technical University, Greensboro, NC, USA
jmgreen12@ncat.edu

**Abstract.** The integrity of democratic elections relies heavily on the security of electronic voting systems. Dominion Voting Systems' ImageCast X and Election Systems & Software's ExpressVote System are among the most widely used electronic voting systems in the United States. This chapter describes efforts to verify reported vulnerabilities and identify new vulnerabilities in the two electronic voting systems at the hardware and software levels. The goal is to increase the understanding of voting system security and identify areas for improvement in order to safeguard upcoming elections.

**Keywords:** Electronic Voting Systems · Election Security · Dominion Voting Systems ImageCast X · Election Systems · Software ExpressVote System · Vulnerability Assessment

## 1 Introduction

Ensuring the integrity of elections is critical to preserving democracy. Therefore, it is vital that electronic voting systems are accurate, transparent and secure [53]. One of the most widely used electronic voting systems in the United States is Dominion Voting Systems' ImageCast X that was used in the 2020 U.S. Presidential Election as well as the 2022 U.S. Midterm Election [13]. However, the ImageCast X system has faced multiple allegations of vulnerabilities, including claims that its vulnerabilities were exploited to steal the 2020 election from President Trump.

This chapter examines the vulnerabilities of the ImageCast X system and their implications with regard to election security. Also, it compares and contrasts the ImageCast X system vulnerabilities with those of Election Systems & Software's ExpressVote System, which was also widely used in the 2020 and 2022 U.S. elections.

To arrive at a thorough and unbiased assessment, the evaluation methodology involved a systematic breakdown of various aspects of the ImageCast X and ExpressVote systems, including their architectures, hardware components, software features and security measures. The comparative analysis has helped clarify


Published by Springer Nature Switzerland AG 2025
J. Staggs and S. Shenoi (Eds.): ICCIP 2024, IFIP AICT 725, pp. 23–39, 2025.
https://doi.org/10.1007/978-3-031-81888-2_2

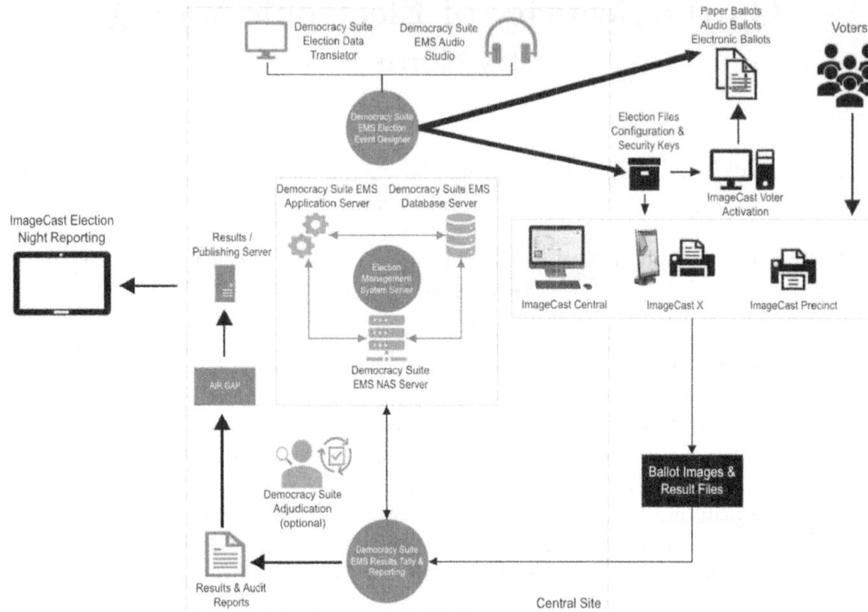


**Fig. 1.** Democracy Suite 5.5-A voting system [49]

nuanced features, operational mechanisms and security attributes of the two electronic voting systems. Identifying vulnerabilities in one system and examining how they have been exploited in the other system provides insights into their potential weaknesses and required security measures. This work does not seek to challenge the results of previous elections. Instead, it attempts to raise awareness about how electronic voting systems could be secured to protect the integrity of future elections.

## 2 Background

Figure 1 shows Dominion Voting Systems' Democracy Suite 5.5-A voting system [49]. It is a modified version of the certified Democracy Suite 5.5 voting system [48], that was primarily developed to meet requirements imposed by the Commonwealth of Pennsylvania. The modifications include the elimination of the ImageCast X DRE (direct vote recording) configuration and ImageCast X Classic 15″ model.

Democracy Suite 5.5-A is a paper-based optical scan voting system comprising four major components: Election Management System (EMS), ImageCast X ballot-marking device (ICX BMD), ImageCast Precinct (ICP) scanner and ImageCast Central (ICC) count scanner. The Election Management System is responsible for all pre-voting and post-voting activities. Its applications execute as front-end clients or as back-end server applications. The system is available in two deployable physical hardware configurations, EMS Express and EMS Standard [9,10,12].

A U.S. Cybersecurity and Infrastructure Security Agency (CISA) report [7] analyzes the ImageCast X Android 5.1 firmware used in the Democracy Suite 5.5-A voting system. The report covers ImageCast X application versions 5.5.10.30 and 5.5.10.32 dating as far back as 2019 [12], with little differences found in subsequent versions. The report identifies vulnerabilities in cryptographic signature verification, reporting data attestation, hidden functionality, alternate path protection and privilege assignment protection. Exploiting these vulnerabilities requires physical access to a voting system or the ability to modify files before they are uploaded to the voting system.

## 3 ImageCast X Vulnerabilities

This section discusses the hardware and software vulnerabilities discovered in ImageCast X systems.

### 3.1 Hardware Vulnerabilities

ImageCast X hardware vulnerabilities relate to commercial-off-the-shelf (COTS) devices, printers, barcode scanners, USB drives, touchscreens and low-level hardware.

**Commercial-Off-The Shelf Devices.** The 2020 California use procedures state that all COTS devices must be wiped with the DBAN utility [10] to securely erase their hard drives, following which, the devices should be started with absolutely no software installed. However, this does not delete firmware and other components of computer hardware. As a result, firmware attacks and malware infections are possible, especially if a computer was infected with malware before being wiped [21]. Malware could also be present in other components such as the basic input/output system (BIOS), firmware and peripherals [41,54]. Interestingly, the DBAN utility has not been updated since 2015 and does not work on solid-state drives [18].

**Printers.** Canon and HP printers used with the ImageCast Central Workstation and ImageCast X systems have potential vulnerabilities, including remote code execution, cross-site scripting (XSS) [29,30], default login credentials, information disclosure [28] and printer hijacking. An attacker could exploit these vulnerabilities to access sensitive information, take control of printers and infect the voting system network. Even if the voting system is air-gapped, a local attacker (e.g., malicious employee) could access a targeted printer via TCP/IP [28].

**Barcode Scanners.** Barcode scanners that tabulate votes are subject to attacks that render them inconsistent with the human-readable portions of paper ballots. Barcodes that are inconsistent with the human-readable portions of paper ballots result in incorrect vote tallies and potential election fraud [1].

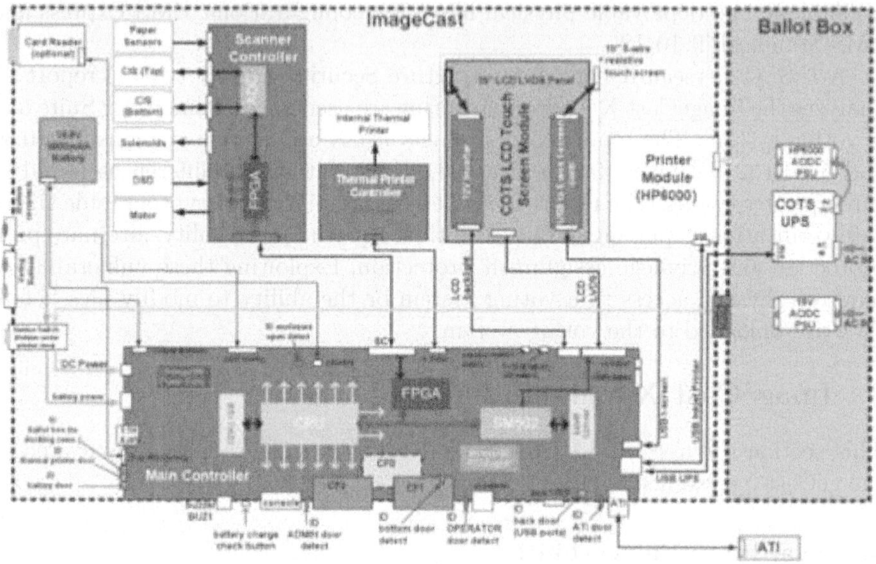


**Fig. 2.** ImageCast Evolution functional block diagram [12]

**USB Drives.** USB drives are used to transport voting data [11]. These devices could be lost, stolen or tampered with. An individual with access to an unencrypted USB drive could modify or delete the data, compromising election integrity. Data on an encrypted drive could also be deleted. Dominion Voting Systems reports that its voting systems are designed to detect and prevent unauthorized actions [40]. However, the possibility exists that a malicious insider could attack the USB drive verification process.

An attacker could also use a USB drive containing malware to exploit vulnerabilities and reprogram firmware as desired. Firmware vulnerabilities can enable an attacker to gain access to a voting system and steal sensitive information or disrupt system operation. A USB drive is a popular vector for introducing malware into a system, which is why firmware vulnerabilities are a concern [31,43].

**Touchscreens.** ImageCast X runs on Samsung Galaxy Tab Pro 12.2 and Samsung Galaxy Note Pro 12.2 tablet devices with touchscreens that are used by voters to enter and check their votes. These devices no longer receive security updates from Samsung [16], which exposes them to attacks that exploit known and unknown vulnerabilities. Caution must be exercised when using the devices. Better still, they should be replaced by newer and more secure devices.

**FPGA Hardware.** The ImageCast Evolution system shown in Fig. 2 [12] has multiple hardware components based on field programmable gate array (FPGA) technology. This opens the door to a class of exploits that compromise hardware operation by inducing suboptimal performance characteristics such as power consumption, energy efficiency and trapped heat [17] that can impact the voting process. For example, high power consumption can degrade the runtime performance and increase voting time.

Hardware Trojans that target hardware components can disrupt system performance and functionality. The Trojans are typically introduced through other components and are often difficult to detect [38,42]. They are activated during system operation and perform various actions depending on the attacker's goals. For example, they may alter stored or transmitted data, or disrupt energy/power consumption [23]. A Trojan can easily target the FPGA hardware in an ImageCast Evolution system. Since Dominion voting systems rely on common-off-the-shelf components [12], it is important to identify and eliminate hardware Trojans because they can introduce small errors that are difficult to detect [19].

Another potential threat is the exploitation of hardware flaws in DRAM chips that can result in data corruption and system compromise. The DRAM chips in the ImageCast Evolution system are attractive targets because they are responsible for data storage and retrieval during device operation. They can be a catalyst for executing software Trojans [37]. This is particularly worrisome because the chips can provide unauthorized access to passwords and other sensitive data. Furthermore, a DRAM vulnerability can be exploited to launch additional attacks or use the compromised system as a foothold for further exploitation.

### 3.2 Software Vulnerabilities

ImageCast X software vulnerabilities relate to external data sources, memory card and security key programming, ballot scanners, scanned ballot images, election result validation and reporting, and Android software.

**External Data Sources.** Importing election definition data can pose problems if the data sources are not vetted. A malicious actor could leverage the importation of election definition data as an attack vector to introduce malware or other malicious code in a voting system [12].

**Memory Card and Security Key Programming.** The integrated programming functionality of memory cards and security keys could be exploited by an attacker to gain access to a voting system [12].

**Ballot Scanners.** Dominion Voting Systems states that the ImageCast Central scanner is not connected directly to any network. However, it is connected to an ImageCast Central workstation that uses a standard gigabit Ethernet port to connect to a local-area network [12]. The ImageCast Central scanner could be vulnerable to attacks if the ImageCast Central workstation is compromised from the local-area network.

**Scanned Ballot Images.** Scanned ballot images could be tampered with or manipulated to affect the outcome of an election. It is important to ensure that ballot scanning and ballot image storage are secured to prevent unauthorized access and tampering [12].

**Election Result Validation and Reporting.** The EMS RTR (results tally and reporting) client application used for validating, tallying, reporting and publishing election results could be compromised if the system is not secured properly [9]. Dominion Voting Systems states that the Democracy Suite platform in its EMS Standard and EMS Express configurations does not use public communications networks for its operation. However, EMS Standard and Express with ImageCast Listeners enable the ImageCast Precinct and ImageCast Evolution systems to use public telecommunications networks to send results to the EMS data center [12]. Therefore, it is important to ensure that the application is only accessible to authorized users and that the data it processes is secured and validated.

**Android Software.** Dominion Voting Systems states that ImageCast X Prime and Classic systems run the Android 8.1 operating system. However, two listed versions of ImageCast X run versions earlier than Android 8.1. Using any version earlier than Android 8 brings increased security risks.

Additionally, the Android 8.1 software used by the voting system has been found to have several vulnerabilities, including Stagefright [52] that enables arbitrary code execution, WebView [36] that enables arbitrary JavaScript code execution and Mediaserver [24] that enables denial-of-service attacks and arbitrary code execution.

## 4 ExpressVote System Vulnerabilities

This section discusses the hardware and software vulnerabilities discovered in the ES&S ExpressVote System (EVS) 6.3.0.0. Also, it examines system versions going back to EVS 6.1.1.1 due to their use since 2020.

### 4.1 Hardware Vulnerabilities

ExpressVote System hardware vulnerabilities relate to unsecured Ethernet ports, audit log exposure, lack of data redundancy, COTS components, administrator passwords and USB drives.

**Unsecured Ethernet Ports.** The ExpressVote HW 1.0, a ballot-marking device with a touchscreen and printer, has an unsecured Ethernet port on its rear side near the power terminal. Although ES&S claims that the port is inactive and not intended for use, it is physically accessible. The concern is that a malicious entity with physical access to the device could exploit the port if its functionality is activated in the future. Although, this is not an immediate threat, security best practices recommend securing unused ports to prevent unauthorized use and tampering [25].

**Audit Log Exposure.** Examiners are given access to ExpressTouch device audit logs in the CSV format. This is problematic because audit logs often contain sensitive information about system activities and user interactions. Unauthorized access to the logs could result in data breaches and election integrity compromises. Proper security measures should ensure that audit logs are protected or all sensitive information is removed [25].

**Lack of Data Redundancy.** The DS450 and DS850 Central Scanners [35,45] rely on a 1 TB hard drive for storage without backup or redundancy [14,51]. If the hard drive were to fail or become corrupted, all the scanned voter selections and ballot images could be lost. Data redundancy is integral to ensuring the availability and reliability of election results. While security mechanisms such as data encryption, hash validation and digital signatures are implemented, mechanisms such as data mirroring and failover mechanisms [14] are not instituted to provide robust data redundancy.

ES&S recommends regular backups to prevent data loss [25]. While backups are essential, relying solely on manual backups introduces the risk of human error or oversight. If regular backups are not performed or are incomplete, data loss could occur in the event of storage media failure. The use of automated backup mechanisms to ensure data redundancy and prevent data loss is not discussed [14,25,45]. Automated backups can reduce the reliance on manual processes and enhance data protection. The lack of data redundancy [14] requires ballot processing to be paused periodically in order to manually export data and backup election results. These interruptions could delay the reporting of results.

**Commercial Off-The-Shelf Components.** The use of COTS software and firmware components in election systems poses security challenges. These widely-used components may have documented vulnerabilities that could be exploited by malicious actors. Moreover, since voting system vendors have limited control of third-party COTS components, it is difficult to respond to new threats and implement customized security measures. The dependence on third-party vendors for timely security updates is a vulnerability in itself and compatibility issues can arise when integrating COTS components in voting systems. The lack of transparency pertaining to COTS components, especially with regard to their source code and security mechanisms, can hinder security assessments of voting systems. While Dominion Voting Systems' COTS printer specifications enhance predictability and control, ES&S's more general descriptions, while offering flexibility, can introduce variability and uncertainty in component selection that negatively impact system security. Therefore, careful consideration and proactive security measures are essential when incorporating COTS components in voting systems to mitigate their inherent security risks [46].

**Administrator Passwords.** The presence of default, unchangeable administrator passwords in ExpressVote System 6.3.0.0 raises security concerns [50]. Also, the default passwords lack complexity, which exacerbates the risk. In fact, ES&S default passwords have been exposed in the past and even a single case of password reuse can enable an attacker to gain access to a voting system [34].

Vulnerabilities in the ExpressVote System 6.3.0.0 can enable unauthorized access and credential theft. While ES&S has instituted improved security and two-factor authentication using Microsoft Bitlocker [4], it does not necessarily imply that these measures are implemented in voting systems. Passwords required to perform specific functions such as changing the date/time and loading firmware could be exploited by a malicious actor who gains physical access to the system.

ES&S and other voting system vendors incorporate modems in tabulators and scanners to relay unofficial election results quickly [26]. The modems are claimed to connect to cellular phone networks and not directly to the public Internet [55]. However, the use of default passwords in the voting systems is problematic due to their indirect connections to the Internet.

**USB Drives.** The use of USB drives in ES&S voting systems introduces several vulnerabilities. A malicious actor can inject malware into the Election Management System via a USB drive to steal data, corrupt files and alter election results [22]. The USB drive threat is exacerbated due to bugs in the reference hashcode. The hash verification process involves the creation of two USB drives, one containing the data to be verified and the other containing verification scripts and a trusted hash file. A host separate from the Election Management System is booted using a DVD with a live Ubuntu operating system. The user can then run Linux from the DVD without altering the non-volatile memory in the host computer [25]. The problem is that the Linux Ubuntu DVD used for USB verification is itself a vector for malware injection [5].

The use of ES&S Delkin USB drives for various purposes, including data storage and loading security codes, are potential avenues for unauthorized access. If the USB drives are not properly secured and controlled, they could be manipulated or stolen, leading to unauthorized access to sensitive election data. ES&S has attempted to address this situation by restricting USB drives to loading election information on voting systems, collecting and storing election results, and transporting election results after polls close. Even with advanced encryption and limited physical access, attackers could leverage social engineering and human error to access and compromise the USB drives. In any case, USB drives are leading vectors for malware insertion [22] and using them for important tasks is a recipe for disaster.

## 4.2 Software Vulnerabilities

ExpressVote System software vulnerabilities relate to application programming interface (API) weaknesses, remote code execution, updates and patches, and the Windows 7 operating system.

**Application Programming Interface Weaknesses.** In 2019, it was discovered that the ExpressVote System, despite ES&S's claims of it being air-gapped, is connected to the Internet. This enables attackers to exploit vulnerabilities in the system APIs, potentially leading to unauthorized access and election result tampering [27].

**Remote Code Execution.** The ExpressVote System is susceptible to remote code execution where an attacker injects and launches arbitrary code on the system without authorization. Several instances of remote code execution vulnerabilities in ES&S voting systems have been reported [39]. In 2020, researchers discovered a remote code execution vulnerability in the Java Runtime Environment (JRE) used by ES&S voting systems [8]. Remote code execution can enable an attacker to gain control of a voting system and steal data, alter election results and disrupt an election.

ES&S has taken steps to address remote code execution vulnerabilities in its voting systems. For example, it has released security updates that address known vulnerabilities. However, the availability of updates does not necessarily mean that they have been installed in voting systems. According to a 2015 report [32], ES&S voting machines used in some U.S. states were not updated from 2005 to 2015. Another concern is that undiscovered remote code execution vulnerabilities may exist in ES&S systems.

**Updates and Patches.** According to a 2015 report [32], ES&S machines in 14 states were still using software that was at least ten years old. Additionally, ES&S had not released security updates for some of its older software. Regular system updates and patches are paramount to maintaining the security of ES&S systems.

While ES&S has released security updates for certain older software, the company has faced censure for the sluggish pace of its update and patch releases. In 2022, researchers discovered that ES&S had failed to release a security update for a critical vulnerability in its software for more than a year. The protracted update process exposes ES&S systems to election result tampering, voter data theft and election disruptions.

**Windows 7 Operating System.** The installation of the Windows 7 operating system on ES&S voting systems introduces security vulnerabilities. Windows 7 is considered to be outdated software and susceptible to known vulnerabilities in the absence of security patches. ES&S has stated that it is taking steps to upgrade to the Windows 10 operating system [20]. However, even with the operating system upgrade, ES&S must establish a track record of diligently providing security updates and patches.

### 4.3 Additional Vulnerabilities

Additional ExpressVote System vulnerabilities relate to contractual restrictions, proprietary interests, security concerns and lack of transparency.

**Contractual Restrictions.** ES&S voting systems are often purchased by U.S. states through contracts that restrict the disclosure of information about the systems. The contracts may include clauses that prohibit states from releasing information about the system source code, security vulnerabilities and/or testing procedures [33].

**Proprietary Interests.** ES&S is a private company that owns the intellectual property rights to its voting systems. The company has a financial interest in protecting its proprietary information, which may restrict disclosures of information about its voting systems.

**Security Concerns.** ES&S may be reluctant to disclose information about its voting systems because it could make the systems more vulnerable to attacks. For example, if ES&S discloses information about voting system vulnerabilities, attackers could exploit the vulnerabilities to impact elections.

**Lack of Transparency.** There is an overall lack of transparency regarding ES&S voting systems that stems from systemic issues that are not necessarily related to the company [55]. For example, there is a lack of public demand for transparency pertaining to ES&S voting systems. Many voters are not aware of the potential security risks posed by voting systems and they may not be concerned about the lack of transparency.

The lack of transparency regarding ES&S voting systems is a concern among election security experts. They argue that the public has the right to know about voting system security and that the lack of transparency makes it difficult to assess the risks posed to elections. In fact, malicious entities who seek to undermine elections are actually enabled by electoral processes that lack transparency and are vulnerable to tampering that is not traceable by audits [2].

## 5 Comparison of ImageCast X and ExpressVote Systems

Dominion Voting Systems' ImageCast and ES&S's ExpressVote are comparable voting systems. Table 1 compares the key features of the ImageCast X and ExpressVote systems. They have common features such as touchscreen technology for electronic ballot marking and paper ballot printing, audio prompts for voters with disabilities and election result auditing.

However, there are some differences in the ImageCast X and ExpressVote features. ImageCast X can be configured as a ballot marking device (BMD) or as a direct recording electronic (DRE) device whereas ExpressVote only functions

**Table 1.** Comparison of ImageCast X and ExpressVote systems [48–50]

| Feature | ImageCast X | ExpressVote |
|---|---|---|
| Machine Type | BMD or DRE | DRE |
| Display | Touchscreen | Touchscreen |
| Paper Ballot Printing | Yes | Yes |
| Audio Prompts | Yes | Yes |
| Result Auditing | Yes | Yes |
| Year Introduced | 2009 | 2012 |

as a direct recording electronic device. A ballot marking device marks votes on paper ballots that are input to a scanner to record votes while a direct recording electronic device only records votes electronically [15]. ImageCast X made its debut in 2009 whereas ES&S ExpressVote is a newer system that was introduced in 2012. However, both systems have undergone revisions and upgrades, with 20 states employing ImageCast X in 2020 and 17 states opting for ExpressVote [47].

**Table 2.** Comparison of ImageCast X and ExpressVote vulnerabilities

| Vulnerability Category | ImageCast X | ExpressVote |
|---|---|---|
| Default Administrator Passwords | No | Yes |
| Outdated Operating Systems | Yes | Yes |
| Data Redundancy | No | No |
| COTS System Vulnerabilities | Yes | Yes |
| USB Drives | Yes | Yes |
| Networked Components | No | Yes |
| API Weaknesses | No | Yes |
| Remote Code Execution | No | Yes |
| Regular Updates and Patches | No | No |
| Transparency | No | No |

Table 2 compares the vulnerabilities identified in the ImageCast X and ExpressVote systems. Default administrator passwords used by ExpressVote introduce risks of unauthorized access and tampering. ImageCast X does not have this vulnerability.

The two systems employ outdated operating systems that increase the risk of vulnerability exploitation. They also lack data redundancy that renders them vulnerable to data loss due to hardware failures. Both systems use COTS components with documented vulnerabilities that could be exploited to gain unauthorized access and disrupt operations. Both systems also use USB drives that can serve as vectors for unauthorized access and malware infection.

ImageCast X fares better than ExpressVote in that it does not have networked components. Additionally, ImageCast X does not have API weaknesses whereas ExpressVote has API weaknesses that enable attackers to gain unauthorized access. ExpressVote also has the risk of remote code execution that can lead to unauthorized access and tampering.

ImageCast X and ExpressVote do not provide regular updates and patches to address security vulnerabilities. Both the voting systems also lack transparency, which makes it difficult to assess their risks.

## 6 Countermeasures

A U.S. Cybersecurity and Infrastructure Security Agency report [7] recommends that election officials adopt and enhance defensive measures to reduce the risk of exploitation of identified vulnerabilities in voting systems. Specifically, election officials are advised to work with voting system vendors to determine the software/firmware updates that should be applied. Dominion Voting Systems has reported to the Cybersecurity and Infrastructure Security Agency that the vulnerabilities have been addressed in various software versions. However, a security researcher [3] has argued that the lack of transparency regarding the implemented fixes persists, stating "no one but Dominion has had the opportunity to test the asserted fixes." This raises concerns about the effectiveness of updates. Additionally, lawsuits such as Curling et al. v. Raffensperger et al. [44] have revealed that voting systems used in Georgia had not been updated since at least 2005 to address security flaws. This highlights the importance of independent testing and verification of security updates. Relying solely on vendors to address the vulnerabilities are inadequate to ensure the voting system security and integrity

Indeed, voting system security is shrouded by obscurity. Open design principles [6] that have provided benefits in other domains must be applied to voting systems. Open designs promote the development of secure and trustworthy systems by adhering to open standards and protocols. They ensure that system components interoperate securely and security best practices are followed throughout the system lifecycle. Ultimately, the implemented systems should be exposed to public scrutiny to create transparency and engender trust between system developers and users.

Certain federal laws and regulations apply to voting systems. The Voting Rights Act of 1965 prohibits discrimination in voting, including discrimination based on race, color or language. Additionally, the Computer Fraud and Abuse Act prohibits unauthorized access to computer systems, including voting machines.

The Help America Vote Act of 2002 established the U.S. Election Assistance Commission (EAC) and gave it the authority to develop and maintain standards for voting systems. The Commission has adopted the Voluntary Voting System Guidelines, a set of specifications and requirements covering functionality, accessibility and security capabilities against which voting systems can be evaluated.

While the Voluntary Voting System Guidelines are voluntary, most U.S. states have adopted them as law. The Commission also has the authority to certify voting systems that meet the guidelines. The certification is not mandatory, but it is often used by states to ensure that their voting systems meet the standards.

Existing regulations are designed to ensure that voting systems are fair, accessible and secure. However, there are concerns that the regulations are not strong enough to prevent hacking and other types of election fraud. Additionally, some states have not adopted the Voluntary Voting System Guidelines or have adopted weaker forms of the guidelines.

At this time, no federal regulations cover the cyber security of voting systems. In 2021, Congress passed the Secure Elections Act that would have established new security requirements for voting machines, but the bill was never signed into law. The responsibility of ensuring voting machine security falls on each state. Unfortunately, the patchwork of cyber security regulations at the state level leaves U.S. voting systems vulnerable to attacks.

## 7 Conclusions

The security and reliability of electronic voting systems are crucial to maintaining the integrity of democratic elections. Dominion Voting Systems' ImageCast X and Election Systems & Software's ExpressVote System are the most widely used electronic voting systems in the United States. This work has leveraged vendor documentation and system evaluations to examine alleged ImageCast X and ExpressVote System vulnerabilities at the hardware and software levels as well as to identify new vulnerabilities. The comparative vulnerability analysis provides insights into the security postures of the two voting systems and identifies areas for improvement.

The vulnerabilities described in this chapter would require physical access to voting systems and/or the ability to modify files before they are uploaded to the voting systems. According to the Cybersecurity and Infrastructure Security Agency, there is no evidence that such vulnerabilities have been exploited in previous elections. But the possibility exists because exploiting voting system vulnerabilities is well within the reach of hostile nation states and sophisticated hacker groups.

## References


1. Appel, A., DeMillo, R., Stark, P.: Ballot-marking devices cannot ensure the will of the voters. Election Law J. Rules Polit. Policy **193**(3), 432–450 (2020)
2. Breedon, K., Bryant, A.: Counting the votes: electronic voting irregularities, election integrity and public corruption. Univ. Memphis Law Rev. **49**(4), 979–1017 (2019)
3. Brumback, K.: Cyber agency: voting software vulnerable in some states. AP News, 31 May 2022

4. Burt, T.: Statement from Tom Burt, President and CEO of Election Systems & Software at the Hearing on 2020 Election Security – Perspectives from Voting System Vendors and Experts, The Committee on House Administration, U.S. House of Representatives, Washington, DC, 9 January 2020. www.essvote.com/media-resources/hearing-election-security-ess-statement
5. Carrillo-Mondejar, J.: Characterizing Linux-based malware: Findings and recent trends. Futur. Gener. Comput. Syst. **110**, 267–281 (2020)
6. Christen, M., Gordijn, B., Loi, M. (eds.): The Ethics of Cybersecurity. TILELT, vol. 21. Springer, Cham (2020). https://doi.org/10.1007/978-3-030-29053-5
7. Cybersecurity and Infrastructure Security Agency, Vulnerabilities affecting Dominion Voting Systems ImageCast X, ICS Advisory, Alert Code: ICSA-22-154-01, Washington, DC, 3 June 2022. (www.cisa.gov/news-events/ics-advisories/icsa-22-154-01
8. Danon and Proofpoint Threat Insight Team, 2020 election threats: An overview of our research. Proofpoint Blog, 30 October 2020. www.proofpoint.com/us/blog/threat-insight/2020-election-threats-overview-our-research
9. Dominion Voting Systems, Democracy Suite EMS Results Tally and Reporting User Guide, Version 5.11-CO:7, Denver, Colorado (2019). https://web-storage1.pilled.net/pdc1/old/proofs/63c500e7-aafb-0979-6aa2-784e19ed8f9b/UG-RTR-UserGuide-5-11-CO.pdf
10. Dominion Voting Systems, Democracy Suite Use Procedures, Version: 5.10-CA:11, Denver, Colorado (2020). https://votingsystems.cdn.sos.ca.gov/vendors/dominion/ds510-use-proc-jan.pdf
11. Dominion Voting Systems, 2.02 – Democracy Suite System Overview, Version: 5.13-CO:8, Denver, Colorado (2021). www.coloradosos.gov/pubs/elections/VotingSystems/DVS-DemocracySuite513/documentation/2-02-SystemOverview5-13.pdf
12. Dominion Voting Systems, Democracy Suite ImageCast X User Guide, Version: 5.13-CO:11, Denver, Colorado (2021). www.coloradosos.gov/pubs/elections/VotingSystems/DVS-DemocracySuite513/documentation/UG-ICX-UserGuide-5-13.pdf
13. Dominion Voting Systems, Setting the record straight: Facts about Dominion, Denver, Colorado (2024). https://www.dominionvoting.com/setting-the-record-straight
14. Election Systems & Software, High-Throughput Scanner and Tabulator DS450, Omaha, Nebraska (2024). https://www.essvote.com/products/ds450
15. Election Systems & Software, Universal Voting System ExpressVote, Omaha, Nebraska (2024). https://www.essvote.com/products/expressvote
16. EndofLife.date, Samsung Mobile – End of life updates, 27 July 2024. https://endoflife.date/samsung-mobile
17. Ferreira da Silva, R., Casanova, H., Orgerie, A., Tanaka, R., Deelman, E., Suter, F.: Characterizing, modeling and accurately simulating power and energy consumption of I/O-intensive scientific workflows. J. Comput. Sci. **44**, 101157 (2020)
18. Fisher, T.: DBAN 2.3.0 (Darik's Boot and Nuke) – A full review of DBAN, a free data destruction software tool, Lifewire, New York, New York, 1 December 2022. https://www.lifewire.com/dban-dariks-boot-and-nuke-review-2619130
19. Fournaris, A., Pyrgas, L., Kitsos, P.: An efficient multi-parameter approach for FPGA hardware Trojan detection. Microprocess. Microsyst. **71**, 102563 (2019)

20. Granger, K.: EAC certifies ES&S Windows-10-based operating systems. Election Systems & Software Blog, Omaha, Nebraska, 24 September 2019. https://www.essvote.com/blog/our-technology/ess-windows-10-based-operating-systems-certified-by-eac
21. IBM X-Force Exchange, Intel NUC BIOS firmware privilege escalation CVE-2022-36370, X-Force Vulnerability Report, Cambridge, Massachusetts, 22 November 2022. https://exchange.xforce.ibmcloud.com/vulnerabilities/239655
22. Joven, R., Kiat, N.: The spies who loved you: infected USB drives to steal secrets. Threat Intelligence Blog, Mandiant, Reston, Virginia, 11 July 2023. https://www.mandiant.com/resources/blog/infected-usb-steal-secrets
23. Li, T., John, L.: Run-time modeling and estimation of operating system power consumption. ACM SIGMETRICS Perform. Eval. Rev. **31**(1), 160–171 (2003)
24. Lu, K.: Deep analysis of CVE-2016-3820 – Remote code execution vulnerability in Android Mediaserver. Fortinet Blog, Fortinet, Sunnyvale, California, 17 August 2016
25. Mechler, B.: Voting System Examination of Election Systems & Software EVS 6.1.1.0, 20 September 2020. https://www.sos.state.tx.us/elections/forms/sysexam/brian-mechler-ESS-exam-report-EVS6110-aug.pdf
26. Monahan, K., McFadden, C., Martinez, D.: Online and vulnerable: experts find nearly three dozen U.S. voting systems connected to Internet. NBC News, 10 January 2020
27. Morris, D.: Swing states voting machines were left connected to the Internet, report says. Fortune, 18 August 2019
28. Muller, J., Mladenov, V., Somorovsky, J. Schwenk, J.: Exploiting network printers. In: Proceedings of the IEEE Symposium on Security and Privacy, pp. 213–230 (2017)
29. National Institute for Standards and Technology, CVE-2019-6332 detail, National Vulnerability Database, Gaithersburg, Maryland, 9 January 2020. https://nvd.nist.gov/vuln/detail/CVE-2019-6332
30. National Institute for Standards and Technology, CVE-2021-20877 detail, National Vulnerability Database, Gaithersburg, Maryland, 14 February 2021. https://nvd.nist.gov/vuln/detail/CVE-2021-20877
31. Nohl, K., Lell, J.: BadUSB – On accessories that turn evil, presented at *Black Hat USA* (2014)
32. Norden, L., Famighetti, C.: America's Voting Machines at Risk, Brennan Center for Justice, New York University School of Law, New York, New York (2015). https://www.brennancenter.org/sites/default/files/publications/Americas_Voting_Machines_At_Risk.pdf
33. North Carolina State Board of Elections, State board unanimously certifies new voting system, Press Release, Raleigh, North Carolina, 6 July 2023. https://www.ncsbe.gov/news/press-releases/2023/07/06/state-board-unanimously-certifies-new-voting-system
34. Porup, J.: Want to hack a voting machine? Hack the voting machine vendor first, *CSO Online Security Blog*, IDG Communications, Needham, Massachusetts, 30 March 2018. https://www.csoonline.com/article/565020/want-to-hack-a-voting-machine-hack-the-voting-machine-vendor-first.html
35. Pro V&V, Test Report for EAC VVSG 1.0 Certification Testing Election Systems & Software (ES&S) Voting System (EVS) 6.5.0.0, Document Number: TR-01-01-ESS-2023-05-01, Huntsville, Alabama. https://www.eac.gov/sites/default/files/2024-07/ESS

36. Redfox Cyber Security, Exploiting Android WebView vulnerabilities. Redfox Cyber Security Blog, Dover, Delawars, 22 December 2022. https://redfoxsec.com/blog/exploiting-android-webview-vulnerabilities
37. Salem, H., Topham, N.: Detecting denial-of-service hardware Trojans in DRAM-based memory systems. In: Proceedings of the Twenty-Eighth IEEE International Conference on Electronics, Circuits and Systems (2021)
38. Sarihi, A., Jamieson, P., Patooghy, A., Badawy, A.: Multi-criteria hardware Trojan detection: a reinforcement learning approach (2023). arXiv: 2304.13232v1
39. Secure77, Voting System 1.0 – Remote code execution (unauthenticated), Exploit Database, OffSec, New York, New York, 7 May 2021. https://www.exploit-db.com/exploits/49846
40. Sganga, N.: U.S. finds no evidence flaws in Dominion voting machines were ever exploited. CBS News, 3 June 2022
41. Sudlow, J.: Moonbounce: The dark side of UEFI firmware, IBM X-Force Exchange, Cambridge, Massachusetts, 21 January 2022. https://exchange.xforce.ibmcloud.com/collection/MoonBounce-the-dark-side-of-UEFI-firmware-1737264e9b084a6e99a35b2148076a11
42. Swierczynski, P., Fyrbiak, M., Koppe, P., Moradi, A., Paar, C.: Interdiction in practice - hardware Trojan against a high-security USB flash drive. J. Cryptogr. Eng. **7**, 199–211 (2017)
43. Tian, J., Scaife, N., Kumar, D., Bailey, M., Bates, A., Butler, K.: SoK: "Plug & Pray" today – Understanding USB insecurity in versions 1 through C. In: Proceedings of the IEEE Symposium on Security and Privacy, pp. 1032–1047 (2018)
44. U.S. District Court (Northern District of Georgia, Atlanta Division), Curling et al. v. Raffensperger et al., Civil Action no. 1:17-CV-2989-AT, Atlanta, Georgia, 21 May 2019
45. U.S. Election Assistance Commission, ES&S EVS 6.3.0.0 Certificate Conformance, Washington, DC. https://www.eac.gov/sites/default/files/voting_system/files/ESS
46. U.S. Election Assistance Commission, Considerations for Implementing Voting Systems with COTS Products, Washington, DC (2023). https://www.eac.gov/sites/default/files/eac_assets/1/28/Considerations_for_Implementing_Voting_Systems_with_COTS_Products.pdf
47. U.S. Election Assistance Commission, System Certification Process, Washington, DC, 10 October 2023. https://www.eac.gov/voting-equipment/system-certification-process
48. U.S. Election Assistance Commission, Democracy Suite 5.5, Washington, DC, 2 January 2024. https://www.eac.gov/voting-equipment/democracy-suite-55
49. U.S. Election Assistance Commission, Democracy Suite 5.5-A (Modification), Washington, DC, 2 January 2024. https://www.eac.gov/voting-equipment/democracy-suite-55-modification
50. U.S. Election Assistance Commission, EVS 6.3.0.0, Washington, DC, 2 January 2024. www.eac.gov/voting-equipment/evs-6300
51. Verified Voting, Election Systems & Software DS850, DC450 and DS950, Philadelphia, Pennsylvania (2023). https://verifiedvoting.org/election-system/ess-ds850-ds450
52. Virgilitto, D.: How to hack Android devices using the Stagefright vulnerability (updated 2021), Resource Center, InfoSec Institite, Chicago, Illinois, 10 January 2021. https://resources.infosecinstitute.com/topics/hacking/hack-android-devices-using-stagefright-vulnerability

53. Wylde, V., et al.: Cybersecurity, data privacy and blockchain: a review. SN Comput. Sci. **3**, 127 (2022)
54. Yin, J., et al.: Finding SMM privilege-escalation vulnerabilities in UEFI firmware with protocol-centric static analysis. In: Proceedings of the IEEE Symposium on Security and Privacy, pp. 1623–1637 (2022)
55. Zetter, K.: Election commission orders top voting machine vendor to correct misleading claims. Politico, 13 August 2020

# Advanced Manufacturing Security

# Detecting Control Injection Attacks Using Energy Data Anomalies in Computer Numerical Control Machining

Jeffrey Kimmell[1,2(✉)], Vladimir Orlyanchik[1,2], Logan Sturm[1,2], Joel Dawson[1,2], and Curtis Taylor[1,2]

[1] Oak Ridge National Laboratory, Oak Ridge, TN, USA
kimmelljc@ornl.gov

[2] Cybersecurity Manufacturing Innovation Institute, San Antonio, TX, USA

**Abstract.** The widespread adoption of networked devices, sophisticated automation and data-driven processes in industry – also known as Industry 4.0 – has boosted the quantity and quality of manufacturing products. However, the benefits come with substantial increases in the attack surfaces of manufacturing processes and systems. In addition to affecting the quality and readiness of critical products, attacks against manufacturing processes and systems can have severe physical consequences, including human injury and death.

This chapter presents the results of remote network-based control injection attacks on a computer numerical control mill. The focus is on the impacts of attacks during computer numerical control mill operation. A machine-agnostic, affordable and scalable solution for attack monitoring is developed by considering the physical effects of the attacks on wax workpieces. A simple threshold-based method for detecting attacks is demonstrated and its effectiveness is evaluated.

**Keywords:** Manufacturing Cyber Security · Attack Detection · Power Analysis · Attack Quantification

## 1 Introduction

Computer numerical control (CNC) machining is a subtractive manufacturing process that removes material from a preform to fabricate a specific geometry. Traditionally, the preform has been a solid piece of material with basic geometry such as a cube or cylinder. Recently, however, preforms have become more complex with the explosion of hybrid manufacturing, which interleaves additive and subtractive processes to create geometries that might not be possible to make using traditional manufacturing processes. This new type of system expands the reach of CNC machines further, and due to the vast numbers of legacy CNC machines already in use, the importance of ensuring that the machines continue to operate as intended cannot be overstated.


Published by Springer Nature Switzerland AG 2025
J. Staggs and S. Shenoi (Eds.): ICCIP 2024, IFIP AICT 725, pp. 43–63, 2025.
https://doi.org/10.1007/978-3-031-81888-2_3

In addition to the national importance of CNC machining, the vast size of the CNC machining market makes it an attractive target for adversaries. Coupled with the introduction of new digital techniques for machine monitoring and control, there are myriad vulnerabilities that can be exploited [2]. Many of the vulnerabilities can be mitigated by basic cyber hygiene, but low cyber hygiene persists in a domain that has only recently become networked and many domain-specific vulnerabilities are not addressed satisfactorily by standard cyber security controls. Meanwhile, numerous examples demonstrate that improper implementations of new technologies can lead to production disruptions [27].

The consequences of breaches in the manufacturing industry are not limited to data leaks and invasions of privacy. In fact, successful attacks could have severe physical impacts that reach beyond the impacted businesses. Process integrity and quality are critical to the fabrication of CNC-machined parts. Although some cyber attacks are easily observable, stealthy CNC-based attacks are a concern. Even slight deviations from the intended toolpaths can introduce defects that impact part performance. This is why strict, industry-specific standards are promulgated for characteristics such as part surface finish that directly impact part certification, performance and durability [21].

Additionally, 90% of United States manufacturing businesses are considered small to medium manufacturers (SMMs) [26]. Such businesses, which have less than 500 employees, often do not have the resources to survive successful cyber attacks. This is a concern because 31% of businesses that fall victim to cyber attacks such as ransomware close down permanently [7]. Since SMMs are the backbone of American manufacturing, it is imperative that adequate cyber security methods are made accessible and are implemented in manufacturing environments.

Depending on the levels of sophistication of the internal networks of machine shops, attackers could obtain and maintain access to the networks for extended periods of time. They could leverage network access to gain insights into shop capabilities and devise attacks that maximize destruction while minimizing their exposure. Indeed, if proper network monitoring is not in place, attackers could have uninterrupted access to the connected machines. It is, therefore, incumbent on human operators and the machines themselves to detect breaches.

This work is motivated by the need to develop attack detection methods that leverage side-channel data generated by manufacturing machine behavior. Power consumption, a common attribute of all manufacturing equipment, is a data source that is capable of supporting attack detection methods that can scale to numerous machines [22,34]. The components required to measure the data are low cost and minimally intrusive, and sensor deployment does not involve significant machine downtime.

This chapter focuses on control packet injection attacks launched by an adversary with remote network-level access on a commercially-available CNC mill. A cost-effective, machine-agnostic method for detecting attacks and assessing their severity using side-channel energy data is presented and evaluated.

## 2 Related Work

Anomaly detection has long been the focus of attention in manufacturing system environments. The ability to detect system behavior outside normal operating conditions prevents defects, limits failures/downtime and supports intelligent scheduling of preventative maintenance and replacement [9]. Traditionally, these efforts have focused on manufacturing-specific concerns such as predicting tool wear [15,16] and planning preventative maintenance [24], with efforts extending to detect behavior outside of nominal operating conditions [33]. While it is not unreasonable to expect that these methods might label cyber attacks as anomalous, the lack of cyber awareness in the manufacturing industry would likely result in attacks being treated as normal process anomalies instead of malicious acts. In fact, cyber attacks, such as those demonstrated in this work, can induce anomalies that are well outside normal machine behavior.

Much research has focused on detecting anomalies such as tool wear [12], breakage [14,15] and predictive maintenance [13]. Other work has investigated fault identification in ultra precision CNC machines [23] and the application of unsupervised machine learning methods for anomaly detection. Many of these approaches use electric current or power consumption sensors to monitor system behavior and detect anomalies [3,11,34]. Electric current sensors are well suited for these purposes because they are non-intrusive, highly sensitive and can be set up to monitor independent system components such as x/y/z-servomotors and spindles. Machine learning approaches are commonly employed due to their flexibility and improved detection. However, while machine learning is often effective at detecting normal failures in manufacturing environments, the design and training methods employed may leave machine learning models vulnerable to sophisticated attacks that cause damage while evading detection.

Interest in cyber security for manufacturing systems and their associated quality monitoring systems is growing. Elhabashy et al. [8] have presented a cyber-physical attack taxonomy from a quality control perspective that provides a high-level outline of how attacks might be executed on manufacturing systems and their quality control systems. However, the work does not provide in-depth evaluations of attacks on any system. Tran et al. [25] have leveraged deep learning and Internet-of-Things-device-based monitoring to identify normal cutting, chatter and false data injection. A dynamometer was used to monitor cutting force, the primary metric employed by their machine learning model to detect anomalies.

Wu et al. [29–32] have developed a cyber security testbed for intrusion detection and employed alert correlation to detect cyber attacks and intrusions. Their work combines traditional cyber (network-based) approaches such as Snort with physics-based approaches [5] to enhance the accuracy of the alerting system. They discuss similarity-, sequence- and case-based alert correlation along with the benefits and drawbacks of each approach. They also present case studies in different domains that demonstrate the effectiveness of their approach.

Other researchers have focused on a variety of side channels using vibration sensors [1,4,17,35], acoustic sensors [1,6,29,35], magnetic sensors [1,4,35] and electric current sensors [1,3,4,10,11,18,20,29,34,35] as well as combinations of these sensors.

A common limitation in the research literature is the paucity of detailed cyber attack scenarios, and sensing and analysis methods for detecting attacks. Works that focus on part quality tend to ignore these considerations completely, and those that do address cyber security concerns often involve limited case studies that consider variations of G-code attacks [1,6,11,18–20,28,29,31,32,34, 35]. Many case studies require large changes to the monitored systems to detect attacks. However, the relatively coarse attacks fail to provide insights into the detection thresholds, i.e., the lowest levels of deviations/attacks that can be detected. Also, because G-code commands are interpreted by firmware to create machine control signals, certain control states cannot be achieved by merely by altering G-code. An example is accelerations outside the allowable ranges caused by attacks with timescales smaller than those of G-code.

Works that address general manufacturing anomaly detection tend to be focused on anomalies that persist over time, not anomalies that occur at a single point in time. Therefore, detecting single-packet control injection cyber attacks, the focus of this work, requires an entirely different approach.

This work attempts to address gaps in the research literature related to network injection attacks during CNC mill operation. It investigates the thresholds at which attacks cause measurable physical effects on parts and the detectability of attacks using electrical current sensors. The objective is to provide additional insights into realistic attack scenarios and identify realistic attack detection thresholds.

## 3 Experimental Setup

This section describes the experimental setup, including the testbed architecture, data collection methods and control protocol.

### 3.1 Testbed Architecture

The experiments were conducted on a low-cost commercial CNC machine used in small manufacturing shops and by machining enthusiasts. The CNC machine uses a proprietary interface built on LinuxCNC (www.linuxcnc.org), an open-source project that provides reliable and configurable controls for CNC machines. Several important components of LinuxCNC are discussed later in this section.

To perform a machining run, LinuxCNC receives a pre-computed G-code toolpath file from a user and then proceeds to execute each G-code command in sequence to perform the desired positioning and cutting operations with the mill's actuators. Motion control of a CNC machine is primarily implemented by two hardware components. One component is a high-level card that interprets user commands, tracks machine status and initiates machining operations by converting G-code commands to direction and rate values, which it distributes. The other component is a low-level, FPGA card that fills the driver role by

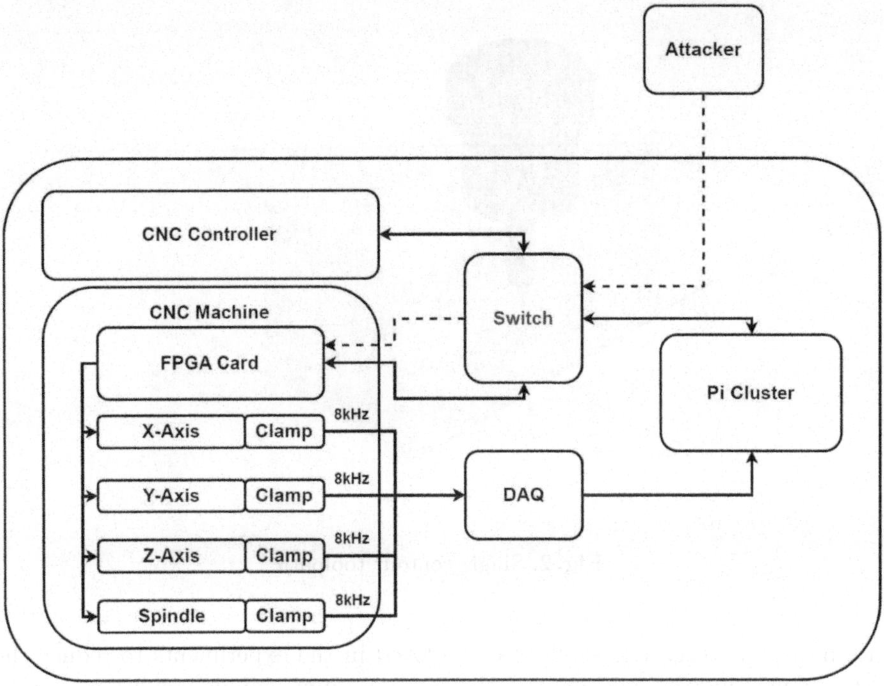


**Fig. 1.** Networked testbed architecture

converting rate commands received from the high-level card to actuator-specific movement commands. The low-level FPGA card also reads, reports on, and in some cases, performs closed-loop control using the machine's built-in sensors. The high-level CNC controller and FPGA card communicate via a switched local-area network (LAN) over Ethernet as shown in Fig. 1.

The experimental machining involved a single G-code execution that implemented a simple contour pass along the front side of a block of material. The single contour toolpath created using Autodesk Fusion 360 was employed in all the experiments.

Figure 2 shows the single contour toolpath. The spindle follows the path along the front side of the block in the direction of the dashed arrow. The attack causes the spindle to move in the perpendicular direction shown by the dashed arrow on the top of the block. The arrows at the top of the tool denote the spindle rotation direction.

Focusing on a single operation minimizes several sources of variability in testbed behavior. A contour pass is common enough to enable a simple relationship to be drawn between the correctness of the operation and a concrete quality metric, in this case, surface roughness.

In addition to the operation, facing operation experiments were executed using a five-flute $\frac{1}{2}$-in bull-nose end mill. Blocks made of machine wax instead

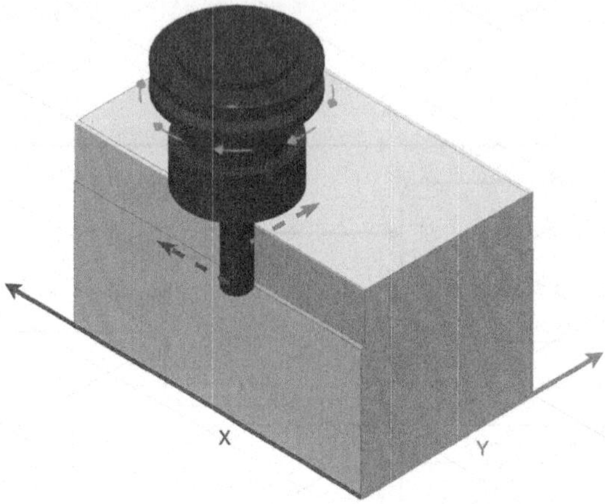


**Fig. 2.** Single contour toolpath

of a harder material like steel were employed in the experiments to reduce the risk of damaging the machine and creating unsafe machining conditions.

### 3.2 Data Collection

LinuxCNC provides access to several machining process data streams. The data can be used to gain insights into how well the machine is performing and provide feedback on how machining strategies can be improved. In addition to the existing data collection capabilities, the experimental machine was outfitted with clamp-on current transducers to measure electrical current (Fig. 1). The sensors were placed on the wires that deliver power to the x-, y- and z-axis servomotors, spindle motor, variable frequency drive, direct current power bus board and main power supply. The sensors were read by a data acquisition (DAQ) unit polled at 8 kHz by a Linux machine over a USB connection. The resulting amperage measurements represent the relationship between the G-code being executed on the machine and the energy required to perform the corresponding movements.

It is important to note that normal energy consumption patterns can vary based on machining strategies and preform material. After these factors were accounted for, the out-of-band data source was able to capture slight deviations from normal machine behavior. This was necessary because the attacks introduce small shifts in machine movements that could go undetected if only the native data streams were being monitored.

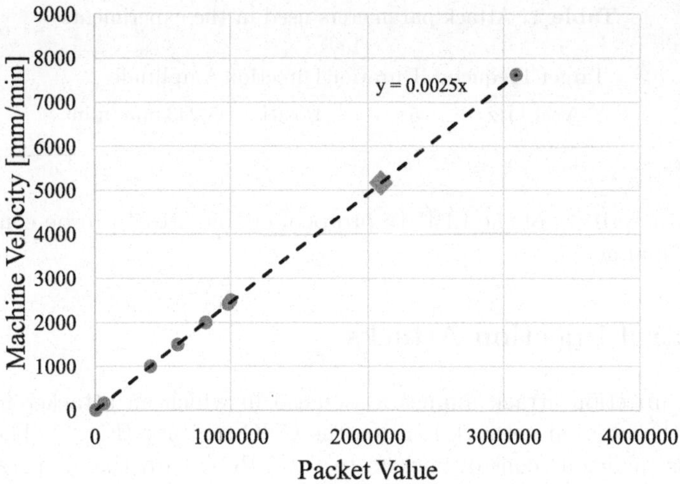


**Fig. 3.** Correlation between machine velocity and packet values

### 3.3 LBP 16 Protocol

In order to inject attack packets into the CNC machine, it was necessary to first dissect the UDP traffic being sent between the controller and FPGA card to determine how the LBP 16 protocol was being used for system control. This was accomplished by capturing the traffic sent from the controller to the FPGA card and analyzing its content.

The LBP 16 protocol controls the movement of the servomotor corresponding to each axis by writing values to the StepGen memory registers associated with the servomotor. The written values comprise a step amount and step direction. LBP 16 supports the writing of values to multiple registers via a single command as well as writing values to a specific register. During normal communications between the controller and FPGA card, the controller performs a bulk write to all the StepGen registers every time a control packet is sent. The structures of the malicious control packets were determined by analyzing how the StepGen values changed during movements along a single axis.

A simple experiment was performed to determine how the values written to the motor registers dictate the velocity of movement along each axis. The dotted line in Fig. 3 shows the linear regression for machine velocity versus packet value in the single-packet attack experiments.

The insights gained from analyzing normal communications traffic between the controller and FPGA card were used to construct an attack script. The script enables an attacker to tamper with machine components such as the x-, y- and z-servomotors and spindle. The LBP 16 protocol does not authenticate the origins of requests, so the FPGA card acts on the requests it receives regardless of their source IP addresses. Additionally, the controller cannot query the FPGA card to determine if additional commands have been injected into the control stream.

**Table 1.** Attack parameters used in the experiments

| Target | Frequency | Duration | Direction | Amplitude |
|---|---|---|---|---|
| Y-Axis | 4 Hz | 5 s | Positive | 5,243 mm/min |

These characteristics of the LBP 16 protocol enable attacks to be conducted in a stealthy manner.

## 4 Control Injection Attacks

A control injection attack mimics a scenario in which an attacker has gained access to the internal network housing the CNC machine (Fig. 1). The attacker then sends malicious control packets to the FPGA card that bypass the controller. Since the FPGA card lacks an authentication mechanism, it cannot differentiate between legitimate and malicious control packets.

The attack script was designed to accommodate various characteristics and parameters of single-packet attacks, such as the axis to be attacked, attack direction and attack amplitude. Additionally, the attack script allows adjustments to the frequency (repetition rate in packets/s) of a single attack packet as well as a block of packets. The ability of the LBP 16 protocol to write to a single register was leveraged to target a specific axis instead of writing to all the registers.

For simplicity and ease of demonstration, the experiments were designed with the machining and attacking directions perpendicular to each other. Attack packets were injected into the constant flow of legitimate commands from the controller to the FPGA card that instructed the machine to move in the positive direction along the y-axis. This caused the spindle to plunge into the part, locally impacting the machined surface finish. Attack packets were sent at a rate of 4 Hz and each attack lasted five seconds.

Table 1 shows the attack parameters used in the experiments. The amplitude of the damage was measured using a profilometer, a common tool for characterizing the surface finishes of machined parts. However, this type of defect measurement is cumbersome and requires an operator to interrupt the machining process. The operator must also select the correct measurement because there are numerous types of surface finish measurements and using an incorrect method would diminish the severity of the defect. For these reasons, it was important to be able to utilize machining process data to determine attack severity.

### 4.1 Machine Response to Attacks

Normal communications between the FPGA card and machine controller are accomplished using cyclic reads and writes to constantly move and verify the positions along the axes. Both the actions are performed by the controller sending write and read requests to the FPGA card.

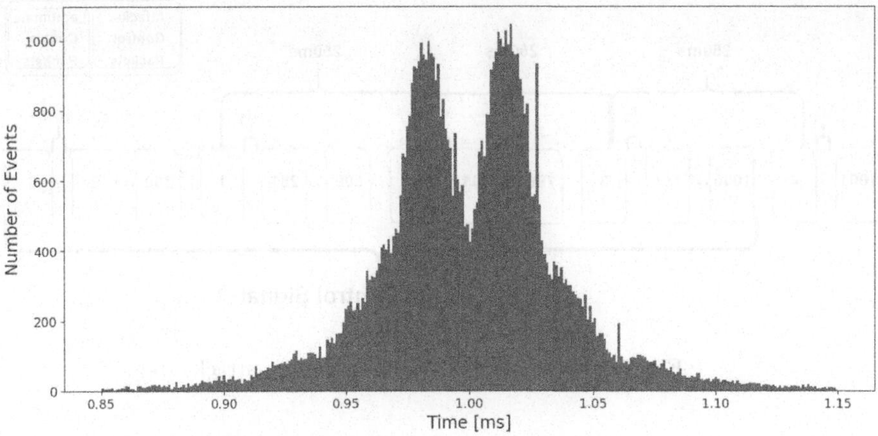


**Fig. 4.** Packet timing distribution measurements

The timing between write commands is an important parameter when measuring attack severity. To better understand this, the timing between packets in the captured traffic was analyzed. Figure 4 shows that the timing between legitimate write packets during normal CNC machine operation is tightly grouped around 1 ms, indicating that the internal position verification loop operates at a rate of 1 kHz. Where an attack packet falls between legitimate write commands determines the attack severity. Details about this issue are provided below with additional analysis.

The machine response is influenced by the attack parameters. If packets are sent at a high enough frequency or if the step amount is too large, a software emergency stop (e-stop) is triggered due to the position exceeding a predetermined error threshold. Therefore, the parameters were selected so as not to cause the machine to e-stop, mimicking a more subtle attack that could cause prolonged damage. The decision to attack at 4 Hz with a moderate step value enables the machine position verification loop to move the spindle back to its expected position along the toolpath after each attack packet. This is the reason why the defects manifest themselves as notch-like features.

### 4.2 Timing Impacts

During an attack, the FPGA card received packets from two sources, the controller and the attacker. Figure 5 provides an overview of the packet control stream during an attack. The 1 kHz control signal resulted in legitimate control packets being sent during a 1 ms period. During the attack, malicious control packets were sent at a period of 250 ms (4 Hz) for five seconds. Due to an imperfect timing loop that ended 0.5 s early, only 18 attack packets were sent over the course of the attack. The timing consideration $\Delta t_n$ measures the time between an attack packet and the next legitimate control packet. Attack packets were

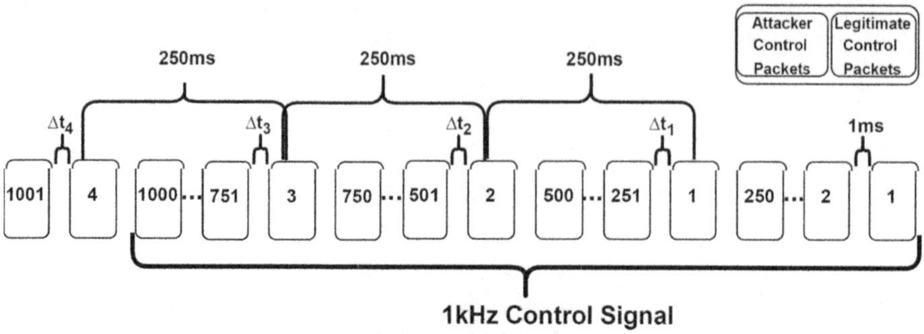


**Fig. 5.** Packet control stream during an attack

not sent in a tightly bound control loop, and thus, varied slightly around to the 250 ms target.

Due to the presence of legitimate and malicious control packets, the machine acted on both types of commands, alternating between legitimate and malicious commands. The arrival time of an attack packet with respect to the next legitimate write command dictated the severity of the corresponding defect. Figure 6 shows the machined surfaces of wax and aluminum workpieces after the attacks. The arrows point to undetectable indentations and deep indentations on the wax workpiece.

The amount of time a malicious control packet resides in the buffer is important to an adversary because it results in a longer execution time before the next control packet. To maximize the attack impact, the adversary would increase $\Delta t$ up to 1 ms, causing the attack packet to arrive immediately after a legitimate control packet. The impact on the manufactured part is minimized as $\Delta t$ approaches 0 ms because the malicious control packet would be overridden by a legitimate control packet.

Since the legitimate communications flow is not observable to a remote adversary, $\Delta t$ is unknown; this makes it difficult for the adversary to maximize the attack impact. Due to this limitation, every time an attack is executed, a slightly different $\Delta t$ is observed and, as a result, the part impact measurement varies. Additionally, the greater the time that a malicious control packet is acted upon, the greater the corrective action needed from the controller. Although it is not shown, each legitimate control packet is followed by a read command from the controller to determine the absolute position from the machine. Because the attack increasingly impacts the part, the controller must adjust the legitimate control messages to account for the deviations caused by the attack. However, at no point does the controller user interface notify the operator of these deviations. A quantitative discussion of this timing phenomenon is provided in Sect. 5.2.

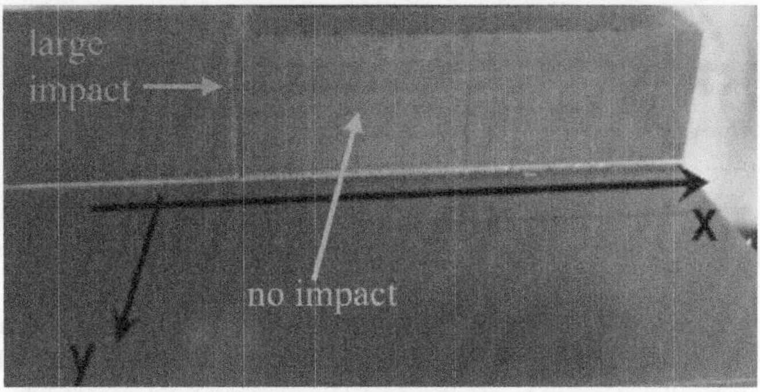


(a) Wax workpiece.

(b) Aluminum workpiece.

**Fig. 6.** Machined surfaces of workpieces after attacks

## 5 Results

To simplify the experimental procedure and to reduce the cost, most of the results were obtained with wax workpieces. However, similar results – in a smaller quantity – were reproduced with aluminum workpieces.

Table 2 shows the machining conditions used in the experiments. In the testing procedure, the spindle, equipped with a $\frac{1}{2}$-inch end mill operated at 5,000 rpm, performed a contour operation along the x-axis at a feed rate of 1,000 mm/min. The attack packet directed the workpiece to move in a perpendicular direction along the y-axis. In each experiment, 18 single attack packets were sent such that the attack packets were separated by 250 ms.

Figure 6 shows a machined surface generated after one of the experiments. A sudden change in the movement direction induced by the attack resulted in an indentation on the machined surface. Due to the periodic nature of the attack, the indentations are equally spaced, but have different amplitudes. The impact of an attack on the machined surface can vary from being invisible to a clearly identifiable deep indentation. The amplitude of the impact was characterized by

**Table 2.** Machine conditions used in the experiments

| Axis | Direction | Velocity | Mill Diameter | Spindle Speed |
|---|---|---|---|---|
| X-Axis | Positive | 1,000 mm/min | 0.5 in | 5,000 rpm |

its peak-to-peak value measured by a profilometry scan taken after the experiment.

During normal operation, a series of legitimate control packets separated from each other by ~1 ms (Fig. 4) instructed the machine to move along the machining direction (x-direction). At the time of the attack, a single attack packet that induced movement along the y-direction (perpendicular to the machining direction) was inserted between two legitimate control packets. Thus, the perpendicular motion due to the attack was naturally interrupted by the next legitimate control command issued by the controller. The duration of the attack $\Delta t$ is the interval between the attack packet arrival time $t_{attack}$ and the arrival time of the next legitimate control packet $t_{write}$:

$$\Delta t = t_{write} - t_{attack}$$

Figure 7 shows the profilometer measurement of each attack. The magnitude of the attack impact $R_T$ is shown as a function of attack duration $\Delta t$. Note that the dashed line depicts the profilometry detection threshold. The increase of $R_T$ with attack duration is intuitive – the longer the machining tool is made to move in the perpendicular direction, the deeper it will cut into a workpiece. The absence of data points below ~0.2 ms is related to an internal parameter of the controller that defines how long the control packet must be present in the FPGA card before a step pulse signal to the stepper motor is issued. In particular, if the legitimate write command arrives within a $\Delta t$ of 0.2 ms from the attack packet, it replaces the attack packet and thus completely eliminates the attack. However, this never occurs with legitimate control write packets because they are always transmitted 1 ms apart.

There are also data points above the 1 ms mark due to the deviation in the 1 ms control signal as shown in Fig. 4. The large spread of the data is partially related to milling operation inconsistency introduced by a relatively short attack time, typically $\Delta t < 1$ ms. During this time, the end mill rotating at 5,000 rpm turns at most 32 degrees, less than 9% of a complete revolution. As a result, the amplitude of the indentation produced on the workpiece strongly depends on the exact positions of the flutes with respect to the workpiece during time $\Delta t$.

### 5.1 Current Monitoring Procedure

To monitor the electric current, appropriately rated standard split core alternating current transformers were connected around the electrical cables leading to the x-, y- and z-servomotors and the spindle. The analog alternating current voltage signals generated by the current transformers were directly proportional

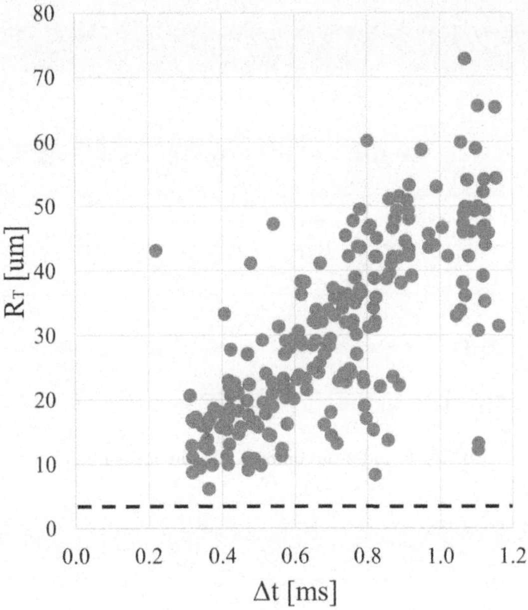


**Fig. 7.** Magnitude of surface degradation as a function of attack time

to the measured alternating current and ranged between −1 to 1 V. These signals were sampled by a Measurement Computing data acquisition device at a frequency of 8 kHz. The sampling frequency was sufficient to resolve the details of any event occurring on a timescale of order 1 ms.

Figure 8(a) shows the current measurements of the x-, y- and z-servomotors during a typical contour machining operation. The current trace of the machining process is visually divided into three regions: (i) $t \leq 6.75$ s during normal operation prior to the attack sequence, (ii) $6.75\,\text{s} < t \leq 12$ s during the attack sequence and (iii) $t > 12$ s during normal operation after the attack sequence. While the two regions of normal operation show smooth variations in the measured current, discrete events in the form of sharp current spikes seen during the time interval $6.75\,\text{s} < t \leq 12$ s for the y-servomotor current in Fig. 8(a) are associated with the sequence of 18 individual single-packet attacks. Due to internal electrical crosstalk, much less prominent current spikes are also seen in the current traces associated with x- and z-axes, although the two axes were not directly subjected to attacks.

Figure 8(b) shows a detailed view of the y-servomotor current measurements during and after each single-packet attack. Importantly, the timescale associated with the event related to a single-packet attack was of the order of 1 ms. The initial current fluctuations associated with the attack are followed by the machine response. The latter is an internal attempt by the controller to correct the position of the machine that was altered by the attack. Detailed analysis

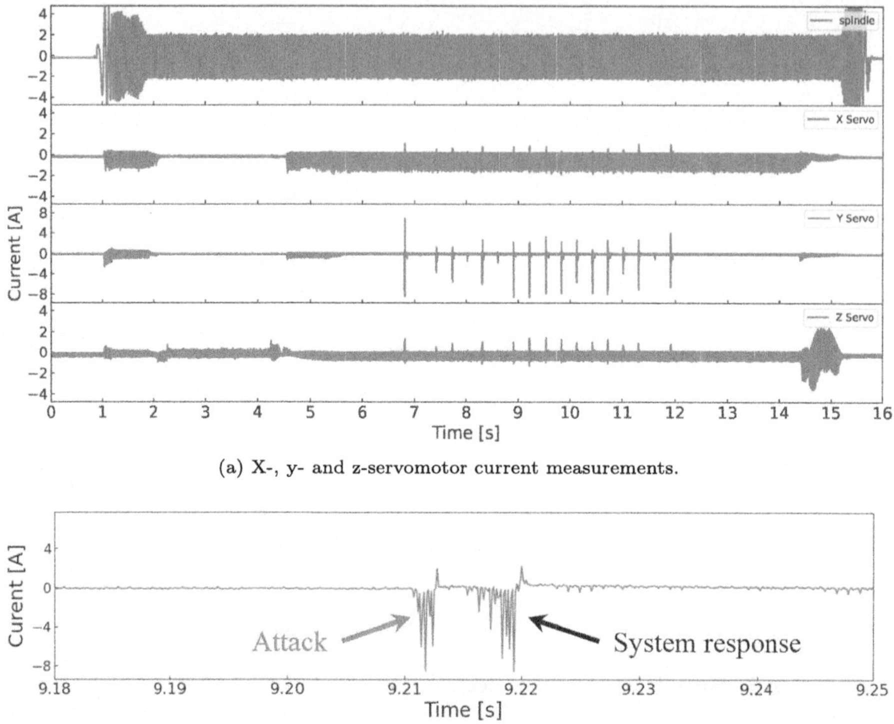


(a) X-, y- and z-servomotor current measurements.



(b) Detailed view of y-servomotor current measurements.

**Fig. 8.** Servomotor current measurements

of the behavior and characteristics of the machine response to the attacks are beyond the scope of this work.

## 5.2 Attack Impact Quantification

As seen in Fig. 8(b), an attack is characterized by a series of downward current spikes with varying amplitudes. The change in current during the attack $I_{max}$ can be defined as a proxy for the amplitude of the attack:

$$I_{max} = f(V_Y, f, \Delta t)$$

where $V_Y$, $f$ and $\Delta t$ are the machine velocity in the y-direction, single-packet attack frequency and attack duration, respectively.

In this study, the dependence of $I_{max}$ was examined only for the parameter $\Delta t$ while keeping $V_Y$ and $f$ constant. Figure 3 and Table 1 provide the reference values.

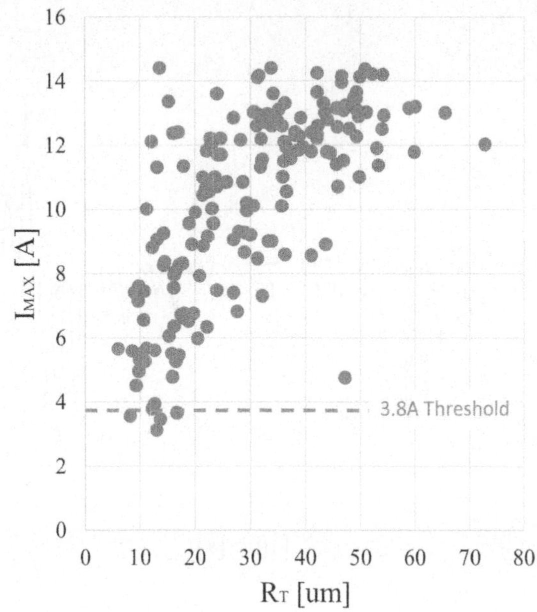


**Fig. 9.** Current change during attack versus surface degradation

Figure 9 shows the correlation between the current change $I_{max}$ to the amplitude of the surface indentation caused by the attack $R_T$. The dashed line depicts the current threshold selected for attack detection. The fast initial increase of $I_{max}$ is followed by almost complete saturation. The saturation is due to restrictions on the electrical system settings imposed by servomotor characteristics (i.e., maximal input current rating). As a result, although the current changes provide visual evidence of attacks, they cannot be used to quantify the damage caused by the attacks.

The fundamental difference between the $I_{max}$ and $R_T$ quantities is that the former reflects the electrical current value at a specific moment during an attack while the latter expresses the damage accumulated over the entire duration of the attack. To create a quantity that reflects the extent of the attack, the current change during the attack is integrated over time as shown by the shaded area enclosed by the current trace in Fig. 10. This metric is referred to as the power of attack ($PoA$).

Figure 11 shows the correspondence between the surface degradation caused by an attack as a function of the power of attack. The dashed line is a linear regression. The baseline values of surface degradation $R_T$ obtained by scanning the freshly-machined surface without attacks are in the range $2.5\,\mu\text{m} < R_T \leq 3.5\,\mu\text{m}$, which are in agreement with linear regression. The linear dependence indicates that the power of attack is a good proxy metric for attack significance.

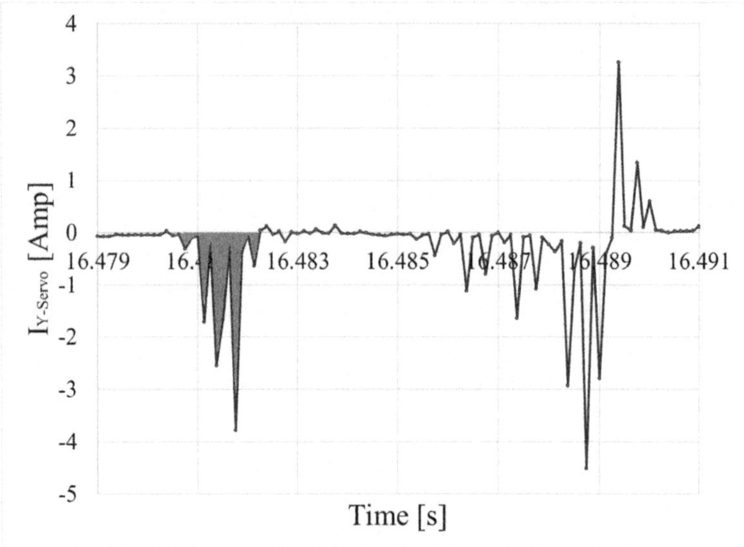


**Fig. 10.** Y-servomotor current during and after the attack

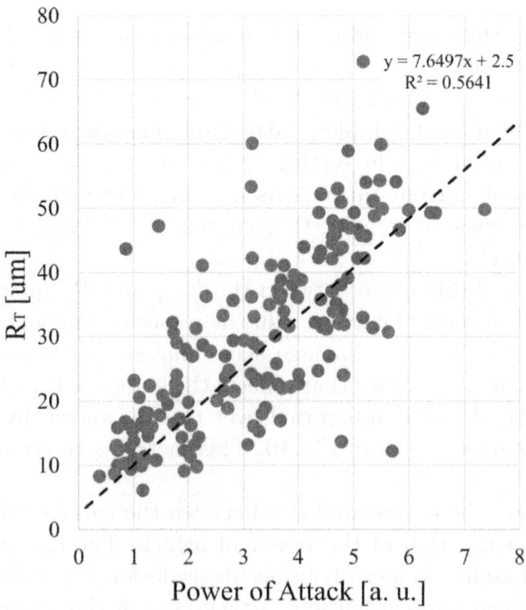


**Fig. 11.** Surface degradation versus power of attack

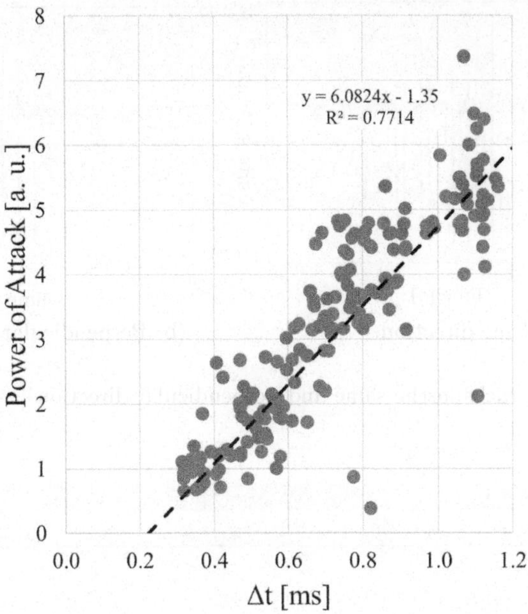


**Fig. 12.** Power of attack versus attack time

Figure 12 the dependence of the power of attack metric $PoA$ on the attack time $\Delta t$. The dashed line is a linear regression. The correlations between surface degradation $R_T$, power of attack $PoA$ and attack time $\Delta t$ render current utilization a suitable parameter for detecting and characterizing packet injection attacks.

Although all the experiments described above were performed under "stationary" conditions when the attacks were executed perpendicular to the machining axis, it must be emphasized that the same analysis and arguments are valid when the attack and machining axes are identical. Figure 13 shows the y-servomotor current during the machining process when the attack packets included commands to move the spindle in the same direction or in a perpendicular direction to the machining direction. In both cases, the current spikes indicating the attacks are clearly visible.

### 5.3 Attack Detection

The simplest detection method is to employ a threshold-based discriminator in which events with amplitudes exceeding the threshold are identified as malicious. The y-servomotor current values were collected during various machining operations to quantify the detection capability and limitations. Energy data was also collected during a CNC engraving operation, one of the most aggressive operations in terms of electrical current changes.

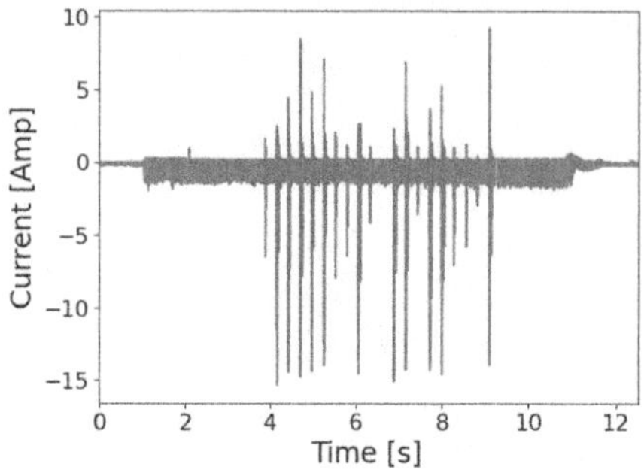


(a) Same direction.

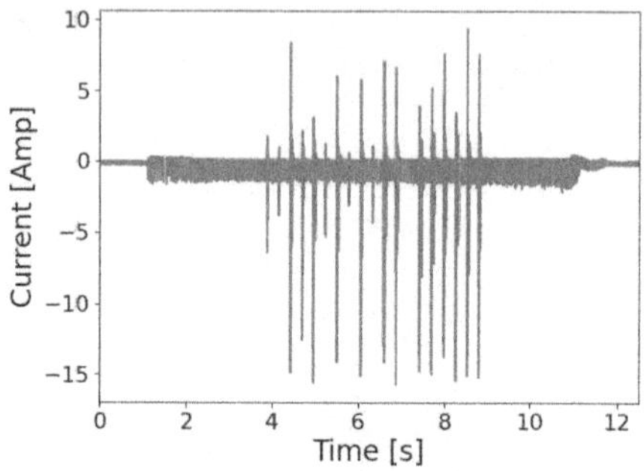


(b) Perpendicular direction.

**Fig. 13.** Attacks in the same and perpendicular directions as machining

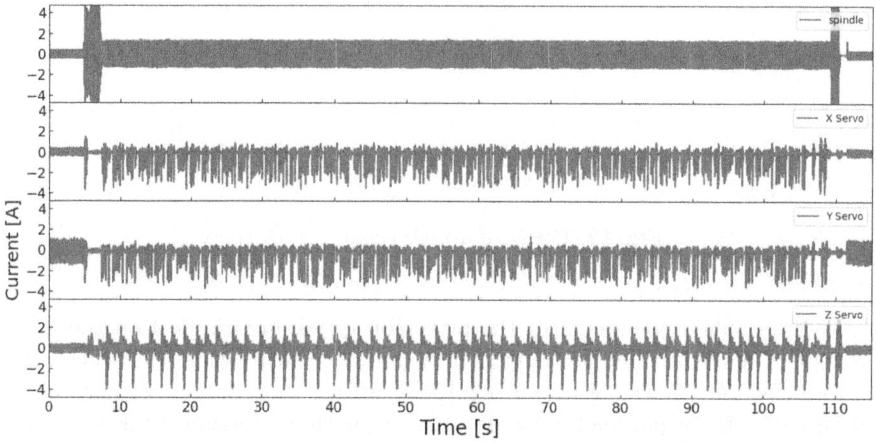


**Fig. 14.** Servomotor and spindle current measurements during an engraving operation

Figure 14 shows the current measurements of the x-, y- and z-servomotors, and spindle during an engraving machining operation without attacks. The engraving operation is an extreme example of fast and abrupt changes in machining direction and, therefore, could manifest similar current characteristics as those observed during attacks. However, even for this fast process, the variations in servomotor current associated with abrupt changes in machining direction on the scale of 30 to 100 ms are considered to be smooth compared with the behavior during single-packet attacks.

Figure 15(a) shows the probability distribution of y-servomotor current measurements for various manufacturing operations. Figure 15(b) shows the tail of the probability distribution. The maximum absolute value of the y-servomotor current recorded is less than 3.8 A. The threshold value could be set to −3.8 A to minimize false positives. Based on the data analysis presented in Fig. 9, the threshold value shown by the horizontal dashed line could potentially miss less

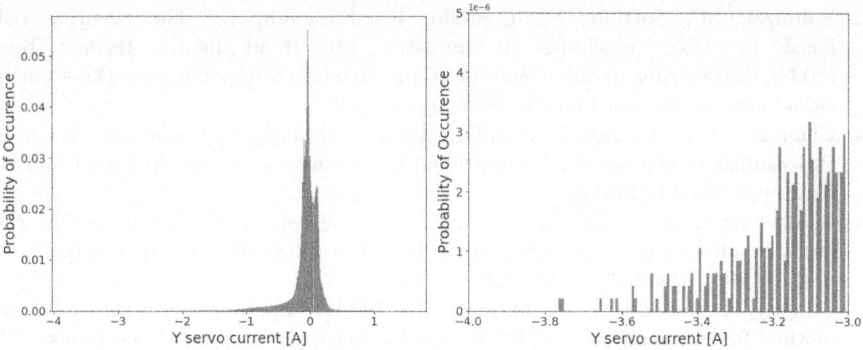


(a) Overall probability distribution. (b) Tail probability distribution.

**Fig. 15.** Probability distributions of y-servomotor current measurements

than 1.5% of the attacks. The attacks that remain undetected are those with the smallest impacts on the machined surface, i.e., below 15 µm.

## 6 Conclusions

This work has analyzed a key CNC machining cyber attack scenario in which an attacker has penetrated the internal network and can inject attack packets directly to the FPGA card, bypassing the CNC machine controller. Certain machine and attack variables clearly influence the severity of the damage inflicted on manufactured parts. This has contributed to the development of a low cost, non-invasive and efficient current measurement solution for monitoring a CNC machine for attacks and quantifying the damage inflicted by attacks. The simple threshold-based method provides measurement-based estimates of attack detection efficiency and the maximal damage inflicted by undetected attacks. The results raise interesting questions about the possibility of more sophisticated attacks and the development of efficient attack detection methods.

The views expressed in this chapter do not necessarily represent the views of the U.S. Department of Energy or the United States Government.

**Acknowledgement.** This material is based on work supported by the U.S. Department of Energy Office of Energy Efficiency and Renewable Energy (EERE) under the Advanced Materials and Manufacturing Technologies Office (AMMTO) Award no. DE-EE0009046.

## References

1. Ahsan, M., Rais, M., Ahmed, I.: SOK: side channel monitoring for additive manufacturing – bridging the cybersecurity and quality assurance communities. In: Proceedings of the Eighth IEEE European Symposium on Security and Privacy, pp. 1160–1178 (2023)

2. Balduzzi, M., Sortino, F., Castello, F., Pierguidi, L.: The security risks faced by CNC machines in Industry 4.0, trend micro, Irving, Texas (2022). https://documents.trendmicro.com/assets/white_papers/wp-the-security-risks-faced-by-cnc-machines-in-industry-4-0.pdf
3. Chen, H., et al.: Energy-consumption-data-based machine anomaly detection. In: Proceedings of the Second International Conference on Advanced Cloud and Big Data, pp. 136–142 (2014)
4. Rokka Chhetri, S., Al Faruque, M.A.: Side channels of cyber-physical systems: case study in additive manufacturing. IEEE Des. Test **34**(4), 18–25 (2017). https://doi.org/10.1109/MDAT.2017.2682225
5. Chhetri, S., Canedo, A., Al Faruque, M.: KCAD: kinetic cyber-attack detection method for cyber-physical additive manufacturing systems. In: Proceedings of the IEEE/ACM International Conference on Computer-Aided Design (2016)
6. Chhetri, S., Lopez, A., Wan, J., Al Faruque, M.: GAN-Sec: generative adversarial network modeling for the security analysis of cyber-physical production systems. In: Proceedings of the Design, Automation and Test in Europe Conference and Exhibition, pp. 770–775 (2019)
7. Connor, J.: 31% of U.S. companies close down after falling victim to ransomware, TweakTown, Camperdown, Australia, 12 August 2021. https://www.tweaktown.com/news/80567/31-of-us-companies-are-forced-to-close-down-after-ransomware-attack/index.html
8. Elhabashy, A., Wells, L., Camelio, J., Woodall, W.: A cyber-physical attack taxonomy for production systems: a quality control perspective. J. Intell. Manuf. **30**, 2489–2504 (2019)
9. Farbiz, F., Yuan, M., Zhou, Y.: A cognitive analytics based approach for machine health monitoring, anomaly detection and predictive maintenance. In: Proceedings of the Fifteenth IEEE Conference on Industrial Electronics and Applications, pp. 1104–1109 (2020)
10. Gatlin, J., et al.: Encryption is futile: reconstructing 3D-printed models using the power side-channel. In: Proceedings of the Twenty-Fourth International Symposium on Research in Attacks, Intrusions and Defenses, pp. 135–147 (2021)
11. Gatlin, J., Belikovetsky, S., Moore, S., Solewicz, Y., Elovici, Y., Yampolskiy, M.: Detecting sabotage attacks in additive manufacturing using actuator power signatures. IEEE Access **7**, 133421–133432 (2019)
12. Ha, H., Min, D., Jeong, J.: A novel clustering anomaly detection of PCA based time series features with CNC machines data. In: Rocha, A., Adeli, H., Dzemyda, G., Moreira, F. (eds.) Information Systems and Technologies: WorldCIST 2022, Volume 1, pp. 22–31. Springer, Cham (2022). https://doi.org/10.1007/978-3-031-04826-5_3
13. Kamat, P., Sugandhi, R.: Anomaly detection for predictive maintenance in Industry 4.0 – a survey. In: Proceedings of the Sixth International Conference on Energy and City of the Future, no. 02007 (2020)
14. Li, E., Bedi, S., Melek, W.: Anomaly detection in three-axis CNC machines using LSTM networks and transfer learning. Int. J. Adv. Manuf. Technol. **127**, 5185–5198 (2023)
15. Li, G., Fu, Y., Chan, D., Shi, L., Zhou, J.: Deep anomaly detection for CNC machine cutting tools using spindle current signals. Sensors **20**(17), 4896 (2020)
16. Liang, Y., Wang, S., Li, W., Lu, X.: Data-driven anomaly diagnosis for machining processes. Engineering **5**(4), 646–652 (2019)

17. Liu, C., Kan, C., Tian, W.: An online side channel monitoring approach for cyber-physical attack detection in additive manufacturing. In: Proceedings of the International Manufacturing Science and Engineering Conference (2020)
18. Moore, S., Gatlin, J., Belikovetsky, S., Yampolskiy, M., King, W., Elovici, Y.: Power consumption-based detection of sabotage attacks in additive manufacturing (2017). arXiv:1709.01822v1
19. Rahman, M., Shafae, M.: Physics-based detection of cyber attacks on manufacturing systems: a machining case study. J. Manuf. Syst. **64**, 676–683 (2022)
20. Rott, M., Monroy, S.A.S.: Power-based intrusion detection for additive manufacturing: a deep learning approach. In: Peñalver, L., Parra, L. (eds.) Industrial IoT 2020. LNICST, vol. 365, pp. 171–189. Springer, Cham (2021). https://doi.org/10.1007/978-3-030-71061-3_11
21. Routara, B., Bandyopadhyay, A., Sahoo, P.: Roughness modeling and optimization in CNC end milling using a response surface method: effect of workpiece material variation. Int. J. Adv. Manuf. Technol. **40**, 1166–1180 (2009)
22. Schirmer, P., Mporas, I.: Non-intrusive load monitoring: a review. IEEE Trans. Smart Grid **14**(1), 769–784 (2023)
23. Selvaraj, V., Min, S.: Real-time fault identification system for a retrofitted ultra-precision CNC machine from equipment power consumption data: a case study of an implementation. Int. J. Precis. Eng. Manuf. Green Technol. **10**, 925–941 (2023)
24. Tanuska, P., Spendla, L., Kebisek, M., Duris, R., Stremy, M.: Smart anomaly detection and prediction for assembly process maintenance in compliance with Industry 4.0. Sensors **21**(7), 2376 (2021)
25. Tran, M., et al.: Reliable deep learning and IoT-based monitoring system for secure computer numerical control machines against cyber attacks with experimental verification. IEEE Access **10**, 23186–23197 (2022)
26. Trombley, D.: One small step for energy efficiency: targeting small- and medium-sized manufacturers. American Council for an Energy-Efficient Economy, Washington, DC (2014). www.aceee.org/research-report/ie1401
27. Verizon Business: 2023 Data Breach Investigations Report, Ashburn, Virginia (2023). www.verizon.com/dbir
28. Wu, D., et al.: Cybersecurity for digital manufacturing. J. Manuf. Syst. **48**(C), 3–12 (2018)
29. Wu, M., Moon, Y.: Intrusion detection system for a cyber-manufacturing system. J. Manuf. Sci. Eng. **141**(3), 031007 (2019)
30. Wu, M., Moon, Y.: Alert correlation for detecting cyber manufacturing attacks and intrusions. J. Comput. Inf. Sci. Eng. **20**(1), 011004 (2020)
31. Wu, M., et al.: Establishment of an intrusion detection testbed for cyber manufacturing systems. Procedia Manuf. **26**, 1053–1064 (2018)
32. Wu, M., Song, Z., Moon, Y.: Detecting cyber-physical attacks on cyber manufacturing systems with machine learning methods. J. Intell. Manuf. **30**, 1111–1123 (2019)
33. Yan, S., Shao, H., Xiao, Y., Liu, B., Wan, J.: Hybrid robust convolutional autoencoder for unsupervised anomaly detection of machine tools under noise. Robot. Comput. Integr. Manuf. **79**, 102441 (2023)
34. Yoginath, S., et al.: Stealthy cyber anomaly detection on large noisy multi-material 3D printer datasets using probabilistic models. In: Proceedings of the ACM CCS Workshop on Additive Manufacturing (3D Printing) Security, pp. 25–38 (2022)
35. Yu, S., Malawade, A., Chhetri, S., Al Faruque, M.: Sabotage attack detection for additive manufacturing systems. IEEE Access **8**, 27218–27231 (2020)

# Security Assessment of an LBP16-Protocol-Based Computer Numerical Control Machine

Yahya Forihat[1], Curtis Taylor[2], Rima Asmar Awad[2], and Irfan Ahmed[1(✉)]

[1] Virginia Commonwealth University, Richmond, VA, USA
iahmed3@vcu.edu

[2] Oak Ridge National Laboratory, Oak Ridge, TN, USA

**Abstract.** Subtractive manufacturing systems, specifically, computer numerical control machines, have revolutionized the manufacturing industry. Computer numerical control machining is the preferred method for producing finished parts due to its efficiency, speed and suitability for high-volume production. Securing computer numerical control machines is a priority. Compromises or disruptions of these machines can result in significant downtime, loss of productivity and financial loss.

This study examines the vulnerabilities and risks associated with computer numerical control machines, in particular, systems utilizing the LBP16 protocol for controller-machine communications. The study reveals that an adversary can execute cyber-physical attacks such as sabotage and denial of service. The potential security threats emphasize the importance of implementing robust security measures to mitigate the cyber risks to computer numerical control machines.

**Keywords:** Subtractive Manufacturing · Computer Numerical Control Machine · Cyber-Physical Attacks · Sabotage · Denial of Service

## 1 Introduction

Subtractive manufacturing creates parts by selectively removing material from workpieces through milling, lathing and drilling techniques. It is versatile in that it accommodates diverse materials and design requirements, produces superior surface finishes and provides cost-effective solutions for high-volume production. The integration of computer numerical control (CNC) technology, an exemplar of subtractive manufacturing, has dramatically improved the precision, consistency, repeatability, efficiency and reliability of machining processes. In fact, CNC machines are indispensable in intelligent manufacturing, especially in precision-critical sectors such as aerospace, healthcare, automotive and defense [15].

CNC has played a pivotal role in shaping new industrial models that adhere to the Industry 4.0 framework. A significant aspect of this progress is the ability of CNC machines to connect to networks. While networking enhances productivity, it also introduces security and privacy risks [3].


Published by Springer Nature Switzerland AG 2025
J. Staggs and S. Shenoi (Eds.): ICCIP 2024, IFIP AICT 725, pp. 65–84, 2025.
https://doi.org/10.1007/978-3-031-81888-2_4

Cyber attacks that target physical systems are on the rise [10]. A prominent example is Stuxnet, which caused significant damage to uranium hexafluoride centrifuges in Iranian nuclear facilities [2,6,12,13,24,25]. In the past, manufacturing systems were isolated, shielding them from remote attacks. However, the ubiquitous deployment of cyber manufacturing systems has made the manufacturing industry highly vulnerable to cyber-physical accidents and attacks [17]. Many cyber-physical attacks are executed by insiders such as disgruntled employees with authorized access to computers and networks [5].

Modern manufacturing relies on a complex mix of digital and physical technologies, including control systems, machining equipment (lathes and mills), assembly tools (pneumatics, welders and robots), post-processing machinery (kilns and paint lines) and inspection devices (digital cameras and measuring machines) [11]. CNC manufacturing systems are encountering industrial viruses and network attacks that have brought cyber security to the forefront [7].

While a large body of research has focused on cyber security vulnerabilities in additive manufacturing systems [1,4,8,9,14,18,19,22,23], studies of subtractive manufacturing systems are notable for their absence. The work described in this chapter fills the gap by shedding light on CNC machine vulnerabilities and providing insights and solutions. In particular, it presents an analysis of vulnerabilities in CNC machines that utilize the LBP16 protocol for controller-machine communications. The vulnerabilities render the systems susceptible to cyber-physical attacks such as sabotage and denial of service. The results, which have been communicated to the affected vendors, are discussed in this chapter along with mitigation strategies that enhance CNC machine security.

## 2 Background and Related Work

This section provides an overview of CNC manufacturing and research related to manufacturing system security.

### 2.1 CNC Manufacturing

In CNC manufacturing, computer software directs the movement of machinery and tools in a factory setting. This enables manufacturers to enhance efficiency by reducing production time, minimizing waste and eliminating potential human errors. Workpiece material is gradually removed by controlled machining until the finished part with the desired shape and dimensions is produced.

Figure 1 provides an overview of the CNC machining process. It begins with the creation of a 2D or 3D computer-aided design (CAD) model that specifies the part shape and dimensions. The CAD model is input to computer-aided manufacturing (CAM) software that creates the tool paths and establishes the machining parameters. The CAM software exports the plans as G-code to a CNC machine controller that dispatches detailed instructions to the CNC machine. The CNC machine follows the instructions to precisely cut, drill and mill the material, producing the final product with high precision and consistency.

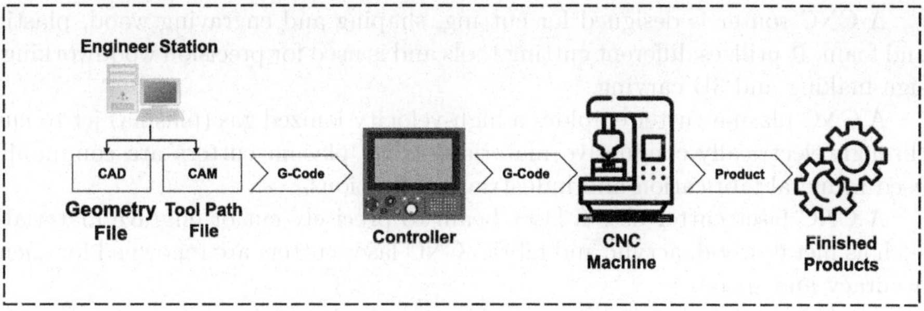


**Fig. 1.** CNC machining process

Commonly-used CAD software includes AutoCAD, SolidWorks and Fusion 360. Popular CAM software includes Mastercam, Fusion 360 CAM and Siemens NX CAM. CAM software generates tool paths and machining instructions based on the input CAD model. The software also enables the optimization of cutting strategies, selection of appropriate tools and simulations of machining processes to identify potential problems. The tool paths and machining instructions produced by CAM software are typically specified in G-code, a program that guides CNC machine operation. The G-code commands and instructions are processed by a CNC machine to dictate its movements, speeds, tooling operations and other parameters. Each line of code represents a specific action or function, such as moving the machine to a particular location, controlling the tooling operation or activating an auxiliary function. G-code enables the precise, automated control of CNC machines, allowing for the creation of complex parts accurately and efficiently.

LinuxCNC is an open-source, real-time operating system engineered to serve as a CNC controller. It is renowned for converting a standard personal computer into a highly adaptable CNC controller that maintains precise timing control over low-level hardware such as stepper motors. While it is not a complete tool for CNC machining, LinuxCNC offers considerable flexibility, ranging from preparing G-code instructions using CAM software to selecting appropriate stepper drivers and managing everything in between.

CNC machines employ G-code instructions for machining operations and applications. A CNC mill employs computer control to cut materials. It utilizes G-code instructions to precisely control the movements of the mill spindle in various directions and patterns. Following the instructions, a CNC mill can accurately shape and cut materials according to the programmed specifications. This level of automation and precision has contributed to the wide use of CNC mills in prototyping and manufacturing.

A CNC lathe secures a workpiece on a spindle and rotates it while various cutting tools are applied to shape the material. The movements and operations of the lathe, including spindle rotation, tool positioning, feed rates and depths of cuts, are controlled using G-code.

A CNC router is designed for cutting, shaping and engraving wood, plastic and foam. It utilizes different cutting tools and is used for precision woodworking, sign-making and 3D carving.

A CNC plasma cutter employs a high-velocity ionized gas (plasma) jet to cut through electrically-conductive materials. CNC plasma cutters are commonly used in metal fabrication and industrial applications.

A CNC laser cutter uses a laser beam to precisely cut or engrave materials such as metal, wood, acrylic and fabric. CNC laser cutters are renowned for their accuracy and speed.

### 2.2 Related Work

Despite their importance in modern manufacturing processes, CNC machines have not been the subject of much security research. The literature primarily concentrates on the broader aspects of industrial control system security, with only a few studies delving into the vulnerabilities and threats associated with CNC machines.

DeSmit et al. [10] have introduced a novel cyber-physical vulnerability assessment method for manufacturing systems. Their two-step method begins by creating intersection maps that represent the diverse processes in a manufacturing setting; potential vulnerabilities are identified by examining how different entities interact. Next, decision tree analysis is employed to evaluate the impact of each exposure at each intersection node. DeSmit and colleagues demonstrated the utility of the assessment method for handling the growing complexity and frequency of attacks targeting manufacturing systems.

Tu et al. [20] have proposed a CNC machine security framework based on Trusted Computing 3.0 technology. The framework automatically recognizes self-instructions and non-self-instructions to protect a CNC/industrial control system (ICS) network from interference. They also introduced a trusted communications monitoring and control scheme that supports real-time monitoring, control and encryption verification of CNC-ICS instructions.

Wu et al. [21] have focused on detecting cyber-physical attacks in computerized manufacturing systems (CMSs) using physical data and machine-learning approaches. They developed and integrated machine learning algorithms to identify and mitigate potential attacks in two manufacturing processes, 3D printing and CNC milling. A vision system was used as the physical data source for 3D-printing and the method for detecting malicious defects yielded 96.1% accuracy. Acoustic signals were used in the case of CNC milling and the random forest algorithm achieved 91.1% accuracy in identifying cyber-physical attacks during manufacturing operations.

Chen et al. [7] have proposed a security protection scheme that incorporates mechanisms such as data encryption, identity authentication, digital signatures, access control, secure communications and key management. Their scheme focuses on protecting CNC system terminal equipment, safeguarding data and securing the network infrastructure.

Li et al. [15] have explored innovative methods for detecting cyber attacks on cyber-physical manufacturing systems in real time. Their MPI-CNC prototype system developed for FANUC CNC machine tools automatically analyzes numerical control programs to detect anomalies by extracting machining process invariants and key parameter rules. The system effectively identifies cyber attack behaviors by comparing real-time data with predefined rules, ensuring that the normal operations of CNC systems are not disrupted. MPI-CNC was rigorously evaluated in several real-world machining scenarios. It displayed superior adaptability and accuracy at detecting attacks compared with other state-of-the-art methods.

In a study related to the work described in this chapter, Balduzzi et al. [3] investigated the security and privacy aspects of CNC machines. They conducted in-depth empirical analyses of modern CNC controllers from several vendors and identified their vulnerabilities. The threat modeling work identified five attack classes: compromise, damage, denial of service, hijacking and theft. The research results have been communicated to the affected vendors along with proposed mitigation strategies.

The research described in this chapter analyzes the communications between controllers and CNC machines. This is significant because a key threat involves adversaries leveraging network access to intercept traffic and gain insights into the communications, enabling them to orchestrate sophisticated attacks. The research has uncovered security weaknesses in CNC machines that employ the LBP16 communications protocol.

## 3 LBP16 Protocol Attack Methodology

This work focuses on attacks on the LBP16 protocol used by CNC machines for controller-machine communications. This section describes the LBP16 protocol, attack methodology and adversary model.

### 3.1 LBP16 Protocol

LBP16 is a simple remote register access protocol designed for swift and efficient interactions with hardware registers over Ethernet [16]. The protocol plays a pivotal role in real-time motion control applications. LBP16 can access eight distinct memory spaces, enabling it to handle a broad range of data. Each memory space is linked to an exclusive read-only info area. The first entry in the info area is a cookie, which is used to confirm that access is proper and authorized; this enhances system security.

**LBP16 Command Structure.** LBP16 commands have a standard structure that enables precise communications with hardware registers. Table 1 shows the LBP16 protocol command structure. Each command is 16 bits long and has several crucial bits.

**Table 1.** LBP16 protocol command structure

| Bit(s) | Description |
|---|---|
| 0 to 6 | `N`: Transfer count (number of transfers) |
| 7 | `I`: Increment address (1 = yes, 0 = no) |
| 8, 9 | `S`: Transfer element size specifier (00b = 8 bits, 01b = 16 bits, 10b = 32 bits, 11b = 64 bits) |
| 10, 11, 12 | `M`: Memory space specifier (000b through 111b) |
| 13 | `C`: Memory space indicator (0 = memory, 1 = info area) |
| 14 | `A`: Includes address (1 = yes, 0 = no) |
| 15 | `W`: Write bit (1 = write, 0 = read) |

**Info Area.** The info area is an essential component of each of the eight possible memory spaces [16]. Three entries in the info area play key roles:

- **COOKIE (Address 0):** This first entry serves as a verification mechanism, ensuring proper and authorized access to the memory space. The cookie is represented as `OX5AON`, where `N` corresponds to the address space (ranging from 0 to 7).
- **MEMSIZES (Address 2):** This entry provides information about the memory sizes in the associated memory space.
- **MEMRANGES (Address 4):** This entry holds data related to the memory ranges of the associated memory space.

Each MEMSIZES and MEMRANGES entry is characterized by specific bits that denote whether the memory space is writeable, the memory space type (register, memory, EEPROM or flash) and the allowed data access size.

Table 2 shows the hexadecimal command structure of the LBP16 protocol info area. `NN` indicates the count/increment field whereas `LL` and `HH` refer to the lower and higher bytes of the address.

Table 3 shows the reading and writing commands for different LBP16 memory spaces. The same notation is used to clarify the structure and functionality of the commands.

### 3.2 Attack Methodology

A vulnerability was identified in the LBP16 protocol, a crucial part of the communications process. While the protocol effectively transmits data between a CNC controller and a CNC machine, it has inadequate mechanisms for authenticating entities that attempt to access and control CNC machines. An adversary exploiting the vulnerability can access the control system of the CNC machine, alter the operational parameters or send harmful commands directly to the machine. The negative impacts include the production of defective parts and physical damage to the CNC machine.

**Table 2.** LBP16 command structure

| Info Memory Space | Command | Description |
|---|---|---|
| Ispace 0: Hostmot2 | NN61LLHH | Read with specified address |
| | NN21 | Read without specified address |
| Ispace 1: Ethernet Chip | NN65LLHH | Read with specified address |
| | NN25 | Read without specified address |
| Ispace 2: Ethernet EEPROM | NN69LLHH | Read with specified address |
| | NN29 | Read without specified address |
| Ispace 3: FPGA Flash EEPROM | NN6DLLHH | Read with specified address |
| | NN2D | Read without specified address |
| Ispace 6: LBP16 R/W | NN79LLHH | Read with specified address |
| | NN39 | Read without specified address |
| Ispace 7: LBP16 R/O | NN7DLLHH | Read with specified address |
| | NN3D | Read without specified address |

**Table 3.** Command structures for memory spaces

| Memory Space | Reading Command | Writing Command |
|---|---|---|
| Space 0: HostMot2 | NN42LLHH | NNC2LLHH |
| | NN02 | NN82 |
| Space 1: Ethernet Chip | NN45LLHH | NNC5LLHH |
| | NN05 | NN85 |
| Space 2: Ethernet EEPROM | NN49LLHH | NNC9LLHH |
| | | D9 Enable EEPROM area writes |
| | NN09 | NN89 |
| Space 3: FPGA Flash EEPROM | NN4ELLHH | NNCELLHH |
| | NN0E | NN8E |
| Space 4: LBP Timer/Utility Area | NN51LLHH | NND1LLHH |
| | NN11 | NN91 |
| Space 6: LBP Status/Control Area | NN59LLHH | NND9LLHH |
| | NN19 | NN99 |
| Space 7: LBP Read-Only Area | NN5DLLHH | Not applicable |
| | NN1D | |

Several actions were executed based on the identified vulnerability to simulate and analyze potential attacks on CNC machines utilizing the LBP16 protocol:

- The initial step involved a comprehensive analysis of the communications protocol between the CNC machine controller and CNC machine. This included a review of the official documentation as well as protocol reverse engineering,

which provided a thorough understanding of the communications dynamics and functionality.
- A parser was developed to facilitate the analysis. The tool dissected network dumps, enabling the accurate association of commands with their memory locations. This step helped plan the attack vectors and understand how commands could be manipulated.
- Next, the key registers and memory locations used by the controller to read and write data were identified and mapped. This established clear links between memory locations and the corresponding commands issued by the controller, providing the foundation for the simulated attacks.
- With a clear understanding of the vulnerability, tools were designed and implemented for its exploitation. The tools accessed and modified device memory, enabling the simulation of controlled attacks on CNC machines to assess their effectiveness and impacts.

### 3.3 Adversary Model

CNC machines are typically integrated into manufacturing networks [3]. Traditionally, these networks were isolated. However, in contemporary manufacturing facilities, CNC machines interface with external servers to facilitate remote programming and process monitoring. Also, CNC machines are often located in corporate networks and are accessible via industrial gateways or mobile networks. Mobile network operators provide CNC machines with Internet connectivity and industrial gateways bridge operational technology and information technology networks [3]. Balduzzi et al. [3] report that interviews with domain experts corroborate these assertions.

Figure 2 shows the adversary model adopted in this research. To a certain extent, the model is inspired by the work od Balduzzi et al. [3]. The adversary is modeled as follows:

- A remote adversary with access to the operational technology network poses a threat. The adversary could be an insider with direct access to the operational technology network housing the CNC machine. Alternatively, the adversary could be an external entity that exploits an enterprise network that lacks segmentation or is improperly configured, exposing the CNC machine to attacks.
- A remote adversary with access to the information technology network to which the CNC machine is connected is a potential threat. The adversary can pivot from the information technology network to access the CNC machine, potentially exploiting misconfigurations or vulnerabilities in the industrial gateway that bridges the information technology and operational technology networks.
- A remote adversary that establishes communications with the machine operator presents a threat. In this scenario, the attacker could employ social engineering techniques to gain access to the CNC machine.
- Insiders, employees as well as contractors, with authorized access to the CNC machine also pose threats.

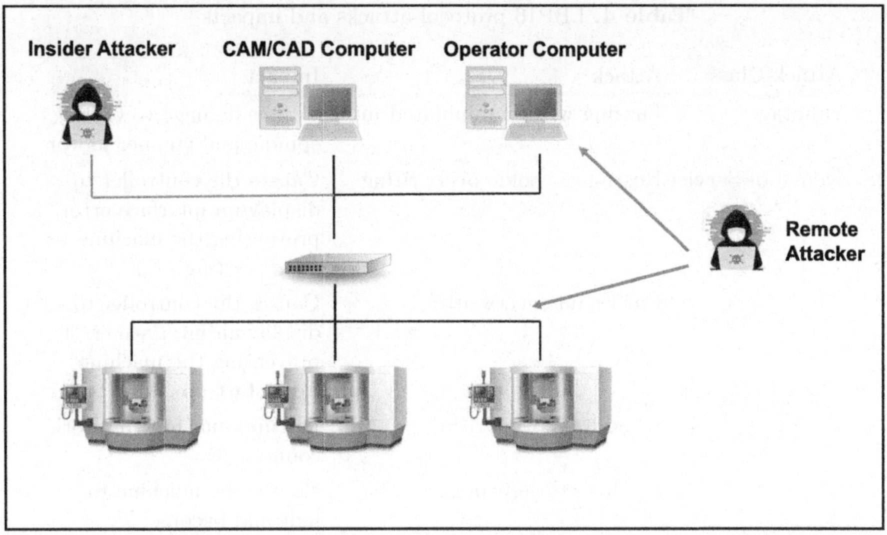


**Fig. 2.** Adversary model

# 4 CNC Machine Attack Case Study

This section describes the CNC machine case study and the attack implementation.

## 4.1 CNC Machine Case Study

For reasons of sensitivity, the CNC machine used in the case study is referred to as Machine X. The CNC machine, which employs the LBP16 protocol for controller-machine communications, incorporates a touchscreen controller, keyboard, mouse, jog shuttle for convenient control and a Wi-Fi module for connectivity.

The controller used in the case study, referred to as Controller Y, is built on LinuxCNC. Controller Y offers an intuitive, user-friendly graphical interface that simplifies CNC machine operation. The LinuxCNC capabilities are augmented with features such as conversational programming, which enables operators to generate G-code directly on the controller instead of being restricted to using pre-written code.

Attacks on Machine X were launched from an Ubuntu 22.04 virtual machine configured to communicate with the CNC machine via Ethernet. In line with the adversary model described above, Machine X was connected to a local network using an industrial switch. This setup mirrors a common industrial configuration where CNC machines in an operational technology network are linked to an information technology network using industrial switches.

**Table 4.** LBP16 protocol attacks and impacts

| Attack Class | Attack | Impact |
|---|---|---|
| Sabotage | Fuzzing with manipulated input | Causes damage to tools, spindle and stepper motor |
| Denial of Service | Hostmot2 cookie overwriting | Causes the controller to display an interface error, preventing the machine from starting |
| | Card name overwriting | Causes the controller to display an interface error, preventing the machine from start-up |
| | IP address overwriting | Disrupts machine network connectivity |
| | Flash sector erasing | Causes the machine to halt and become unresponsive |

The adversary in the model has network access and is assumed to have adequate knowledge of the LBP16 protocol that enables it to send potentially malicious commands to the CNC machine. Specifically, the adversary can launch targeted attacks that exploit protocol-specific vulnerabilities, such as sending malformed or unauthorized commands, testing the resilience of the CNC machine under simulated threat conditions.

Table 4 provides details about the five attacks developed to target the LBP16 protocol vulnerability described in Sect. 3.2. The attacks are classified into two categories based on their impacts on CNC machine functionality – sabotage and denial of service.

## 4.2 CNC Machine Attack Implementation

This section describes the implementation of the CNC machine attacks, including the memory mapping analysis required to develop the sabotage and denial-of-service attacks.

**Memory Mapping Analysis.** In order to elucidate the command structure and memory interactions of the LBP16 protocol, a parser was developed to deconstruct the packet payloads extracted from network dumps. The analysis revealed that each payload comprises a sequence of regularly-transmitted protocol commands. The commands initially write to specific memory locations followed by read operations, which continue cyclically. The systematic analysis provided a deep understanding of the protocol's operational dynamics related to network communications.

It was observed that during idle periods the protocol overwrites specific memory locations with zeros. These locations are subsequently populated with hexadecimal values upon executing a G-code file. G-code commands were executed in order to monitor and analyze the resulting network traffic. This enabled the correlation of registers and their values. For example, when a G-code instruction was issued to reposition the spindle, analysis of the network traffic enabled the identification of the memory locations that were overwritten with the corresponding $x$-, $y$- and $z$- coordinate values.

These efforts enabled the mapping of the critical memory locations used by protocol to overwrite memory. However, the mapping could vary depending on the CNC machine model. In any case, the analysis provided a precise understanding of how the protocol interacts with the machine's operational parameters.

**Sabotage Attack.** The first attack category involved the sabotage of tools, spindles and stepper motors. Fuzzing techniques that evaluate protocol implementations were employed to identify flaws that could be exploited to gain control of the system. Fuzzing involves generating and transmitting malformed packets to a device under test and evaluating the impacts.

A fuzzer for testing CNC machine responses was created to manipulate command inputs extracted from captured a network dump utilizing the parser. Specifically, the protocol values in memory location `0x0598` that stores the $x$-, $y$- and $z$- coordinate values were manipulated using a byte-flipping technique. For example, an original packet `84c2980598a2ffff9c6c000003fbffff00000000` was changed to `84c2980598a2ffff9c6c000003fbff0000ff0000` and stored in the memory location.

Two tests were conducted to assess the influence of altered data on Machine X. The first test was performed when the machine was idle and the second test was conducted during model creation. During the first test, the CNC machine emitted a startling sound because the fuzzed value caused the stepper motor to drive the spindle beyond its operational limit. Simultaneously, an error message appeared on the Controller Y screen indicating a machine malfunction and suggesting a review of the power supply and cable connections (Fig. 3). Despite the warning, the spindle persisted in its bidirectional movements and attempted to exceed its constraints even after the emergency stop button was activated.

In the second test conducted during model design, the controller engine halted unexpectedly (i.e., the spindle switched off), causing the machine to become unresponsive. The controller displayed an identical error message as in the first test, but the spindle continued to move beyond its limit. Maintaining this attack on the CNC machine would damage critical components such as the machine tool and stepper motor. Recognizing and mitigating such attacks promptly are crucial to avoid significant equipment damage and associated operational disruptions. Equipment damage is a concern because CNC machine costs range from a few thousand to millions of U.S. dollars [3]. Even if the damage is restricted to tools or specific machine components, delays due to replacement and

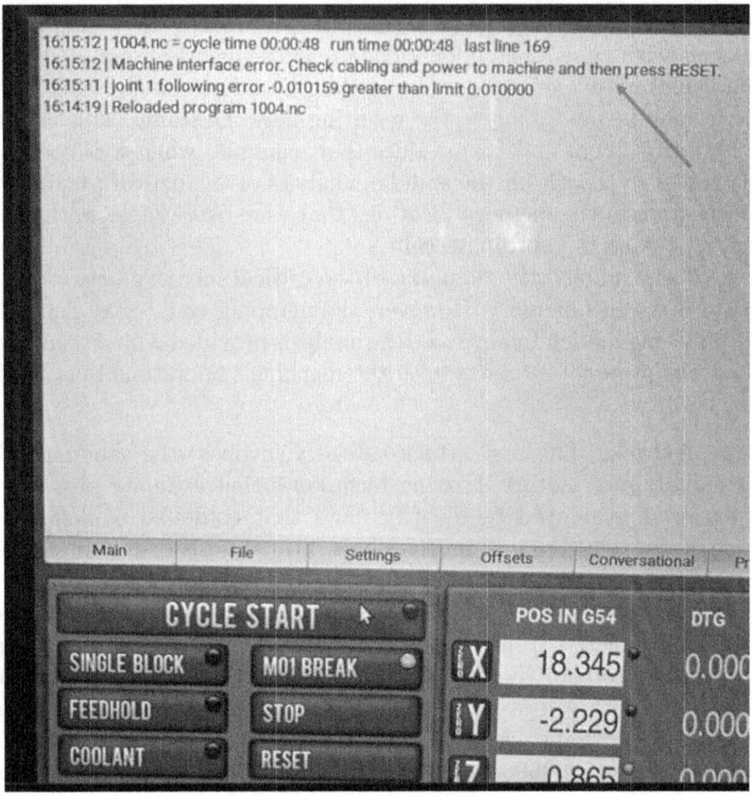


**Fig. 3.** Controller error message

maintenance could result in production line stoppage and significant economic losses.

**Denial-of-Service Attacks.** Four distinct denial-of-service attacks were developed: Hostmot2 cookie overwriting, card name overwriting, IP address overwriting and flash sector erasing:

- **Hostmot2 Cookie Overwriting Attack:** This denial-of-service attack targets the Hostmot2 cookie located in the Hostmot2 memory space [16]. The cookie value should not be manipulated or overwritten because the protocol uses it for authentication to confirm authorized access. Figure 4 shows that the initial LBP16 protocol command reads the cookie to confirm proper access – `01420001` is the command used to read the cookie and `fecaaa55` denotes the cookie itself. The objective of the Hostmot2 cookie overwriting attack is to corrupt the authentication process that relies on the integrity of the Hostmot2 cookie, undermining CNC machine security.

```
0000  02 80 e1 11 74 0c 68 ed  a4 5d 95 26 08 00 45 00   ····t·h· ·]·&··E·
0010  00 20 c7 18 40 00 40 11  4b 8e 0a 0a 0a 09 0a 0a   · ··@·@· K·······
0020  0a 0a bf 18 6a 2d 00 0c  ad 26 01 42 00 01 00 00   ····j-·· ·&·B····
0030  00 00 00 00 00 00 00 00  00 00 00 00               ········ ····
```

**(a) Initial command requesting the Hostmot2 cookie.**

```
0000  68 ed a4 5d 95 26 02 80  e1 11 74 0c 08 00 45 00   h··]·&·· ··t···E·
0010  00 20 00 01 00 00 ff 11  93 a5 0a 0a 0a 0a 0a 0a   ········ ········
0020  0a 09 6a 2d bf 18 00 0c  05 49 fe ca aa 55 00 00   ··j-···· ·I···U··
0030  00 00 00 00 00 00 00 00  00 00 00 00               ········ ····
```

**(b) Hostmot2 cookie.**

**Fig. 4.** LBP16 protocol request for the Hostmot2 cookie

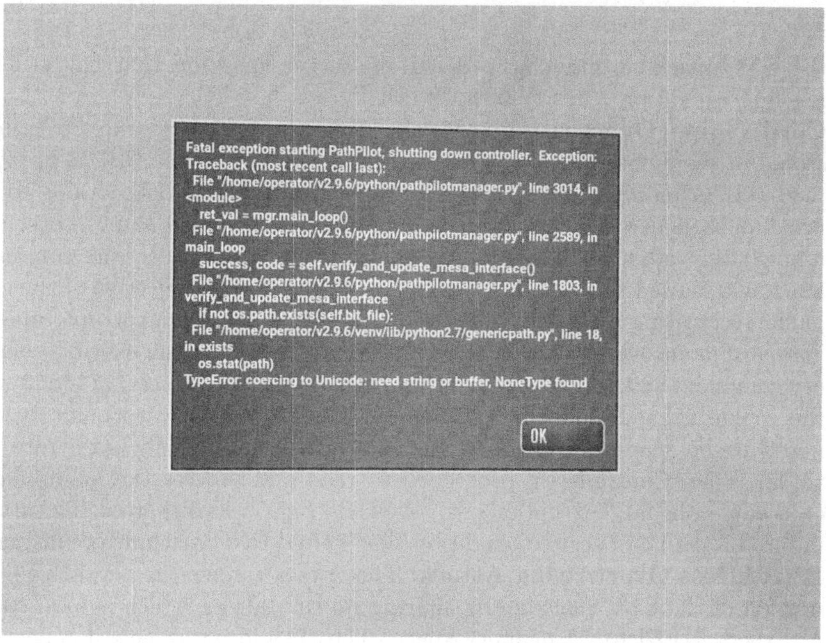


**Fig. 5.** Fatal exception error displayed by the controller

The Hostmot2 cookie overwriting attack was executed by issuing an overwrite memory command `01c20001fecc55aa` in which `fecc55aa` denotes the manipulated cookie value. The memory that holds the cookie is supposed to be read-only memory, but the attack successfully overwrote the cookie.
After Controller Y proceeded to read and process the manipulated cookie value, a fatal exception error shown in Fig. 5 was displayed. The error indicated the controller's inability to correctly interpret the manipulated cookie value. The attack terminated the connection between the controller and

```
0000  02 80 e1 11 74 0c 68 ed  a4 5d 95 26 08 00 45 00   ····t·h· ·]·&··E·
0010  00 20 c7 19 40 00 40 11  4b 8d 0a 0a 0a 09 0a 0a   · ··@·@· K·······
0020  0a 0a bf 18 6a 2d 00 0c  26 0c 88 5d 00 00 00 00   ····j-·· &··]····
0030  00 00 00 00 00 00 00 00  00 00 00 00               ········ ····
```

(a) Command requesting the card name.

```
0000  68 ed a4 5d 95 26 02 80  e1 11 74 0c 08 00 45 00   h··]·&·· ··t···E·
0010  00 2c 00 02 00 00 ff 11  93 98 0a 0a 0a 0a 0a 0a   ·,······ ········
0020  0a 09 6a 2d bf 18 00 18  cd 79 73 74 6d 63 00 00   ··j-···· ·ystmc··
0030  00 00 00 00 00 00 00 00  00 00 00 00               ········ ····
```

(b) Card name.

**Fig. 6.** LBP16 protocol request for the card name

the CNC machine, inducing a denial-of-service condition that halted CNC machine operation.

- **Card Name Overwriting Attack:** This attack targets the card name stored in the device memory. The card name, located in the LBP16 protocol read-only memory space, is crucial for device identification. According to the protocol sequence in Fig. 6, the command to read the card name is executed immediately after the Hostmot2 cookie is read. Specifically, the command `885d0000` is used to read the card name `73746d63`. The objective of the card name overwriting attack is to replace the card name with a corrupt value.
  The card name overwriting attack was executed by issuing an overwrite memory command `88dd0000feccaa55` that replaces the card name `73746d63` with the cookie value `feccaa55`. The memory that holds the card name is supposed to be read-only memory, but the attack successfully overwrote the value. When Controller Y proceeded to read and process the manipulated card name, the fatal exception error shown in Fig. 5 was displayed. The attack induced a denial-of-service condition that halted CNC machine operation.
- **IP Address Overwriting Attack:** This attack targets the network configuration of the CNC machine by altering its IP address, which is hard-coded in Ethernet EEPROM memory space. The IP address is vital for network communications and identity verification.
  The IP address overwriting attack was executed by setting the value of the write-enable register `EEPROMEna` to `5A02` to enable writing or erasing. Importantly, the `EEPROMEna` value and the command to replace the IP address `82c92000(190a0a0a)` must be sent together in a single packet. Accordingly, the packet `01D91A00025A82c92000190a0a0a` is sent to change the IP address from `0a0a0a0a` (hard-coded in memory) to the new IP address `190a0a0a`.
  The IP address overwriting attack disrupted the network connection between Controller Y and the CNC machine, resulting in denial of service. As shown in Fig. 7, Controller Y continually attempts to establish communications with the CNC machine using its IP address, but the efforts are unsuccessful. The attack is feasible because the LBP16 protocol, which supports IP address updates, lacks a robust authentication mechanism.

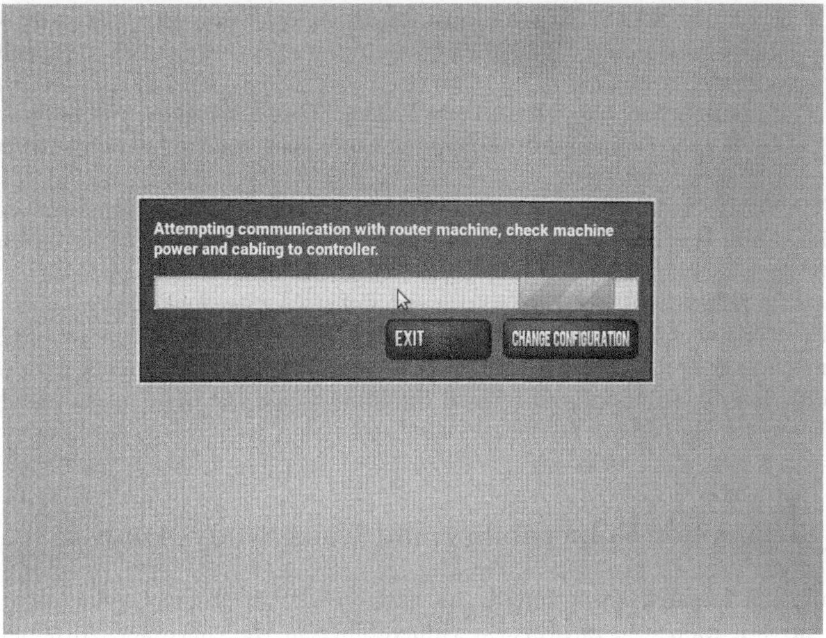


**Fig. 7.** Communications error displayed by the controller

- **Flash Sector Erasing Attack:** This attack targets the FPGA flash memory of the CNC machine, which holds critical data and configurations necessary for normal operation. Due to the absence of authentication mechanisms in the LBP16 protocol, an adversary who gains network access to the CNC machine can issue LBP16 protocol commands to delete specific sectors of the FPGA flash EEPROM memory space.
  Access to the flash EEPROM using the LBP16 protocol is mediated via direct interactions with designated registers [16]. The primary mechanism involves the flash address register `FL_ADDR` and flash data register `FL_DATA`. In order to initiate an operation on the EEPROM, the target address is first written to the `FL_ADDR`. Subsequent read and write operations are executed via `FL_DATA`, facilitating precise control over data manipulation. Additionally, certain operations, especially erasing, require the EEPROM write function to be enabled via the EEPROM write-enable register `EEPROMWEna`.
  The flash sector erasing attack requires four commands to be issued, all of which must be sent in a single packet:
  - **Enable EEPROM Write:** The EEPROM write-enable register is set to allow erasing by issuing the command `01D91A00(035A)` where `5A03` is the enabling code.
  - **Specify Target Flash Address:** The target sector address for the erase operation is specified by issuing the command `01CE0000(00000100)`, which points to `0x00010000` in the EEPROM.

- **Execute Sector Erase Command:** Sector erasure is initiated by issuing the command `01CE0C0000000000` that effectively erases the specified address.
- **Synchronize the Host Post-Erase:** The flash address is re-read by issuing the command `014E0000` to ensure host synchronization and verify the erase operation.

The flash sector erasing attack removed crucial network configuration data, including the IP address, resulting in the corruption of the CNC machine firmware. Following the restart of the CNC machine, Controller Y displayed a communications error on its screen, indicating it could not reconnect to the CNC machine (Fig. 7). The erasure led to a significant disruption of CNC machine operations that rendered standard recovery methods ineffective. The only feasible solution is to re-flash the firmware on the CNC machine circuit board, which is not a trivial process.

# 5 Controller Vulnerability and Case Study Analysis

While the research has primarily focused on LBP16 protocol vulnerabilities, the investigation also identified a vulnerability in the controller. Although it is not directly linked to the LBP16 protocol, the vulnerability underscores the multifaceted nature of security challenges related to CNC machines.

## 5.1 Controller Vulnerability Analysis

The analysis of the controller revealed a significant security risk stemming from unfettered access to the G-code shared folder. Specifically, the vendor-provided access feature expedites the transfer of G-code files directly from a CAD/CAM system to a CNC machine. While this mechanism is intended to enhance operational efficiency, it inadvertently introduces a significant vulnerability due to the absence of a robust authentication mechanism. The vulnerability can be leveraged by an adversary to gain access to a shared G-code folder, resulting in security breaches such as data theft, data corruption, system hijacking and denial of service.

## 5.2 G-code Encryption Case Study

The attack is linked to the controller feature that supports network-based sharing of G-code files. An experiment was conducted to replicate the behavior of an adversary that exploits the vulnerability. The experiment involved two steps:

- **Network Connection Establishment:** A Windows 10 virtual machine was employed to emulate a typical CAM/CAD computer system in a manufacturing environment. The virtual machine was connected to the shared G-code drive on the controller, replicating a realistic network scenario in which G-code files are commonly accessed and modified.

**Algorithm 1:** G-code file encryption.

**Input**: Path to G-code file *file_path*.
**Output**: Encrypted G-code file.

*key* ← Generate secure 16-byte encryption key
*IV* ← Generate 16-byte initialization vector
*file_path* ← Path to the G-code file in the shared folder
*original_data* ← Read binary data from *file_path*
*encrypted_data* ← **Encrypt**(*original_data*, *key*, *IV*)
**open** *file_path* **in write mode**
**write** *IV* **followed by** *encrypted_data* **to** *file_path*
**close** *file*
**output** "Encryption completed for" *file_path*

- **Attack Script Development and Execution:** A Python script was developed to encrypt the G-code file on the shared drive. Algorithm 1 specifies the G-code file encryption script.

Execution of the attack script encrypted the G-code file, rendering it unusable by the CNC machine. The G-code file encryption illustrates the vulnerability of the shared drive to unfettered access and manipulation due to the lack of authentication. The vulnerability could also be leveraged by an adversary to steal G-code files containing proprietary manufacturing information, potentially resulting in a competitive disadvantage and financial loss. Furthermore, the access enables the adversary to inject malicious instructions into a G-code file, leading to a hijacking attack. The adversary could also alter the operation of CNC machinery, potentially leading to the creation of defective parts that could severely impact safety and brand reputation.

The case study demonstrates the impact of the lack of authentication vulnerability, highlighting how effortlessly critical manufacturing data can be compromised. It also draws attention to the need to implement robust security measures to protect shared network resources in CNC systems and safeguard the confidentiality of proprietary information and the integrity of manufacturing processes.

## 6 Disclosure and Mitigation

The security analysis of a CNC machine utilizing the LBP16 communications protocol has identified vulnerabilities that threaten the operational integrity and security of CNC machines and controllers. Recognizing the severity of the vulnerabilities, steps were taken to inform the vendor and engage in a collaborative effort to address the problems. Comprehensive reports were provided that included descriptions of the vulnerabilities, the methodologies used to expose and exploit the vulnerabilities, and the potential risks. Additionally, the following mitigation strategies were devised.

- **LBP16 Protocol Vulnerability Mitigation:** It is imperative to ensure that firmware and software of the CNC machine and other components utilizing the LBP16 protocol are updated with the latest security patches. A rigorous patch management process must be implemented to resolve known vulnerabilities. Additionally, the implementation of strong authentication mechanisms is crucial.
- **Controller Vulnerability Mitigation:** It is important to ensure that controller is secured. Robust software updates and patch management processes must be instituted. Also, strong access controls with strong password policies and multi-factor authentication must be implemented to safeguard CNC machines and associated systems.

## 7 Conclusions

The investigation of the security vulnerabilities of CNC machines using the LBP16 protocol for controller communications has yielded significant insights into the potential risks to subtractive manufacturing systems. These advanced machines, which are efficient and indispensable to high-volume production, are prone to cyber-physical attacks that include sabotage and denial of service. It is vital to integrate robust cyber security measures in CNC systems. The integration of cyber security measures is not just a technical requirement, but a fundamental aspect that should be instituted in the manufacturing industry's culture.

The views expressed in this chapter do not necessarily represent the views of the U.S. Department of Energy or the United States Government.

**Acknowledgement.** This research was supported by the U.S. Department of Energy Office of Energy Efficiency and Renewable Energy under the Advanced Materials and Manufacturing Technologies Office (AMMTO) Award no. DE EE0009046.

## References

1. Ahsan, M., Rais, M., Ahmed, I.: SOK: side channel monitoring for additive manufacturing – bridging the cybersecurity and quality assurance communities. In: Proceedings of the Eighth IEEE European Symposium on Security and Privacy, pp. 1160–1178 (2023)
2. Ayub, A., Yoo, H., Ahmed, I.: Empirical study of PLC authentication protocols in industrial control systems. In: Proceedings of the IEEE Security and Privacy Workshops, pp. 383–397 (2021)
3. Balduzzi, M., Sortino, F., Castello, F., Pierguidi, L.: A security analysis of CNC machines in Industry 4.0. In: Gruss, D., Maggi, F., Fischer, M., Carminati, M. (eds.) Detection of Intrusions and Malware, and Vulnerability Assessment, pp. 132–152. Springer, Cham (2023). https://doi.org/10.1007/978-3-031-35504-2_7

4. Bi, E.: Detection and intrusion of attacks in cyber-physical security for additive manufacturing, Ph.D. Dissertation, Department of Industrial and Systems Engineering, Auburn University, Alabama (2023)
5. Cardenas, A., Amin, S., Sinopoli, B., Giani, A., Perrig, A., Sastry, S.: Challenges for securing cyber physical systems. In: Presented at the Workshop on Future Directions in Cyber-Physical Systems Security (2009)
6. Chen, T., Abu-Nimeh, S.: Lessons from Stuxnet. IEEE Comput. **44**(4), 91–93 (2011)
7. Chen, X., Wang, Z., Yang, S.: Research on information security protection of industrial-internet-oriented CNC system. In: Proceedings of the Sixth IEEE Information Technology and Mechatronics Engineering Conference, pp. 1818–1822 (2022)
8. Chhetri, S.: Novel side-channel attack model for cyber-physical additive manufacturing systems, M.S. Thesis, Department of Electrical and Computer Engineering, University of California, Irvine, Irvine, California (2016)
9. Cultice, T., Thapliyal, H.: Vulnerabilities and attacks on CAN-based 3D printing/additive manufacturing. IEEE Consum. Electron. Mag. **23**(1), 54–61 (2023)
10. DeSmit, Z., Elhabashy, A., Wells, L., Camelio, J.: Cyber-physical vulnerability assessment in manufacturing systems. Procedia Manuf. **5**, 1060–1074 (2016)
11. Elhabashy, A., Wells, L., Camelio, J., William, H.: A cyber-physical attack taxonomy for production systems: a quality control perspective. J. Intell. Manuf. **30**, 2489–2504 (2019)
12. Falliere, N., Murchu, L., Chien, E.: W32.Stuxnet Dossier, Version 1.4, Symantec, Mountain View, California (2011)
13. Fidler, D.: Was Stuxnet an act of war? Decoding a cyberattack. IEEE Secur. Priv. **9**(4), 56–59 (2011)
14. Graves, L., King, W., Carrion, P., Shao, S., Shamsaei, N., Yampolskiy, M.: Sabotaging metal additive manufacturing: powder delivery system manipulation and material-dependent effects. Add. Manuf. **46**, 102029 (2021)
15. Li, Z., et al.: Detecting cyber-attacks against cyber-physical manufacturing system: a machining process invariant approach. IEEE Internet Things J. **11**(10), 17602–17614 (2024)
16. Mesa Electronics, 7I94 Ethernet Anything I/O Manual, Version 1.0, El Sobrante, California (2024). www.mesanet.com/pdf/parallel/7i94tman.pdf
17. Prasad, R., Moon, Y.: Architecture for preventing and detecting cyber attacks in a cyber-manufacturing system. IFAC-PapersOnLine **55**(10), 2246–2251 (2022)
18. Rais, M., Ahsan, M., Ahmed, I.: FRoMEPP: digital forensic readiness framework for a material-extrusion-based 3D printing process. Forensic Sci. Int. Digit. Invest. **44**, 301510 (2023)
19. Rais, M.H., Ahsan, M., Sharma, V., Barua, R., Prins, R., Ahmed, I.: Low-magnitude infill structure manipulation attacks on fused filament fabrication 3D printers. In: Staggs, J., Shenoi, S. (eds.) Critical Infrastructure Protection XVI: 16th IFIP WG 11.10 International Conference, ICCIP 2022, Virtual Event, March 14–15, 2022, Revised Selected Papers, pp. 205–232. Springer, Cham (2022). https://doi.org/10.1007/978-3-031-20137-0_8
20. Tu, S., Liu, G., Lin, Q., Lin, L., Sun, Z.: Security framework based on trusted computing for industrial control systems of CNC machines. Int. J. Perform. Eng. **13**(8) (2017)
21. Wu, M., Song, Z., Moon, Y.: Detecting cyber-physical attacks in cyber manufacturing systems with machine learning methods. J. Intell. Manuf. **30**, 1111–1123 (2019)

22. Yampolskiy, M., et al.: Security of additive manufacturing: attack taxonomy and survey. Addit. Manuf. **21**, 431–457 (2018)
23. Yampolskiy, M., Schutzle, L., Vaidya, U., Yasinsac, A.: Security challenges of additive manufacturing with metals and alloys. In: Rice, M., Shenoi, S. (eds.) ICCIP 2015. IAICT, vol. 466, pp. 169–183. Springer, Cham (2015). https://doi.org/10.1007/978-3-319-26567-4_11
24. Zetter, K.: Blockbuster worm aimed for infrastructure, but no proof Iran nukes were target. Wired, 23 September 2010
25. Zubair, N., Ayub, A., Yoo, H., Ahmed, I.: Control logic obfuscation attack in industrial control systems. In: Proceedings of the IEEE International Conference on Cyber Security and Resilience, pp. 227–232 (2022)

# An End-to-End Framework for Verifying and Validating Manufacturing Design Integrity

Matthew Jablonski[1], Kyle Everett[2], Gabriela Ciocarlie[2(✉)], Zoran Duric[1], Chris Hathhorn[3], Jeffrey Kimmell[4], Vladimir Orlyanchik[4], John Prevost[2], Gordon Robertson[4], Curtis Taylor[4], Duminda Wijesekera[1], and Kyle Saleeby[5]

[1] George Mason University, Fairfax, VA, USA
[2] University of Texas at San Antonio, San Antonio, TX, USA
gabriela.ciocarlie@utsa.edu
[3] Two Six Technologies, Arlington, VA, USA
[4] Oak Ridge National Laboratory, Oak Ridge, TN, USA
[5] Georgia Institute of Technology, Atlanta, GA, USA

**Abstract.** Cyber attacks on networked automated manufacturing systems can severely impact part quality. In fact, malicious modifications may be introduced at any point during the manufacturing lifecycle. Therefore, it is vital to verify and validate that manufactured parts conform to their designs.

This chapter describes a formal, end-to-end framework that verifies and validates the design integrity of manufactured parts by considering all potential points of alteration during precision manufacturing processes. The framework prevents unauthorized changes to computer-aided designs, verifies the correctness of translations from CAD models to G-code, maintains the integrity of G-code transferred to manufacturing machines, verifies the runtime execution of G-code and part geometry, and considers the contexts of manufacturing machine operations and how manufactured parts could be altered.

**Keywords:** Additive Manufacturing · Subtractive Manufacturing · Design Integrity · G-Code Verification

## 1 Introduction

Precision manufacturing processes contribute to items that are vital to global supply chains. Manufacturing systems with the ability to add (deposit) and subtract (machine) materials create end-use products as well as molds, dies and auxiliary equipment used in manufacturing lines. These manufacturing systems almost exclusively rely on G-code, a text-based information encoding protocol developed in the 1960s.

Like many purpose-built systems, additive and subtractive manufacturing systems often outlast the lifecycles of the software on which their digital security


Published by Springer Nature Switzerland AG 2025
J. Staggs and S. Shenoi (Eds.): ICCIP 2024, IFIP AICT 725, pp. 85–109, 2025.
https://doi.org/10.1007/978-3-031-81888-2_5

is predicated and employ outdated communications protocols to support backward compatibility. While the systems have robust physical construction, they often have ineffective security measures and their designs and parts are vulnerable due to the lack of verification and validation. As a result, there are no guarantees that the final products conform to the intended input files or designs due to unintended design alterations and/or wasted time and material.

This chapter describes a novel end-to-end formal verification framework for maintaining the design integrity of additive and subtractive manufacturing systems. The framework considers all potential points of alteration of manufacturing designs, including the creation of base STEP files, transformation to STL files, communications and runtime execution of G-code. It takes into account the cyber and physical aspects of manufacturing processes from files, compilers and networks to the differential logic formalisms of the cyber-physical systems.

## 2 Background

This section discusses cyber-physical manufacturing, the manufacturing information flow and attack considerations.

### 2.1 Cyber-Physical Manufacturing

Discrete manufacturing operations rely on integrated digital and physical processes executed on disparate platforms, resulting in a network of cyber-physical systems. Rarely are these systems of the same brand or age – production lines are continuously-changing compilations of machines from multiple original equipment manufacturers. The complex nature of modern production lines makes it difficult to protect the physical and digital integrity of manufactured parts as they transit from system to system during manufacturing processes.

A solution that securely manages manufacturing information must be capable of accepting and distributing information to diverse systems. While commercial additive manufacturing systems rely on modern hardware and software that incorporate security mechanisms such as encryption and virtual private networks, legacy manufacturing equipment such as computer numerical control (CNC) machines often do not support modern security mechanisms. Furthermore, the legacy machines have known vulnerabilities that persist due to the lack of updates.

In contrast, mainstream additive manufacturing systems developed over the last decade have been designed with information security in mind. For example, it is common to update the firmware of additive manufacturing systems to enable new deposition strategies. Instructions for software updates and firmware patches for many commercial additive systems are readily available online. The situation is very different for commercial machining systems for which software updates are discouraged, requiring site visits by skilled technicians. Newer additive manufacturing systems, unlike traditional manufacturing equipment, can support modern information transfer methodologies. However, legacy information transfer practices are still heavily used in the newer systems.

One of the most notable outdated practices is the reliance on G-code for machine instructions. G-code is an archaic text-based language that was developed in the 1960s [24]. G-code defines machine actions, providing information about positions, rates of travel and processing parameters. Initially developed for CNC machining operations, G-code has been widely adopted by the additive manufacturing community [19]. Unfortunately, at this time, CNC machining systems as well as additive manufacturing systems provide little if any security, and no verification or validation mechanisms for the acceptance and execution of G-code programs.

## 2.2 Manufacturing Information Flow

A manufacturing workflow relies on multiple computational systems and physical machines as a part passes through the stages of design, production and quality control. The process for creating an additively-manufactured part begins with the digital design of a physical object. Computer-aided design (CAD) platforms such as SolidWorks [10], Autodesk Fusion 360 [2] and Siemens NX [46] are used to model relevant geometric shapes through parametric or feature-based definitions. The model is typically exported in a common file format such as STL, which is transferred to a computer-aided manufacturing (CAM) software package that slices the model into discrete layers and generates the appropriate toolpath for a manufacturing system. A custom post-processor converts the toolpath and selected process parameters into G-code. At this stage, the G-code file inherently contains information such as solid model slicing, toolpath strategy and process parameters that are specific to the production machine. While some commonalities exist between systems of the same category, the exact processing parameters and toolpath strategy are tuned to the specific build system that realizes the digital geometry.

After a toolpath and the relevant process parameters have been generated, the G-code file is transferred from the CAD/CAM system to the production machine. Email, USB flash drives or networked storage may be employed for transferring production information. Often, the infrastructure is not standardized or has little or no access control.

## 2.3 Attack Considerations

Figure 1 summarizes the information flow in commercial additive and CNC machining systems. An attacker can alter the integrity of a part at different stages, starting with the CAD design and ending with the run-time environment of the manufacturing machine. The dependent hardware, software and networking components for each stage are targeted by various attack vectors and exploited to achieve the attack objectives. Specific to manufacturing, the attack objectives include intellectual property theft, sabotage and illegal part manufacturing.

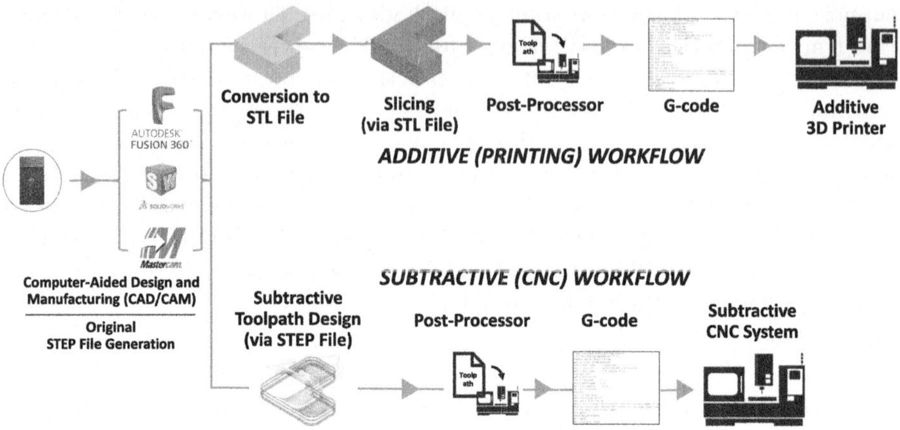


**Fig. 1.** Information flow in commercial additive and CNC machining systems

This work focuses on detecting and mitigating sabotage perpetrated by manipulating design and G-code files during the manufacturing lifecycle. Sabotage through design manipulation can have several intended effects. G-code instruction modification may alter the form, fit and/or function of manufactured parts, maliciously control and/or disrupt various mechanical and/or cyber aspects of manufacturing equipment, disrupt manufacturing process environments (e.g., driving the spindle uncontrollably) and make manufactured parts unsafe during production [50].

Belikovetsky et al. [4] demonstrated the sabotage of an additive manufacturing workflow. In order to weaken the 3D-printed propellers of a quadcopter unmanned aerial vehicle (UAV), Belikovetsky and colleagues inserted defects in the propeller designs. A social engineering attack involving phishing was employed to gain code execution privileges on a designer workstation running CAD software used to design propellers. Next, they manipulated local STL files on the workstation so that the inserted defects propagated into the G-code file specifying the toolpath. The sabotage attack weakened the propeller sufficiently to cause it to break during flight, causing the quadcopter to crash. The security controls applied by the proposed G-code verification framework, specifically through CAD design watermarking and integrity checking, can prevent such sabotage attacks.

## 3 G-Code-Verify Framework

Figure 2 shows the G-code-Verify framework that addresses threats over the design lifecycle by verifying and validating that the design integrity of manufactured parts is preserved at multiple cyber and physical levels:

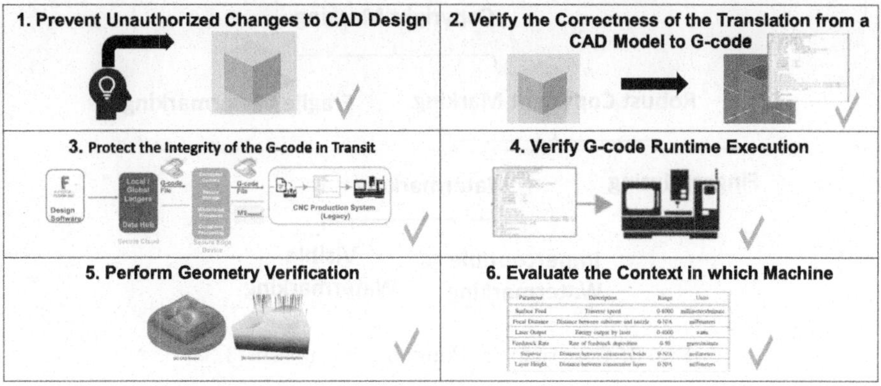


**Fig. 2.** G-code-Verify framework

- **CAD Design Watermarking and Integrity:** G-code-Verify provides the ability to prevent unauthorized changes to a CAD design using cryptographic watermarking techniques while also tracking the provenance of changes made by authorized designers in a collaborative environment.
- **CAD-to-G-Code Translation Integrity:** G-code-Verify verifies the correctness of the translation of a CAD model to G-code for a particular program, relying on a G-code simulator and a certifying G-code synthesizer. This prevents attacks that target the translation process and introduce flaws in G-code.
- **G-Code In-Transit Integrity:** G-code-Verify secures the transfer of generated G-code to a manufacturing machine using a secure file monitoring and management device that receives signed G-code from the CAD design system and writes it to secure storage as the entity with write rights. The G-code residing in secure storage is accessed in a read-only mode by the controller embedded in the manufacturing device.
- **Runtime Verification:** G-code-Verify assesses the integrity of G-code running on a manufacturing machine using a runtime verification mechanism that extracts the current running and the next block of G-code, and sends them to a file monitoring and management device that verifies them against the G-code stored in secure storage.
- **Geometry Verification:** G-code-Verify offers a physics perspective that performs path-correctness verification using kinematic and dynamic methods.
- **Context Impact:** G-code-Verify acknowledges the fact that small perturbations can impact the end result of a manufacturing process even if G-code integrity is preserved.

G-code-Verify focuses on maintaining the integrity of a part design from CAD to production. Other attacks such as tampering with material stock and intellectual property theft are outside the scope of the G-code-Verify framework.

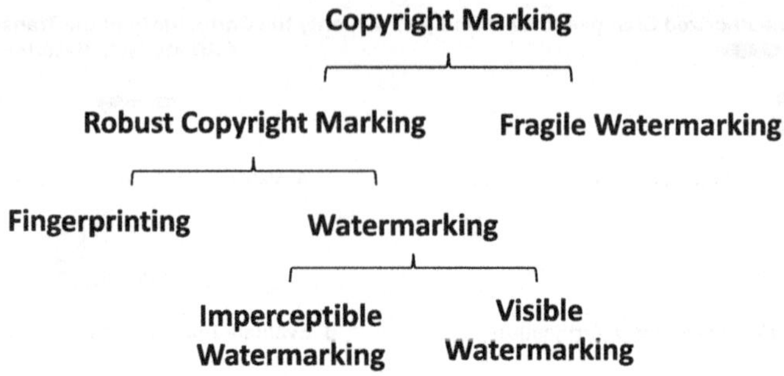


**Fig. 3.** Copyright marking and its subsets [3,38]

### 3.1 CAD Design Watermarking and Integrity

Digital watermarking is a subset of copyright marking [3,38] (Fig. 3). Fragile watermarking techniques are used to detect unauthorized changes to watermarked objects based on changes to their watermarks. A watermark is typically created from the perceptually significant parts of an object and embedded in the parts that are perceptually insignificant. Since it is assumed that the watermark creation and embedding methods are known, asymmetric cryptography is used to create and/or embed a watermark.

Robust watermarking makes changes to the objects such that removing the watermark would damage the protected object. Watermarks may be visible or invisible. Harte and Bors [17] have proposed an approach for watermarking 3D models that modifies the locations of some 3D vertices to embed bits of information. Lee and Kwon [28] have developed an approach for watermarking CAD drawings. The approach groups geometric objects into 3D faces, polylines and arcs. A watermark is embedded by modifying surface areas, angles along polylines and lengths of arcs.

In the case of the G-code-Verify framework, it is necessary to ensure that no unauthorized changes have been made to the original designs. A secondary goal is to incorporate provenance tracking for collaborative designs. The STEP file format [21,31] is considered because it is the dominant CAD design format. A STEP file is a large text file with a header and data part. The header contains metadata, including the file name, creation date and author/owner information. The data part is a sequence of numbered objects, i.e., list of elements $\#n = name(list)$; where $\#n$ is the command number, *name* is its name and *list* is the list of fields. Compound objects such as complex spline curves and spline surfaces have the form $\#n = (objects)$;.

Numbered objects are geometric objects or special instructions that describe objects and manufacturing processes. Geometric objects can be simple (derived from simple objects by extension) or compound. Simple objects include Cartesian point (*CARTESIAN_POINT*) and unit vector (*DIRECTION*) that are expressed using three floating point numbers. Derived objects include *VERTEX_POINT*, an instantiation of a Cartesian point; vector (*VECTOR*) comprising a direction and magnitude value; and 3D coordinate system *AXIS2_PLA-CEMENT_3D* comprising a Cartesian point and two orthogonal directions; plane (*PLANE*) specified by a 3D coordinate system; simple surface such as a circle (*CIRCLE*) comprising a 3D coordinate system and radius, and other simple surfaces such as *SPHERICAL_SURFACE*, *TOROIDAL_SURFACE*, *CONICAL_SURFACE* and *CYLINDRICAL_SURFACE*. Compound objects, such as spline surfaces and spline curves, may have multiple fields that describe them.

The process for watermarking a STEP file begins by creating the digital signature of the file. This involves generating a cryptographic hash $h_0$ of the file, (e.g., SHA-256), and signing the hash with an asymmetric private key $priv_D$ belonging to the CAD designer $D$ to create the signature $sig_0$. The digital signature is 32 bytes long and is saved as a 64-digit hexadecimal number. A simple method is to save the signature as a field in the *FILE_DESCRIPTION* segment of metadata, such as a line /* *sig* */ ($sig_0$). Information pertaining to the designer's identity $D$ may be stored in a similar manner.

When the watermarked file is opened, the authentication procedure is performed in reverse. The line with the digital signature /* *sig* */ ($sig_0$) is removed from the file, the hash of the file $h_1$ is recomputed, and the CAD software compares the recomputed hash value with the results of decrypting $sig_0$ using the original CAD designer's public key from the trusted certificate $pub_D$ to produce $h_0$. If $h_0$ and $h_1$ are identical, then the file has not been tampered with and the designer's identity provides authenticity.

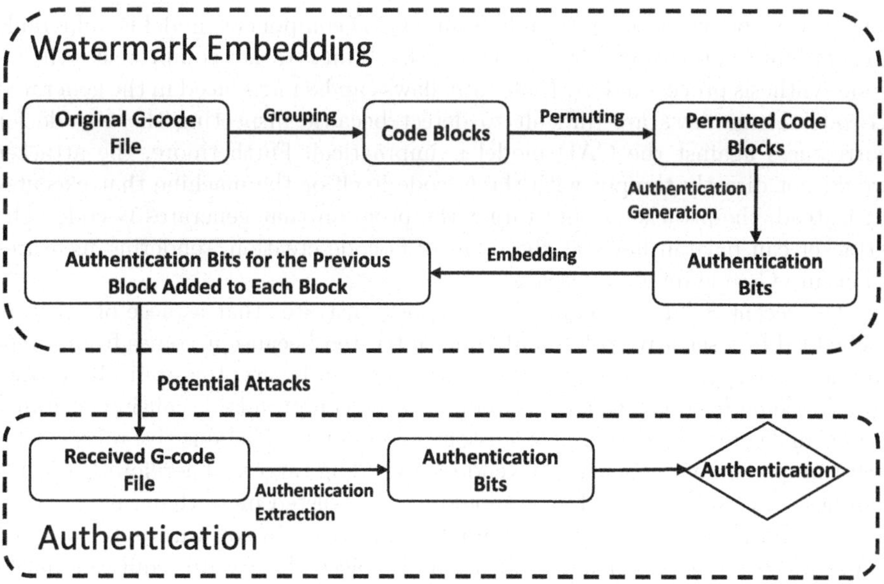


**Fig. 4.** Fragile watermarking [30]

Alternatively, a more complex method that mimics fragile watermarking of images may be employed [30]. Figure 4 provides a graphical representation of the fragile watermarking process. First, the `G0` and `G1` commands of G-code that control linear movements are grouped into smaller code chunks, each comprising several lines of G-code. A permutation function with a random seed $P_s$ is used to permute and rearrange the code chunks. Then, the six most- and least-significant bits of the $x$ and $y$ coordinates in the first line of each code chunk are input to a Fowler-Noll-Vo hash function to generate authentication bits. The authentication bits are embedded into a chunk and the previous chunk is verified. $P_s$ can then be used to rearrange the G-code file and the authentication bits. Additionally, the method generates recovery bits that can be used to restore lines of code that have been tampered with.

The fragile watermarking method has two advantages. First, tampering with any of the significant digits in a single movement line of G-code is detected. Second, the method protects intellectual property in the G-code file from man-in-the-middle attacks; this is because the intercepted file would be convoluted and unusable. Key limitations with the method are that it only processes `G0` and `G1` commands and only validates the $x$ and $y$ coordinates. A simple extension that includes other commands such as arc movement, spline movement and changing axis would address the first limitation. The second limitation can be eliminated by validating the additional axes used by the manufacturing machine.

### 3.2 CAD-to-G-Code Translation Integrity

The process of synthesizing G-code from a CAD component model is vulnerable to subtle but potentially devastating attacks. If an attacker compromises the G-code synthesis process in CAM software, flaws can be introduced in the generated G-code. These flaws are difficult to detect because inspecting the G-code for correctness against the CAD model is impractical. Furthermore, the attacker would not directly tamper with the G-code itself or the machine that executes it; instead, the attacker would target the program that generates G-code. The attacker can bake in flaws at the point of G-code creation, rendering measures to ensure G-code integrity useless.

The recent Solar Winds incident [37] demonstrates that a piece of software embedded in a sensitive role should not be trusted because it comes from a reputable vendor, even if it is digitally signed and can be cryptographically proven to have come from the vendor. Vendors can be compromised, causing digitally-signed malware to be deployed on customer computers. The sensitive roles vendor software play may, in fact, make vendors appealing targets. Therefore, a G-code synthesizer could be used, but it should not be trusted more than necessary.

The most thorough way to eliminate blind trust in software is to formally verify its correctness. Formal verification of a piece of software requires a mathematical proof that the software implements its specification completely and nothing more. An example is CompCert [29] that is used to verify compilers.

In the case of a G-code program, the 3D object model is the specification. Therefore, formally verifying a G-code synthesizer would require proving that every G-code program it generates must implement its 3D object model specification. The difficulty of the task is compounded by the variations in G-code semantics between different machines and even between different configurations of a single machine. The formalization of the proposition to be proved, specifically, what it means for a G-code program to implement its CAD model, is the subject of ongoing research (see, e.g., recent work on spatiotemporal logics [9,41]).

Full formal verification of the G-code synthesizer would provide the most confidence about its correctness, but the task is intractable. Therefore, a lightweight approach leveraging G-code simulators and a certifying G-code synthesizer may be employed.

G-code simulators are widely used in industry [1,8,13]. If the simulator is independent from the G-code synthesizer, its results can increase the confidence in the G-code produced by the synthesizer. However, subtle internal defects introduced by a compromised G-code synthesizer may not be obvious by merely simulating G-code. A sophisticated attacker that uses a compromised G-code synthesizer to inject flaws is likely to hide them in the internal structure of a manufactured part. Therefore, it is necessary to use a G-code analyzer intended specifically for detecting intentionally-hidden defects.

Analyzing G-code for defects is challenging because its meaning depends on the target machine. The G-code synthesizer must produce instructions, for example, to regulate the speed and temperature of the material being extruded based on the physical properties of the material as well as a model of how the target machine interprets each instruction. The analyzer should be as simple and as machine-independent as possible to provide confidence in its correctness.

The approach for creating such an analyzer is inspired by the idea of a certifying compiler [32,33]. Instead of verifying the correctness of a compiler for all possible high-level program inputs, it is easier to verify the correctness of the translation of a particular program [34,40]. Furthermore, the compiler should have justifications for the transformations it performs when producing low-level assembly code, evidence of which could be produced along with the assembly code. A compiler paired with a verifier for checking the evidence is called a certifying compiler.

G-code-Verify engages a G-code synthesizer that presents its work to be checked by a less-sophisticated and target-machine-independent program (Fig. 5). Instead of checking the correctness of the synthesizer, it is necessary only to check the justifications it presents for consistency. Several synthesizers include metadata in the comments of G-code programs they produce. Examples include embedded thumbnails, program settings for generating G-code and pointers for delineating layer transitions and part perimeters. Similar annotations are leveraged in this work to render G-code analysis more tractable.

As an example, consider slicer software for a fused deposition modeling (FDM) 3D printer. Slicer software synthesizes G-code for 3D printers by dividing an object model into flat layers, typically stacked on the $z$-axis. The slicer then generates G-code for printing each layer sequentially, with the printer transition-

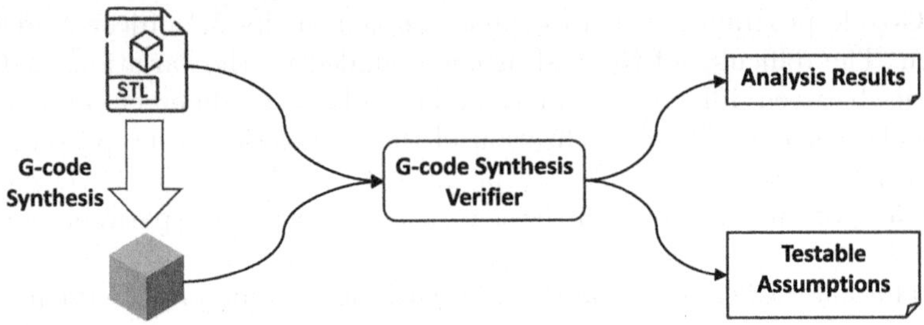


**Fig. 5.** G-code translation integrity checking

ing to the next layer by raising the print head. An attacker could introduce subtle internal structural defects into parts by changing the $z$-axis mass distribution. The printed part would still have the same dimensions, exterior geometry, mass and volume, but because new internal voids are introduced, sections of the part could be weakened and fail prematurely.

G-code-Verify prevents this class of defects with a slicer that certifies the correctness of the $x$-axis mass distribution. During synthesis, the slicer produces annotations that justify the expected $z$-axis mass distribution in the G-code. Annotations include a preamble with the layer height, filament density and infill density. Each layer transition is identified as well as sections in the layer that result in mass deposition corresponding to a part. Not all the instructions that extrude filament would correspond to a part in the CAD object model, because there may be extra scaffolding or supports included in the G-code program.

Consider the following G-code excerpt that prints a triangle on a layer near the top of a tetrahedron:

```
; LAYER_CHANGE
G1 E-2.00000 F3000.000
G1 Z1.150 F9000.000
G1 Z1.200
G1 X89.395 Y89.256
G1 E2.00000 F2400.000
M204 S80
G1 F900
; BEGIN_PART 1 4.584E-4
G1 X90.605 Y89.256 E0.04784
G1 X90.000 Y90.466 E0.05349
G1 X89.422 Y89.310 E0.05112
; END_PART
M204 S1250
G1 X89.195 Y89.602 F9000.000
```

The annotation in line 1 denotes the beginning of a new layer. The `G1` instructions in lines 10–12, which describe a short triangular toolpath, account for all the mass deposited on the layer. `BEGIN_PART` and `END_PART` delineate the G-code extruding filament for a part with id `1` and a computed mass of 4.584E-4g for the section. The computed mass should correspond to $d \times (0.4784 + 0.05349 + 0.5112)$, where $d$ is the filament density in g/mm of filament and the numbers correspond to mm of filament extruded in lines 10–12.

The annotations describe the slicer model that specifies how the machine and filament respond to each G-code instruction. Thus, verifying the $z$-axis mass distribution reduces to two problems. The first is to verify that the slicer has applied its machine model consistently while generating G-code. The second is to verify that the machine model is correct for the particular target machine.

The first problem is to check that the annotations are consistent with themselves and the 3D object model. The verifier must independently compute the expected mass of the object, number of layers and expected mass of each layer and each section within the layer. The verifier then checks the annotations and G-code for consistency with these results.

Because the details of how G-code is interpreted is highly dependent on the target machine and its configuration, the second problem – verifying that the assumptions made by the slicer about the target machine are correct – is difficult if the verifier has no special knowledge about the target machine. Instead of directly checking that the machine model described by the annotations accurately models the target machine, the verifier has two options. It could produce a concise report of the inferred machine model for a human user to check. Alternatively, it could produce test G-code based on the inferred model that is executed by the target machine. The test G-code should produce a simple object for easy inspection, intended only to test the rate of filament mass deposition by the G-code instructions reported by the slicer. If the object produced by the test G-code is consistent with the model inferred from the slicer, then the $z$-axis mass distribution of the original G-code should be correct. Verifying the $z$-axis mass distribution would only catch one class of possible defects that an attacker could introduce. However, the same techniques can be extended to catch other classes of possible defects.

### 3.3 G-Code In-Transit Integrity

After a toolpath and relevant process parameters have been generated, they are transferred from a CAD/CAM designer system to a manufacturing machine. As shown in Fig. 6, the transfer is often done via email, USB flash drive or networked storage locations. However, it is often the case that access control mechanisms are not employed.

Figure 7 shows the G-code-Verify architecture for transferring G-code to production machines. It uses a secure networked storage mechanism and an integrity service that verifies the public key infrastructure (PKI) digital signature of the G-code file and ensures the read-only guarantee to the secure networked storage

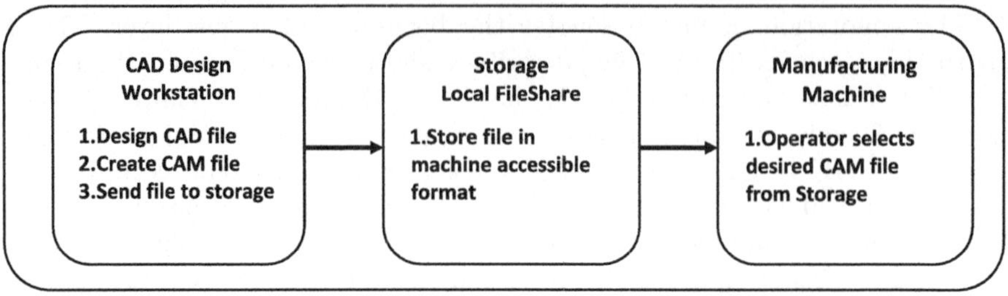


**Fig. 6.** Legacy architecture for transferring G-code to production machines

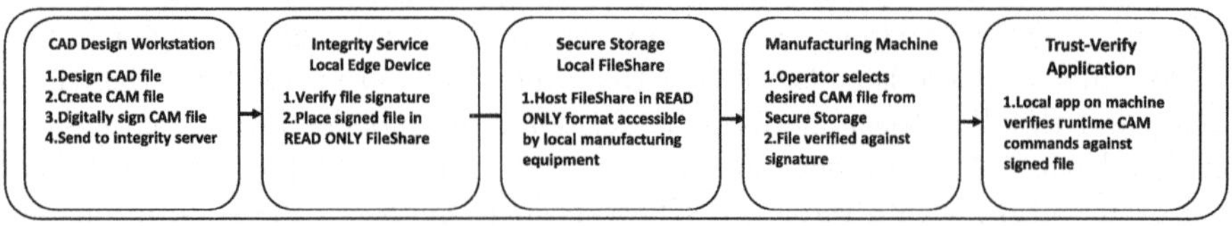


**Fig. 7.** G-code-Verify architecture for transferring G-code to production machines

for the production machine. The signature of the G-code file is also verified along with the runtime commands on the manufacturing machine.

G-code-Verify expands on the networked storage approach and provides guarantees that the integrity of the G-code is preserved in transit. As shown in Fig. 7, two separate network segments must be secured to provide confidence that the G-code file created by a CAD designer is indeed the file used on the targeted manufacturing device. The first segment to consider is the connection from the CAD designer's development workstation to the network storage area designated by the manufacturer as the site for storing G-code files. The second network segment is the pathway from the storage area to the local manufacturing machine.

G-code-Verify uses a file monitoring and management device (also referred to as an "integrity service") that provides an access interface for a CAD designer to securely access a digitally-signed G-code file from the CAD designer's system and place it in a secure storage area that can be accessed by the manufacturing machine in a read-only manner. The G-code file is verified against the signature file after which it is placed in the secure storage area.

To securely access the verified G-code file, the network interface of the manufacturing device uses mutual TLS (mTLS) to establish a secure network channel between the device and secure storage area (item 3 in Fig. 2). All external access to files in the secure storage area is restricted to read access by authorized accounts. The verified G-code file can then be transferred via the secure mTLS network channel to the manufacturing device. By restricting the connectivity of the manufacturing device to secure storage, encrypting the network channel and requiring an authenticated account with only read access to the G-code file, it is ensured that the correct G-code file is delivered to the manufacturing device and that the file has not been altered during transit. Having delivered the G-code file to the manufacturing machine, the next step is to ensure that no process on the machine can inject unverified instructions at runtime.

### 3.4 Runtime Verification

Figure 8 shows the G-code-Verify runtime verification mechanism that validates G-code executed on a manufacturing machine. Each segment of G-code executed on the manufacturing machine is accessed via an application programming interface (API) located on the local manufacturing machine. The API is used to poll the current running block of G-code and the next block. The API then sends the current and next block of G-code to the file monitoring and management device that compares the current and next executed blocks of G-code with the verified signed file located in secure storage. Any deviations observed during the verification process are passed as alerts to the CAD designer or end user.

The runtime verification method is superior to other machine operation monitoring protocols such as MTConnect and OPC-UA due to its direct verification on the controller. This is because machine monitoring data is transferred at a higher frequency whereas monitoring protocols operate at a lower frequency, resulting in unreported G-code blocks. However, if the machine has been compromised and a segment of malicious G-code were to be sent to the monitoring service, the attacker would also have to compromise the signed G-code file because the service also monitors the integrity of the signed file. This method is designed to minimize the attack surface and not to perform mitigation actions on an already-compromised machine.

### 3.5 Geometry Verification

G-code is translated to sequences of machine executable instructions. An example sequence is `M03`: spindle start forward clockwise, `M05`: spindle stop, `M08`: coolant on, `M78`: tailstock advancing and `M79`: tailstock reversing [22], which causes the toolhead to traverse in a specified geometric shape. The toolhead traversals manufacture the part – carving the part in the case of subtractive manufacturing or building it in the case of additive manufacturing. The geometric shapes that are traversed have to be within an acceptable degree of accuracy. Therefore, the verification should ensure that the specified and created curves are within acceptable deviations. This requires the traversal path of the toolhead to be validated slice by slice against an ideal curve created from the ideal geometry specified in the G-code.

Such geometric verification requires a metric for the distance between two shapes that captures the direction and speed of traversal on curves and surfaces. The correctness of the toolpath traversal can be verified at the kinematic level, which considers only the properties of paths, or at the dynamic level, which is based on equations of motion of toolheads. Previous work has proposed the digitization of a system workspace into three-dimensional volumes called "voxels" [26].

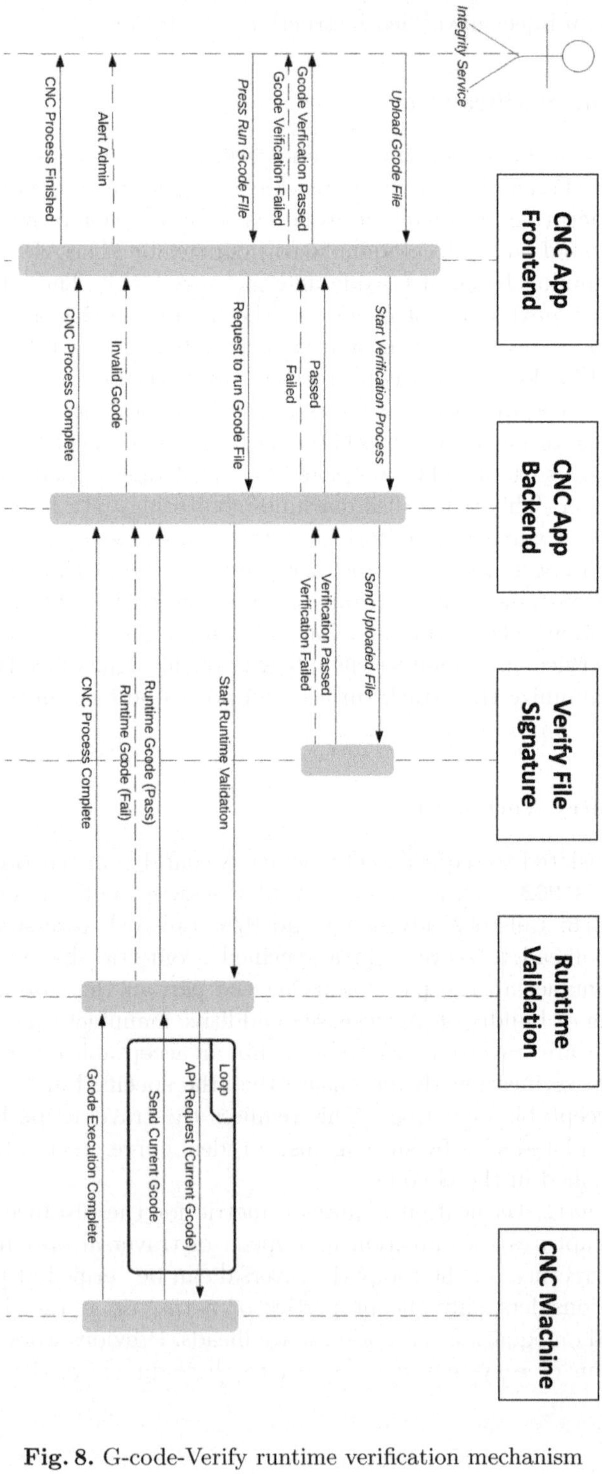


**Fig. 8.** G-code-Verify runtime verification mechanism

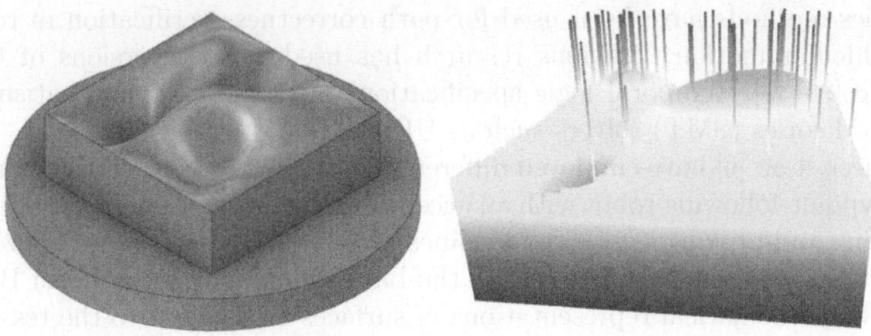

**Fig. 9.** Voxel model (right) created from a CAD model (left)

Figure 9 shows a voxel model created from a CAD model with a 5 mm discretized machine workspace for additive and subtractive manufacturing operations. Given an existing machine monitoring architecture, the voxels are sequentially turned on and off to correspond with additive or subtractive processes [35,44]. However, the geometric verification resolution of 5 mm greatly exceeds the dimensional tolerance of 0.127 mm that is commonly encountered in CNC machining. This renders the technology unsuitable for security applications.

Computing the deviations between the designed and executed paths based on the design and observed curves requires a metric to measure deviations and an algorithm that computes the deviations. While path correctness has been well-addressed in robotics and vehicular motion with respect to kinematics and dynamics, few sources exist for geometric verification for cyber security applications. Most studies on additive manufacturing focus on verifying individual segments of STL files or transmitted G-code. The research literature largely ignores the base STEP files that are required to produce G-code for subtractive manufacturing.

This work engages three well-known distance measures between curves, Hausdorff distance, Frachet distance and Procrustes analysis [18]. The Hausdorff distance [48] is the longest distance to any point on one curve and any other point on another curve. Hence, the Hausdorff distance is not directional, but it is easy to compute. The Frechet distance [45] measures the distance between two curves based on a path that has a specific upper bound of variation between them. The Frechet distance can be visualized as the distance between a dog walker and a dog on a leash as the two move. The Frechet distance is directional like a toolpath and has a known upper bound based on the mechanical limitations of the toolhead. Procrustes analysis [23] measures the shape deformation required to transform one curve to fit to another curve.

The second aspect is the formalization of the manufacturing machine paths and to create a verification and validation system to reason about the correct behavior of machines [41] in following the designed paths. Kinematics and dynamics methods have been used for path correctness verification in robotics and vehicular motion. Previous research has used various versions of temporal logic [25,39]. Temporal logic specifications are translated into satisfiability modulo theories (SMT) solvers such as UPPAAL [5,49].

Bohrer et al. [6] have employed differential dynamic logic to verify the motion of a waypoint-following robot with an acceptable deviation from its specified path by stating and proving safety and liveliness properties. This is more appropriate for subtractive manufacturing due to the base spline and non-uniform B-spline (NURB) mathematical representations of surfaces as opposed to the tessellated triangles in STL files used for additive manufacturing.

The proposed logical formulation uses two fundamental syntactic constructs to model the evolution of a cyber-physical system as a first-order differential equation: $S \models [f(x)]\psi$ and $S \models \langle f(x)\rangle\psi$, where $s$ is a system state, $f(x)$ is the first-order equation of evolution of the state space (i.e., toolhead motion) and $\psi$ is a requirement that is expressed as a sentence interpretable in any system state. The intended intuitive meanings of the two statements $S \models [f(x)]\psi$ and $S \models \langle f(x)\rangle\psi$ are respectively, that all states that $s$ evolves to under $f(x)$ satisfy $\psi$, and that there is some state that $s$ evolves to under $f(x)$ that satisfies $\psi$. These two logical constructs along with others from predicate logic can be used to specify safety and liveliness conditions under the equation $f(x)$.

In this work, $f(x)$, the differential equation that governs the motion of a toolhead, can be used to state the acceptable deviation of the toolhead within a value $\epsilon$. The limitation is that the $\epsilon$ under consideration is a 2D Euclidean distance and not a measure of deviation as discussed above. The second logical limitation is that the base syntax expresses a point property whereas a path property would be better suited for toolheads moving under curves different from Dubins curves [12]. Lastly, a toolhead can reverse its direction and traverse 3D curves in/on material for subtractive manufacturing or in free space for additive manufacturing. To do so, would require controller code that executes a translation of every G-code (or M-code) instruction. The trajectory traversed would then be the reference/ideal trajectory of toolhead movement described by the differential equation. This may be a challenging task for a machine whose translator and controller code are black boxes unless a translator and controller simulator are available.

## 4 Formal Verification of End-to-End Flow

Within an ideally secured manufacturing design process, the integration of the methods described above should limit the possible failures and/or attacks during the G-code design lifecycle. However, the inclusion of various subsystems along with their underlying hardware and software components, and communications to meet the requirements, may lead to other opportunities for failure or for attackers to exploit vulnerabilities inherent in areas such as credential management, network transport and the supply chain. Therefore, it is also necessary to employ established systems engineering methods that incorporate safety best practices (e.g., IEC 61508 [20]) and security best practices (e.g., NIST SP 800-160 [42]) throughout the system development lifecycle. These best practices focus on identifying and tracking risks, with the intent of providing assurance that changes introduced by human behavior or complexity do not lead to their realization.

To demonstrate the formal verification that the G-code design integrity security properties are met throughout the system development lifecycle, a target subtractive manufacturing system architecture is modeled using the Architecture Analysis and Design Language (AADL) [43]. Using AADL, a model is developed based on the data flow diagram (DFD) of the target system before the G-code-Verify framework is introduced, following which G-code-Verify is applied to the model to analyze the security properties of the modified architecture. The benefit of this approach is that the AADL model can analyzed to formally identify potential weaknesses early in the design process when it is most cost effective to develop and apply remediation and mitigation strategies.

In an AADL system model, each DFD subsystem is formally defined using typed software components such as processes, threads, subprograms and data structures, which run on specified hardware components such as processors, physical memory, buses and devices. Each hardware, software and system component may be refined through features that define component types, subcomponents that show dependency relationships within component implementations, and properties that assist with analysis. Supporting libraries, called annexes, have also been developed to augment the SAE AS5506C standard, allowing for automated analysis of system behaviors when it comes to the risks associated with safety and security relative to the DFD (e.g., fault tree analysis, failure modes and effects analysis, and tracking security assurance cases) [14].

An analytical example that models a real LinuxCNC-based CNC machine is developed by introducing the G-code-Verify architecture components in Sect. 3 as well as the relevant details in Figs. 1, 7 and 8 to the target CNC system architecture.

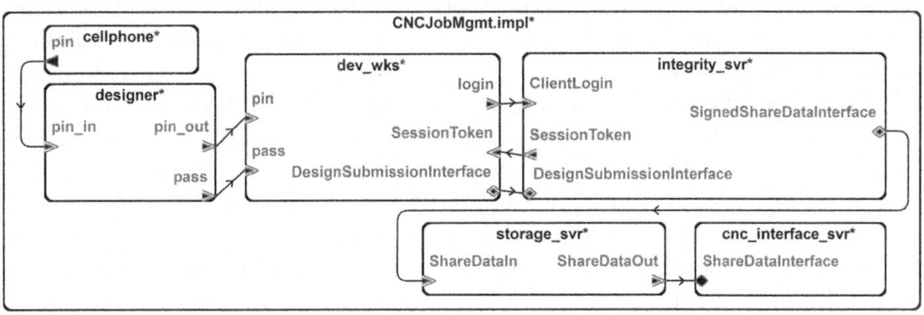


**Fig. 10.** End-to-end flow of G-code submission process from AADL modeling

The process of AADL modeling in OSATE [7] begins by creating a high-level end-to-end data flow of the G-code file from the designer to the desired CNC machine as shown in Fig. 10. The AADL model shows a human designer using a workstation running a browser, logging into a file monitoring and management (integrity) server using a password and a PIN from a smartphone as a second authentication factor. The designer receives a session token after being authenticated and submits a signed design file. The file monitoring and management device (integrity server) verifies the G-code signature and stores the G-code file in secure storage. Finally, the CNC machine reads the G-code file from secure storage. Understanding that each of the boxes represents a subsystem that handles a portion of the end-to-end flow, the AADL model is augmented to add software that manages all the flows and underlying hardware that physically binds their connections.

Figure 11 shows the resulting software (logical) view of the augmented model, which includes processes, internal threads and connections between each subsystem, but hides the underlying hardware from view due to space. Two threads are used within the client_session process on the development workstation to log into the integrity server and pass the signed design, three threads are used by the webserver to handle client sessions and submitted designs on the integrity server, two threads are used by the Samba server to read and write files on the storage server, and one thread is used by the Samba client to retrieve files on the CNC interface server.

Having constructed the model, properties of interest and assurance cases are added to support further analysis. Specifically, the components are augmented with security properties from the AADL Security Annex [16] to include cryptographic algorithms, keying materials and relevant properties such as trust. Using the Architecture-Led Incremental System Assurance (ALISA) built into OSATE, assurance cases are developed that analyze the security properties and map back to the system development processes throughout the system development lifecycle. Integrating ALISA in the system development lifecycle helps formalize conceptual stakeholders and their goals, map the goals to technical requirements and relate the requirements back to the system model as assurance cases for verification as design changes are made using another language named Resolute [11,15].

The results of the assurance case analyses are presented through JUnit checks in OSATE to analyze the application of G-code-Verify and the possible need for additional security controls. Figure 12 shows an example JUnit view of assurance cases that manifest some results of interest for the model. Specifically, two cases pass showing that HTTPS is configured for messages from the workstation to the integrity server and that the integrity server is considered trusted. One case (expanded in the figure) fails because the development workstation is not trusted.

From the results, it was identified that, although the designer workstation stores the signing private key used to watermark G-code files, the workstation is considered untrusted and flagged for further review. In this case, despite the steps taken to assure G-code integrity throughout its lifecycle, if an attacker

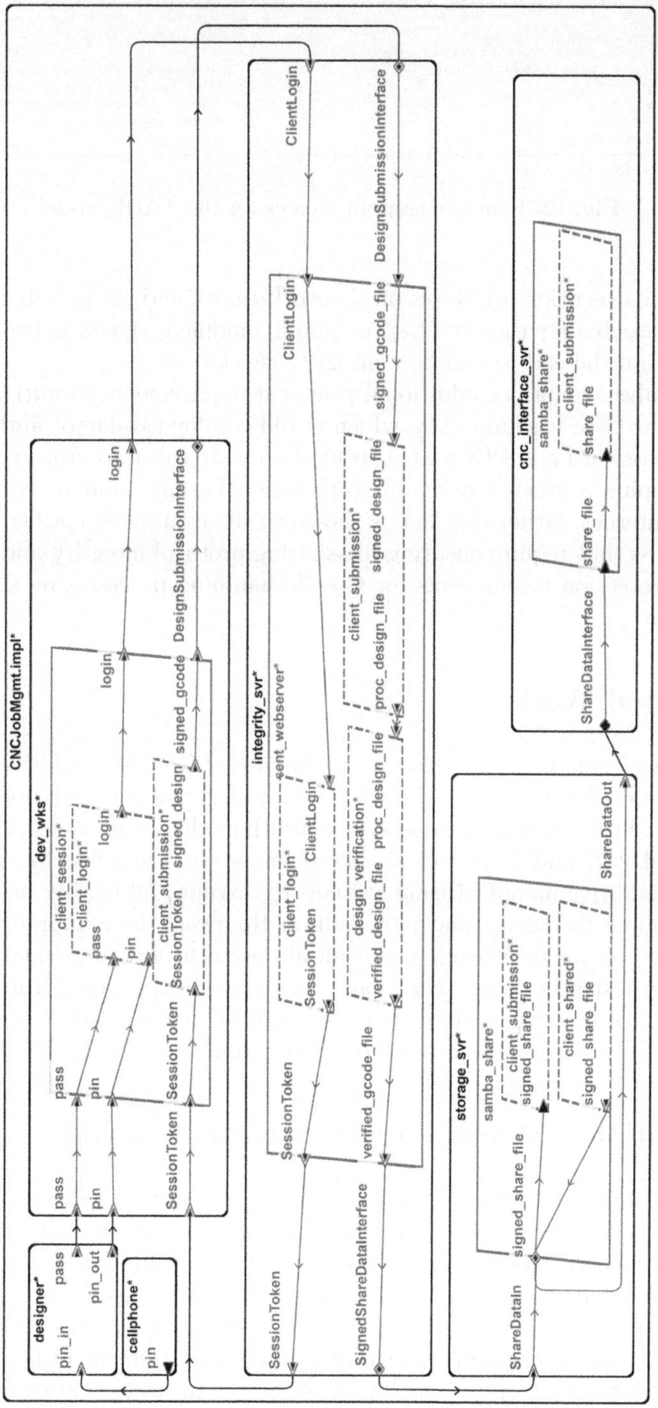


Fig. 11. Augmentation of end-to-end flow with software components

| Evidence | Pass | Fail | Error | Todo | Description |
| --- | --- | --- | --- | --- | --- |
| Case CNC_Job_Submission_Implementation_Assurance | 3 | 1 | | | |
| Plan CNC_Job_Submission_Implementation_Assurance_Plan(CNCJobMgr | 3 | 1 | | | |
| Claim R_CJS_HTTPS_1(HTTPS_Integrity) | 2 | | | | The Developer Workstation shall establish a mutually authentica... |
| Claim R_CJS_TRUST_1(dev_wks) | | 1 | | | The G-Code signing key should only be used or verified within a ... |
| Evidence TrustCheck | | 1 | | | This check confirms the component is trusted. |
| Failure: is_trusted_component | | | | | Trusted component dev_wks : Developer::DevWorkstation.impl |
| Claim R_CJS_TRUST_2(integrity_svr) | 1 | | | | Edge verification of G-Code signature should only occur on a tr... |

**Fig. 12.** Example assurance cases for the AADL model

obtains code execution privileges on the workstation and the private key, then it would be possible for the attacker to submit modified, signed G-code files that would pass all the end-to-end flow integrity checks.

The analysis identifies additional practical requirements to mitigate threats targeting the G-code signing key, which would employ two-factor authentication such as a password and PIN with a secure hardware token to protect the signing key, developing a trusted designer workstation baseline and/or segmenting it from the Internet. Other checks not shown in the example identified additional security gaps that require ensuring file-sharing protocol integrity and leveraging memory protection mechanisms for G-code handling processes on the designer workstation.

## 5 Related Work

Previous studies have largely focused on the use of G-code in additive manufacturing systems. Kurkowski et al. [27] demonstrated the manipulation of G-code in desktop additive manufacturing systems with modern controllers and software. Sturm et al. [47] and Pearce et al. [36] demonstrated attacks that intercepted G-code in additive manufacturing systems to disrupt and modify machine commands, leading to defects and part failure. However, these approaches do not consider the complete lifecycle from initial design to formal geometry verification during post-processing operations. Furthermore, they are not applicable to traditional manufacturing methods involving CNC machines that constitute the vast majority of operations in the precision manufacturing supply chain.

## 6 Additional Manufacturing Security Controls

Additional protections and verification methods specific to the manufacturing process on a given commercial production system could be considered. Each process parameter provides an independent pathway for attacks, where small defects that are extremely difficult to detect can be engineered in the manufactured part. Some of these attacks can be detected through multiple methods such as on-board machine sensors and external monitoring systems. Other attacks are more difficult to detect, requiring highly calibrated measurement equipment that is not commonly employed in production operations. Additionally, the vulnerabilities have various levels of criticality that depend on the process and equipment. These machine- and process-specific vulnerabilities must be considered to ensure secure manufacturing operations.

Metal additive manufacturing processes are susceptible to a number of attacks that affect the performance and quality of the manufactured parts. Structural performance of a part produced by metal additive manufacturing is highly dependent on the material microstructure formation, which in turn depends on the rate of cooling. Small perturbations in the deposition process, such as laser power modulation, metal feed stock gaps or trajectory changes, dramatically affect part strength, hardness and residual stress. Each of these factors can be set and controlled by the process parameter choices embedded in the G-code file. However, they can also be changed via machine parameters, hardware overrides and other open inputs to manufacturing systems. Table 1 shows the common process parameter ranges for a metal additive laser-based directed energy deposition (DED) manufacturing system.

Observing some process parameters is straightforward, but others such as laser power and feed rate are very difficult to observe. In some cases, external monitoring methods can be used to verify the deposition parameters. Given the geometry and deposition process profile, laser backscatter can be measured using external monitoring equipment to detect changes from normal operations. However, monitoring the powder capture efficiency (i.e., ratio of the powder mass welded to the substrate to the powder mass fed to the process) is almost impossible to accurately measure in near real-time.

**Table 1.** Parameter ranges for metal additive laser-based DED system

| Parameter | Description | Range |
|---|---|---|
| Surface Feed | Traverse speed | 0–8,000 mm/min |
| Focal Distance | Distance between substrate and nozzle | 0–N/A mm |
| Laser Output | Energy output by laser | 0–4,000 W |
| Feedstock Rate | Rate of feedstock deposition | 0–50 g/min |
| Stepover | Distance between consecutive beads | 0–N/A mm |
| Layer Height | Distance between consecutive layers | 0–N/A mm |

Attacks involving analogous processing parameters can be executed on standard machining systems that are widely used in high-precision manufacturing. Although the internal material properties are not inherently changed through surface machining processes (i.e., when geometry is machined from existing stock) as they are in additive manufacturing, the final geometric profiles and surface characteristics are exposed to modification.

Variables such as toolpath velocity (feed rate), spindle speed and trajectory smoothing (interpolation resolution) directly affect the physical shape and outer surface finish of manufactured parts, thereby affecting their performance. Some process parameters are easier to monitor than others. Trajectory information such as linear feed rate and spindle rotational speed can be monitored using external power sensors. While slight variations are to be expected, the overall "energy signature" of a subtractive manufacturing process can be used for anomaly detection. Additionally, on-board machine inspection units can be used to measure and verify specific performance-critical geometric features after the manufacturing process has terminated. This method can illuminate surface level defects in standard machining such as gouges and incorrect surface finishes. Machine- and process-specific considerations such as these must be identified and accounted for when securing commercial manufacturing operations.

## 7 Conclusions

Developing security protocols for data communications to and from machine tools in manufacturing operations is a critical step towards verifying and validating the design integrity of manufactured parts. In the modern manufacturing industry, there is little to no verification that the intended designs are properly realized in the manufactured parts. The lack of verification can result in wasted resources due to human error as well as undetected cyber attacks on the manufacturing process.

The proposed G-code-Verify framework can provide the additive and subtractive manufacturing communities with assurance that the design intentions can be securely transferred from CAD/CAM systems to machine tools in order to manufacture parts that satisfy the design specifications. This capability protects large manufacturers who may be targets of cyber attacks and enables small manufacturers to verify the integrity of their manufacturing processes and manufactured parts. The G-code-Verify framework also provides opportunities for securing advanced paradigms such as distributed manufacturing.

The views expressed in this chapter do not necessarily represent the views of the U.S. Department of Energy or the United States Government.

**Acknowledgement.** This research was supported by the U.S. Department of Energy Office of Energy Efficiency and Renewable Energy under the Advanced Materials and Manufacturing Technologies Office (AMMTO) Award no. DE EE0009046.

## References

1. Arthaya, B., Setiawan, A., Sunardi, S.: The design and development of a G-code checker and cutting simulator for CNC turning operation. J. Mech. Eng. Res. **2**(3), 58–70 (2010)
2. Autodesk, Autodesk Fusion, San Rafael, California (2024). www.autodesk.com/products/fusion-360
3. Bauer, F.L.: Decrypted Secrets. Springer, Heidelberg (2002). https://doi.org/10.1007/978-3-662-04736-1

4. Belikovetsky, S., Yampolskiy, M., Toh, J., Gatlin, J., Elovici, Y.: dr0wned – cyber-physical attack with additive manufacturing. In: Proceedings of the Eleventh USENIX Workshop on Offensive Technologies (2017)
5. Belmonte, G., Ciancia, V., Latella, D., Massink, M.: `VoxLogicA`: a spatial model checker for declarative image analysis. In: Vojnar, T., Zhang, L. (eds.) TACAS 2019. LNCS, vol. 11427, pp. 281–298. Springer, Cham (2019). https://doi.org/10.1007/978-3-030-17462-0_16
6. Bohrer, B., Tan, Y., Mitsch, S., Sogokon, A., Platzer, A.: A formal safety net for waypoint-following in ground robots. IEEE Robot. Autom. Lett. **4**(3), 2910–2917 (2019)
7. Carnegie Mellon University, Welcome to OSATE, Pittsburgh, Pennsylvania (2024). www.osate.org
8. Chen, Z.: Development of OpenGL-based 3D simulator for computer numerical control. In: Proceedings of the International Conference on Artificial Intelligence and Computational Intelligence, pp. 319–321 (2010)
9. Ciancia, V., Gilmore, S., Grilletti, G., Latella, D., Loreti, M., Massink, M.: Spatio-temporal model checking of vehicular movement in public transport systems. Int. J. Softw. Tools Technol. Transf. **20**, 289–311 (2018)
10. Dassault Systems – SolidWorks, SolidWorks, Maltham, Massachusetts (2024). www.solidworks.com
11. Delange, J., Feiler, P., Neil, E.: Incremental lifecycle assurance of safety-critical systems. In: Proceedings of the Eighth European Congress on Embedded Real Time Software and Systems (2016)
12. Dubins, L.: On curves of minimal length with a constraint on average curvature and with prescribed initial and terminal positions and tangents. Am. J. Math. **79**(3), 493–516 (1957)
13. Duong, T., et al.: G-code visualization and editing program for inexpensive metal 3D printing. Procedia Manuf. **17**, 22–28 (2018)
14. Feiler, P., Gluch, D.: Model-Based Engineering with AADL: An Introduction to the SAE Architecture Analysis and Design Language. Addison-Wesley, Upper Saddle River, New Jersey (2012)
15. Gacek, A., Backes, J., Cofer, D., Slind, K., Whalen, M.: Resolute: an assurance case language for architecture models. ACM SIGAda Ada Lett. **34**(3), 19–28 (2014)
16. Greenhouse, A., Hansson, J., Wrage, L.: Modeling and Validating Security and Confidentiality in System Architectures, Technical Report CMU/SEI-2021-TR-004, Software Engineering Institute, Carnegie Mellon University, Pittsburgh, Pennsylvania (2021)
17. Harte, T., Bors, A.: Watermarking 3D models. In: Proceedings of the International Conference on Image Processing, pp. 661–884 (2002)
18. Holladay, R., Srinivasa, S.: Distance metrics and algorithms for task space path optimization. In: Proceedings of the IEEE/RSJ International Conference on Intelligent Robots and Systems, pp. 5533–5540 (2016)
19. Horvath, J.: Mastering 3D Printing. Apress, Berkeley, CA (2014). https://doi.org/10.1007/978-1-4842-0025-4
20. International Electrotechnical Commission: Functional Safety of Electrical/Electronic/Programmable Electronic Safety-Related Systems, IEC 61508:2010, Geneva, Switzerland (2010)
21. International Organization of Standardization: ISO 10303-21: Industrial Automation Systems and Integration - Product Data Representation and Exchange, Part 21: Implementation Methods: Clear Text Encoding of the Exchange Structure, Geneva, Switzerland (2016)

22. IQS Directory, Computer Numerical Control (CNC) and CNC M-Codes, Grand Rapids, Michigan (2024). www.iqsdirectory.com/articles/cnc-machining/m-code.html
23. Klingenberg, C.: Analyzing fluctuating asymmetry with geometric morphometrics: concepts, methods and applications. Symmetry **7**(2), 843–934 (2015)
24. Kramer, T., Proctor, F., Messina, E.: The NIST RS274NGC Interpreter - Version 3, NIST Interagency/Internal Report 6556, National Institute of Standards and Technology, Gaithersburg, Maryland (2000)
25. Kroger, F., Metz, S.: Temporal Logic and State Systems. Springer, Heidelberg (2008)
26. Kurfess, T., Lynn, R., Saleeby, K., Tucker, T., Saldana, C.: Multi-axis voxel-based CNC machining of centrifugal compressor assemblies. In: Presented at the AHS International Seventy-Fourth Annual Forum and Technology Display (2018)
27. Kurkowski, E., Van Stockum, A., Dawson, J., Taylor, C., Schulz, T., Shenoi, S.: Manipulation of G-code toolpath files in 3d printers: attacks and mitigations. In: Staggs, J., Shenoi, S. (eds.) Critical Infrastructure Protection XVI: 16th IFIP WG 11.10 International Conference, ICCIP 2022, Virtual Event, March 14–15, 2022, Revised Selected Papers, pp. 155–174. Springer Nature Switzerland, Cham (2022). https://doi.org/10.1007/978-3-031-20137-0_6
28. Lee, S., Kwon, K.: CAD drawing watermarking scheme. Digit. Sig. Process. **20**(5), 1379–1399 (2010)
29. Leroy, X., Blazy, S., Kastner, D., Schommer, B., Pister, M., Ferdinand, C.: CompCert – a formally verified optimizing compiler. In: Proceedings of the Eighth European Congress on Embedded Real Time Software and Systems (2016)
30. Li, Z., Gong, D., Tan, L., Luo, X., Liu, F., Bors, A.: Self-embedding watermarking method for G-code used in 3D printing. In: Proceedings of the IEEE International Workshop on Information Forensics and Security (2021)
31. Library of Congress, STEP-File, ISO 10303-21, Washington, DC (2023). www.loc.gov/preservation/digital/formats/fdd/fdd000448.shtml
32. Morrisett, G., et al.: TALx86: a realistic typed assembly language. In: Proceedings of the ACM SIGPLAN Workshop on Compiler Support for System Software (1999)
33. Necula, G.: Compiling with Proofs, Ph.D. Dissertation, School of Computer Science, Carnegie Mellon University, Pittsburgh, Pennsylvania (1998)
34. Necula, G.: Translation validation for an optimizing compiler. ACM SIGPLAN Not. **35**(5), 83–94 (2000)
35. Newman, D., Parto, M., Saleeby, K., Kurfess, T., Dugenske, A.: Development of a digital architecture for distributed CNC machine health monitoring. Smart Sustain. Manuf. Syst. **3**(2), 68–82 (2019)
36. Pearce, H., Yanamandra, K., Gupta, N., Karri, R.: FLAW3D: a Trojan-based cyber attack on the physical outcomes of additive manufacturing. IEEE/ASME Trans. Mechatron. **27**(6), 5361–5370 (2022)
37. Peisert, S., et al.: Perspectives on the SolarWinds incident. IEEE Secur. Priv. **19**(2), 7–13 (2021)
38. Petitcolas, F., Anderson, R., Kuhn, M.: Information hiding - a survey. Proc. IEEE **87**(7), 1062–1078 (1999)
39. Platzer, A.: Differential dynamic logic for hybrid systems. J. Autom. Reason. **41**, 143–189 (2008)
40. Pnueli, A., Siegel, M., Singerman, E.: Translation validation. In: Steffen, B. (ed.) TACAS 1998. LNCS, vol. 1384, pp. 151–166. Springer, Heidelberg (1998). https://doi.org/10.1007/BFb0054170

41. Rais, M., Li, Y., Ahmed, I.: Spatiotemporal G-code modeling for secure FDM-based 3D printing. In: Proceedings of the Twelfth ACM/IEEE International Conference on Cyber-Physical Systems, pp. 177–186 (2021)
42. Ross, R., McEvilley, M., Oren, J.: Systems Security Engineering: Considerations for a Multidisciplinary Approach in the Engineering of Trustworthy Secure Systems, NIST Special Publication 800-160, Volume 1, National Institute of Standards and Technology, Gaithersburg, Maryland (2016)
43. SAE International, Architecture Analysis and Design Language (AADL), AS5506D, Warrendale, Pennsylvania (2018). www.sae.org/standards/content/as5506d
44. Saleeby, K.: Multi-agent open architecture for process monitoring and part certification, Ph.D. Dissertation, George W. Woodruff School of Mechanical Engineering, Georgia Institute of Technology, Atlanta, Georgia (2021)
45. Schafer, P.: Frechet view – A tool for exploring Frechet distance algorithms. In: Proceedings of the Thirty-Fifth International Symposium on Computational Geometry, pp. 66-1–66-5 (2019)
46. Siemens, NX CAD Software, Plano, Texas (2024). www.plm.sw.siemens.com/en-US/nx/cad-online
47. Sturm, L., Williams, C., Camelio, J., White, J., Parker, R.: Cyber-physical vulnerabilities in additive manufacturing systems: a case study attack on the .STL file with human subjects. J. Manuf. Syst. **44**(1), 154–164 (2017)
48. Tuzhilin, A.: Who invented the Gromov-Hausdorff distance? arXivarXiv:1612.00728 (2016)
49. UPPAAL, UPPAAL, Uppsala, Sweden (2024). www.uppaal.org
50. Yampolskiy, M., et al.: Security of additive manufacturing: attack taxonomy and survey. Addit. Manuf. **21**, 431–457 (2018)

# Industrial Control System Security

# Multiple-Bayesian-Network-Based Risk Assessment Methodology for Industrial Control Systems

Simone Guarino[1], Silvia Ansaldi[2], and Roberto Setola[1](✉)

[1] University Campus Bio-Medico of Rome, Rome, Italy
R.Setola@unicampus.it
[2] National Institute for Insurance Against Accidents at Work, Rome, Italy

**Abstract.** Cyber attacks on industrial control systems have increased dramatically due to the adoption of open, heterogeneous industrial protocols that enable remote connectivity to industrial plants. Of particular concern are attacks that impair physical processes, leading to production loss, service outages, equipment damage, human injury and environmental pollution. Given the plethora of consequences induced by cyber attacks on industrial control systems, it is vital to compute the risks associated with the attacks to enable operators to implement appropriate recovery measures. This chapter presents a probabilistic risk assessment methodology that leverages multiple Bayesian networks to measure the risks associated with cyber attacks on industrial control systems. The Bayesian networks are designed to compute the probabilities of detected cyber attacks propagating to cyber and physical assets that have not yet been compromised, thereby providing an estimate of the overall risk to the integrity of the entire industrial control system. The proposed risk assessment methodology is evaluated using a real hardware-in-the-loop case study involving a water distribution testbed.

**Keywords:** Industrial Control Systems · Cyber Attacks · Risk Assessment · Bayesian Networks

## 1 Introduction

Industrial control systems (ICSs) is a general term that encompasses a variety of control systems, including supervisory control and data acquisition systems, distributed control systems and programmable logic controllers that are deployed in industrial facilities and critical infrastructures to ensure the safe and reliable execution of cyber-physical processes that provide critical services such as electricity, water and natural gas distribution [4,22].

Industrial control systems were relatively secure in the past because they were isolated [10,20]. However, due to the Industry 4.0 phenomenon, industrial control systems are now connected to the Internet to facilitate remote supervision


Published by Springer Nature Switzerland AG 2025
J. Staggs and S. Shenoi (Eds.): ICCIP 2024, IFIP AICT 725, pp. 113–130, 2025.
https://doi.org/10.1007/978-3-031-81888-2_6

and control of distributed industrial facilities [18]. This situation renders industrial control systems highly vulnerable to cyber attacks launched remotely via the Internet, potentially disrupting vital services that could lead to debilitating effects on societal wellbeing and national economic security [15,16,21].

Due to the criticality of industrial control systems, it is important to assess the risks associated with directed cyber attacks. Such assessments are crucial to understanding the potential damage as well as devising effective recovery and mitigation strategies [6,11,12,14].

This chapter presents a probabilistic risk assessment methodology that leverages multiple Bayesian networks to measure the risks associated with cyber attacks. Each Bayesian network computes the probability that a detected cyber attack propagates to the not-yet-compromised cyber and physical assets of an industrial control system, providing valuable insights into the cascading impacts of the attack on the cyber and physical assets. This assessment is very useful during the incident management phase to apply the most effective countermeasures to address service degradation and other physical consequences. The proposed risk assessment methodology is evaluated by executing scanning, man-in-the-middle and denial-of-service attacks on programmable logic controllers in a water distribution testbed.

## 2 Background

Bayesian networks are probabilistic graphical models [13]. They are a useful tool for assessing industrial control system risks [1,5].

A Bayesian network is a directed acyclic graph $G = (V, A)$ where $V$ is a set of nodes and $A \subseteq V \times V$ is a set of arcs. Each $v_i \in V$ represents a random variable $X_i$ and each arc $(v_i, v_j) \in A$ represents a causal relationship between nodes. The causal relationships are encoded as conditional probability tables (CPTs). Each node $v_i$ has an associated conditional probability table that specifies the conditional probability of each possible value that $X_i$ may have given the values of $v_i$'s parent nodes.

The value of a Bayesian network node that is known *a priori* is referred to as evidence. Upon receiving new evidence, a Bayesian network computes the probabilities for all the other nodes using the conditional probability tables.

The global joint distribution $P(X_1, \ldots, X_n)$ is given by:

$$P(X_1, \ldots, X_n) = \prod_{i=1}^{n} P(X_i | pa(X_i))$$

where $n$ is the total number of nodes, $X_i$ is the random variable associated with $v_i$, $pa(X_i)$ is the set of random variables of $v_i$'s parent nodes and $P(X_i|pa(X_i))$ is $v_i$'s conditional probability distribution.

Zhang et al. [24] have proposed a fuzzy probability Bayesian network (FPBN) approach for assessing the dynamic cyber security risks posed to industrial control systems. Their model employs a single Bayesian network that captures the propagation of cyber risk due to cyber attacks that target an industrial control system and the subsequent chain reactions the attacks might trigger on cyber and physical assets. The approach is demonstrated using a simplified simulated chemical reactor.

The Bayesian network model of Peng et al. [19] is also designed for cyber security risk assessments of industrial control systems. The model incorporates three types of nodes: vulnerability nodes, function nodes and accident nodes. A vulnerability node models a vulnerability that an attacker may exploit, a function node models the function associated with a specific cyber or physical asset and an accident node models a possible accident. The approach has been applied to assess the risks posed to the well-known Tennessee Eastman chemical production process.

Lyu et al. [17] have proposed a Bayesian network model for cyber-to-physical (C2P) risk assessment of industrial control systems. Their model captures the impairment probabilities of physical assets given the exploitation of known vulnerabilities in the cyber assets of an industrial control system. The risk assessment model is evaluated using a simulated industrial cyber-physical system.

Xie et al. [23] have developed a risk assessment method using Bayesian attack graphs that describe the relationships between attacks and the behavior of targeted systems. Attacks are modeled based on the exploited vulnerabilities and the relationships between compromised nodes and target nodes. The risk assessment method is evaluated using a Simulink simulation of a three-phase synchronous motor in a power plant.

Barua et al. [3] have proposed a Bayesian-network-based operational risk assessment methodology for dynamic systems with a focus on chemical processes. A level control system case study is employed to demonstrate the ability of the methodology to capture dynamic operational changes to a process due to the sequential dependencies of equipment/components on each other.

A review of the scientific literature reveals that current risk assessment approaches leverage a single Bayesian network that models all the possible attack paths leveraged by an adversary to compromise an industrial control system. This leads to problems related to scalability and the identification of all the possible vulnerabilities that an attacker may exploit. To address these limitations, the proposed methodology employs a set of Bayesian networks, each network modeling the probability that a specific attack class occurred and was detected at a given cyber asset. Collectively, the set of Bayesian networks model the spread of attacks in an industrial control system over time, compromising physical components and ultimately the cyber-physical system. The methodology handles the scalability problems arising from using different Bayesian networks to model different attacks by reducing the number of nodes required in each Bayesian network.

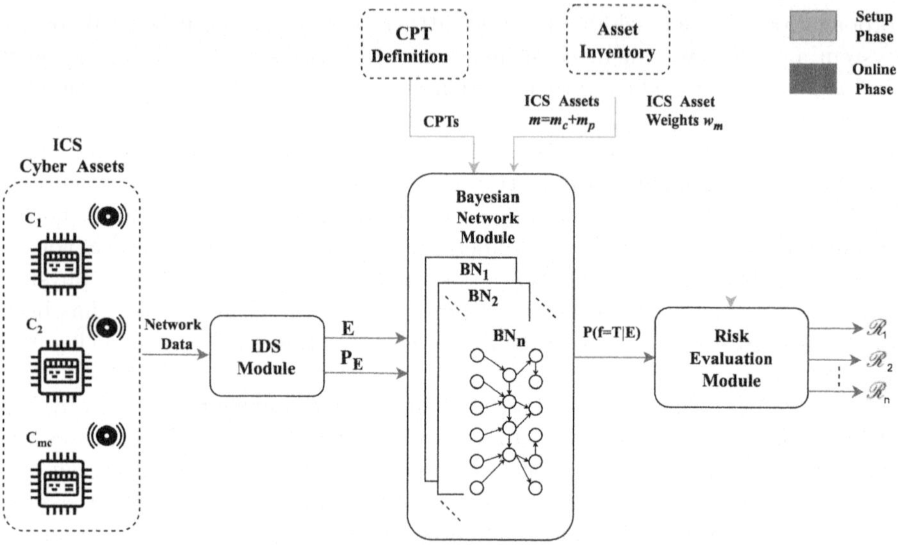


**Fig. 1.** Proposed risk assessment methodology.

## 3 Risk Assessment Methodology

Figure 1 provides an overview of the proposed risk assessment methodology for industrial control systems. The methodology incorporates three main modules: intrusion detection system (IDS) module, Bayesian network module and risk evaluation module. The methodology involves two phases, a setup phase and an online phase. The setup phase initializes the parameters in the Bayesian network and risk evaluation modules. The online phase handles the real-time provision of risk values based on the detected cyber attacks.

### 3.1 Intrusion Detection System Module

The intrusion detection system module detects cyber attacks on industrial control system assets in real time. It monitors network data acquired from the cyber assets and outputs a tuple $(E, P_E)$ where $E$ is the set of detected cyber events and $P_E$ is the set of the detection probabilities associated with the cyber events. The intrusion detection system module implements signature- or anomaly-based detection techniques that may leverage machine learning or deep learning algorithms.

Let $n$ be the number of cyber attack classes detected by the intrusion detection system module and $m_c$ be the set of industrial control system cyber assets at which cyber attacks are detected. A cyber event $E_j^i \in E$ associated with the cyber attack class $n_i \in n$ detected at cyber asset $m_c^j \in m_c$ is defined as:

$$E_j^i = \begin{cases} 1, & \text{if } n_i \text{ is detected on cyber asset } m_c^j \\ 0, & \text{if } n_i \text{ is not detected on cyber asset } m_c^j \end{cases}$$

When cyber event $E_j^i$ is triggered (i.e., $E_j^i = 1$), the intrusion detection system module also provides its detection probability $P_{E_j^i} \in [0, 1]$.

Let $n$ be the number of detectable cyber attack classes, $m_c$ be the number of cyber assets and $t \in [1, T]$ be an online-phase time step in which $T$ is the time horizon. Then, the maximum number of events triggered by the intrusion detection system module at time step $t$ is $m_c \times n$. This is because each cyber attack class may be detected at each cyber asset in the industrial control system.

### 3.2 Bayesian Network Module

The Bayesian network module is the core of the risk assessment methodology. The module comprises a set of Bayesian networks, each of which evaluates the probability that a detected cyber attack propagates to cyber and physical assets that have not yet been compromised. This yields the overall risk to the integrity of the cyber-physical system. Since $n$ is the number of cyber attack classes detectable by the intrusion detection system module, the Bayesian network module incorporates exactly $n$ Bayesian networks, each modeling the propagation of a specific cyber attack class $n_i \in n$ over the cyber and physical assets.

Figure 1 shows that the Bayesian network module receives two inputs from the setup phase: number of cyber and physical assets in the industrial control system ($m = m_c + m_p$) and conditional probability tables for the Bayesian network nodes. The number of cyber and physical assets is specified after conducting a detailed asset inventory. The conditional probability tables, which quantify the probabilities of specific cyber attack classes propagating in the industrial control system, are crucial to assessing the joint conditional probabilities that relate the Bayesian nodes to each other.

Figure 2 shows the Bayesian network topology comprising three main layers: event layer, trustworthiness layer and fault layer. The event layer models the occurrence of events $E_j^i$ related to the specific cyber attack class $n_i$ that impacts $m_c$ cyber assets. Consequently, the layer contains a total of $m_c$ nodes, each representing the occurrence of event $E_j^i$ involving the $j^{th}$ cyber asset ($j \in [0, m_c]$).

The trustworthiness layer models the performance of the intrusion detection system module. The nodes in this layer adjust the outputs generated by the event layer, modifying them according to the attack detection probability associated with a particular event. Each trustworthiness layer node has one parent node from the event layer – the relationship, which is encoded in its conditional probability table, specifies the likelihood of an attack occurring on a particular cyber asset given that the attack is detected by the intrusion detection system module.

Table 1 shows the conditional probability table for trustworthiness layer node $P_{E_j^i}$. $P(E_j^i = 1)$ denotes the detection probability of event $E_j^i$ provided by the intrusion detection system module (i.e., probability that event detection is a true positive). In contrast, $1 - P(E_j^i = 1)$ denotes the probability that the detected event $E_j^i$ is a false alarm (i.e., probability that event detection is a false positive).

The fault layer collects all the nodes representing the probabilities that cyber and physical assets are compromised given the occurrence of cyber events

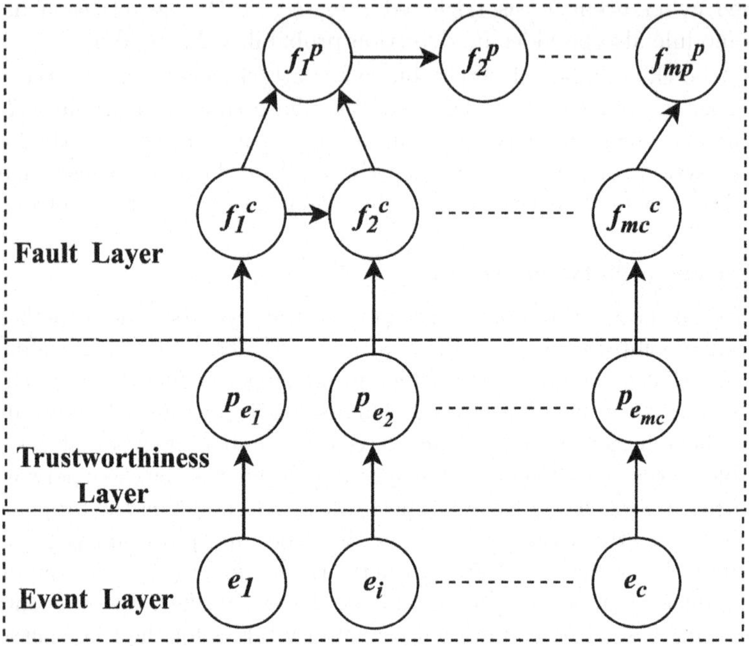


**Fig. 2.** Bayesian network topology with event, trustworthiness and fault layers.

**Table 1.** CPT for trustworthiness layer node $P_{E_j^i}$.

| $E_j^i$ | 0 | 1 |
|---|---|---|
| $P_{E_j^i} = 0$ | 1 | $1 - P(E_j^i = 1)$ |
| $P_{E_j^i} = 1$ | 0 | $P(E_j^i = 1)$ |

detected at the cyber assets. Unlike the nodes in the event and trustworthiness layers, the fault layer nodes model cyber ($F^c$) and physical ($F^p$) assets because a cyber attack may propagate to the physical components (compromising the physical industrial process). Consequently, the number of nodes in the fault layer is equal to the total number of cyber and physical assets in the industrial control system ($m = m_c + m_p$).

Each fault layer cyber node has only one parent node from the trustworthiness layer whose relationship conveys the conditional probability that the occurrence of an event will cause a fault at the associated cyber asset. Additional parent nodes may originate from the same fault layer because an industrial control system asset could be disrupted not only by a cyber event, but also by malfunctions of other industrial control system assets during a cascading failure. This is especially true for physical fault layer nodes that model the probabilities of physical assets being compromised due to failures of other assets in the aftermath of a cyber attack.

Overall, each Bayesian network $BN_i$ outputs the conditional probabilities of cyber and physical assets being compromised given the set of events $E_j^i$ triggered by the intrusion detection system module for a specific cyber attack class $n_i$ and detected at $m_c^*$ of the $m_c$ cyber assets $(P(F_j = T|E_1^i, \ldots, E_{m_c^*}^i), j \in [1, m])$. These conditional probabilities are employed to evaluate the risk value associated with each attack class $n_i$.

### 3.3 Risk Evaluation Module

The risk evaluation module evaluates the risk values for each detected cyber attack class over assets in the industrial control system infrastructure. The module requires two sets of inputs. The first set of inputs comprises the asset weights evaluated and provided during the setup phase. The second set of inputs comprises the conditional probabilities of the fault layer nodes that are computed during the online phase.

The asset weights are computed at setup time after examining all the cyber and physical assets during an asset inventory. The weights are used to quantify the levels of criticality or importance of assets with regard to the overall operation and security of the industrial control system. Factors considered in determining the weights include the potential for production loss, monetary loss, human injury and environmental pollution that could result from asset impairment. Indeed, asset weights increase in proportion to the criticality of cyber and physical assets to the entire industrial control system infrastructure.

Given the asset weights and conditional probabilities of the fault layer nodes, the overall risk value related to each detected cyber attack class $n_i$ is computed as:

$$\mathcal{R}_i = \sum_{j=1}^{m^c} w_j \times P(F_j^c = T|E_1^i, \ldots, E_{m_c^*}^i) + \sum_{j=1}^{m^p} w_j \times P(F_j^p = T|E_1^i, \ldots, E_{m_c^*}^i)$$

where $m_c$ is the number of cyber fault layer nodes, $m_p$ is the number of physical fault layer nodes, $m_c^*$ is the number of cyber assets where cyber attacks are detected and $w_j$ is the weight associated with the $j^{th}$ asset.

Specifically, the risk value $\mathcal{R}_i$ is computed by assessing the probability that cyber and physical industrial control system assets are compromised $(P(F_j^p = T|E_1^i, \ldots, E_{m_c^*}^i)$, $P(F_j^c = T|E_1^i, \ldots, E_{m_c^*}^i))$ given the occurrence of events $E_j^i$ detected with probabilities $P(E_j^i)$ on the $m_c^*$ cyber assets.

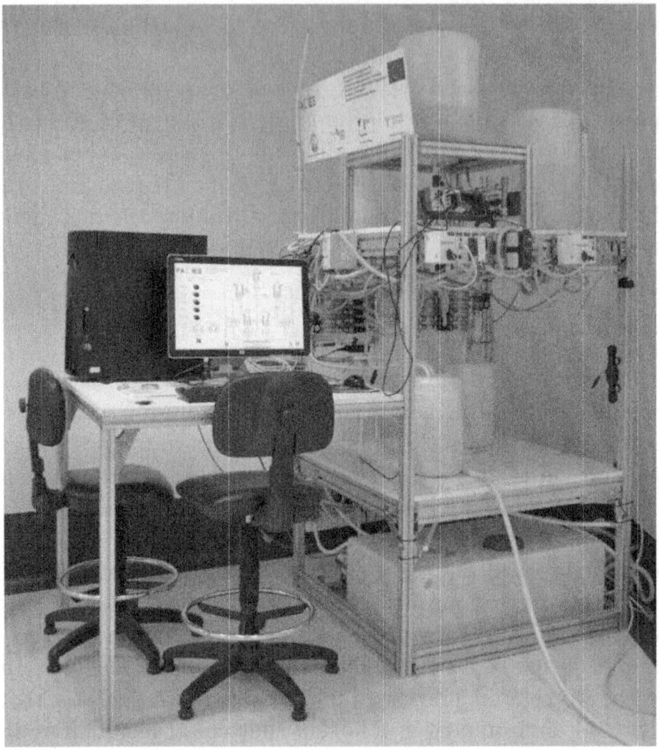

**Fig. 3.** Water distribution testbed overview.

# 4 Case Study

This section evaluates the effectiveness of the proposed risk assessment methodology using a laboratory-scale water distribution testbed.

## 4.1 Water Distribution Testbed

The water distribution testbed shown in Fig. 3 is a scaled-down version of a realistic industrial control system with a hardware-in-the-loop water distribution infrastructure [7]. The testbed has a real partition and a software-simulated partition. The real partition shown in Fig. 3 has five tanks ($T_1^r, \ldots, T_5^r$), 20 solenoid valves ($V_1^r, \ldots, V_{20}^r$), four pumps ($P_1^r, \ldots, P_4^r$) and five pressure sensors ($S_1^r, \ldots, S_5^r$), one sensor under each tank. The water flow is controlled by a real programmable logic controller ($PLC_1^r$).

The simulated partition comprises a total of three tanks ($T_6^s, T_7^s, T_8^s$), two pumps ($P_5^s, P_6^s$), four flow sensors ($F_1^s, \ldots, F_4^s$), two solenoid valves ($V_{21}^s, V_{22}^s$) and three pressure sensors ($S_6^s, S_7^s, S_8^s$), one for each tank. The water flow is controlled by three virtual programmable logic controllers ($PLC_2^s$, $PLC_3^s$, $PLC_4^s$).

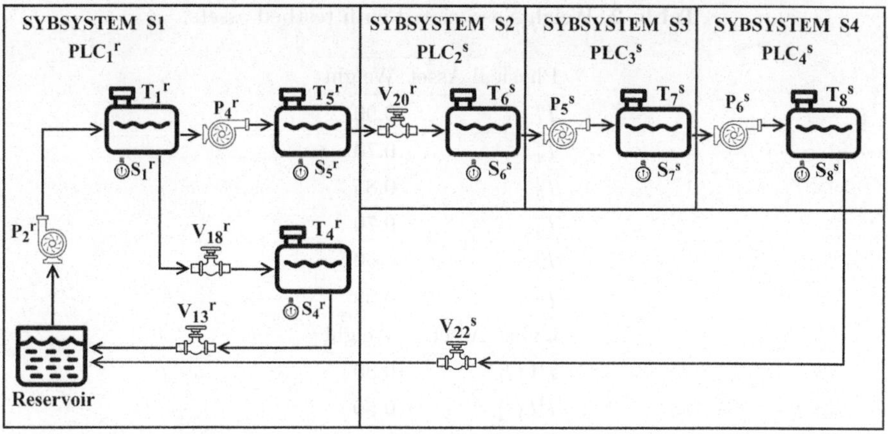


**Fig. 4.** Water distribution testbed physical process.

Figure 4 shows the water distribution testbed physical process. The physical process is divided into four main subsystems, each controlled by a separate programmable logic controller. Water from the reservoir flows to tank $T_1^r$ and then to tanks $T_5^r$ and $T_4^r$ in the first subsystem. Subsequently, water flows from tank $T_5^r$ to tank $T_6^s$ in the second subsystem, then to tank $T_7^s$ in the third subsystem and finally to tank $T_8^s$ in the last subsystem.

## 4.2 Experimental Setup

As discussed in Sect. 3, the risk assessment methodology requires three inputs, two inputs as a result of the asset inventory and the third involving conditional probability tables.

The asset inventory listed $m_c = 4$ cyber assets corresponding to the four PLCs ($PLC_1^r$, $PLC_2^s$, $PLC_3^s$, $PLC_4^s$) and $m_p = 6$ physical assets corresponding to the six tanks ($T_1^r$, $T_4^r$, $T_5^r$, $T_6^s$ $T_7^s$, $T_8^s$) involved in the physical process. Thus, the numbers of event layer and trustworthiness layer nodes for each Bayesian network equal the number of cyber assets ($m_c = 4$) and the number of fault layer nodes equals the number of cyber and physical assets ($m_c + m_p = 10$).

Each identified asset was assigned a weight $w_j$ quantifying the degree of criticality of the asset to the cyber-physical process – the greater the asset importance, the greater its asset weight.

To understand the weight assignments, consider the water flow in the testbed. Water flow starts in the first subsystem and water successively flows to the second, third and fourth subsystems. The assets in the first subsystem have the highest weights because they are responsible for initiating and maintaining water flow in the testbed. The asset weights become progressively lower in the successive subsystems. Table 2 shows the final weights assigned to the physical and cyber assets in the testbed.

**Table 2.** Weights associated with testbed assets.

| Physical Asset | Weight |
|---|---|
| $T_1^r$ | 0.90 |
| $T_4^r$ | 0.70 |
| $T_5^r$ | 0.85 |
| $T_6^s$ | 0.70 |
| $T_7^s$ | 0.60 |
| $T_8^s$ | 0.50 |
| Cyber Asset | Weight |
| $PLC_1^r$ | 0.80 |
| $PLC_2^s$ | 0.60 |
| $PLC_3^s$ | 0.40 |
| $PLC_4^s$ | 0.20 |

**Table 3.** Conditional probability table for fault layer node $F_{T_8}^p$.

| $F_{T_7}^p$ | $F$ | $F$ | $T$ | $T$ |
|---|---|---|---|---|
| $F_{PLC_3^p}$ | $F$ | $T$ | $F$ | $T$ |
| $F_{T_8}^p = T$ | 0 | 0.75 | 0.8 | 0.9 |
| $F_{T_8}^p = F$ | 1 | 0.25 | 0.2 | 0.1 |

After identifying the number of nodes per Bayesian network, the conditional probability tables must be defined to convey the causal relationships between connected nodes. The conditional probability tables for trustworthiness layer nodes express the probabilities that attacks are occurring at specific cyber assets given an event triggered by the intrusion detection system module upon detecting a cyber attack. In contrast, the conditional probability tables for fault layer nodes specify the probabilities of faults occurring when a cyber attack on a specific cyber asset is detected. The conditional probability tables also consider the potential cascading effects a fault in a parent node might have on its child nodes. Cascading effects are apparent in the cyber-physical process implemented by the testbed. A fault in $PLC_1^r$ can compromise water flow from $T_1^r$ and $T_5^r$ to the other tanks in the next three subsystems causing increased anomalies.

In general, the conditional probability tables are based on empirical analysis of historic process data and/or insights from plant operators. In the case study, the conditional probability tables were determined by interviewing ten water distribution experts. Each expert was asked to assess the failure probability of each node (i.e., single asset) given the states of its parent nodes when they were impaired by cyber attacks.

Table 3 shows the conditional probability table associated with fault layer node $F_{T_8}^p$. As mentioned in Sect. 3.2, the conditional probability tables of trust-

**Table 4.** Detectable cyber attack classes.

| Cyber Attack Class |
|---|
| Scanning Attacks |
| Man-in-the-Middle Attacks |
| Denial-of-Service Attacks |

worthiness layer nodes are not established during the initial setup phase. Instead, they are dynamically updated during the online phase based on the attack detection probabilities provided by the intrusion detection system module.

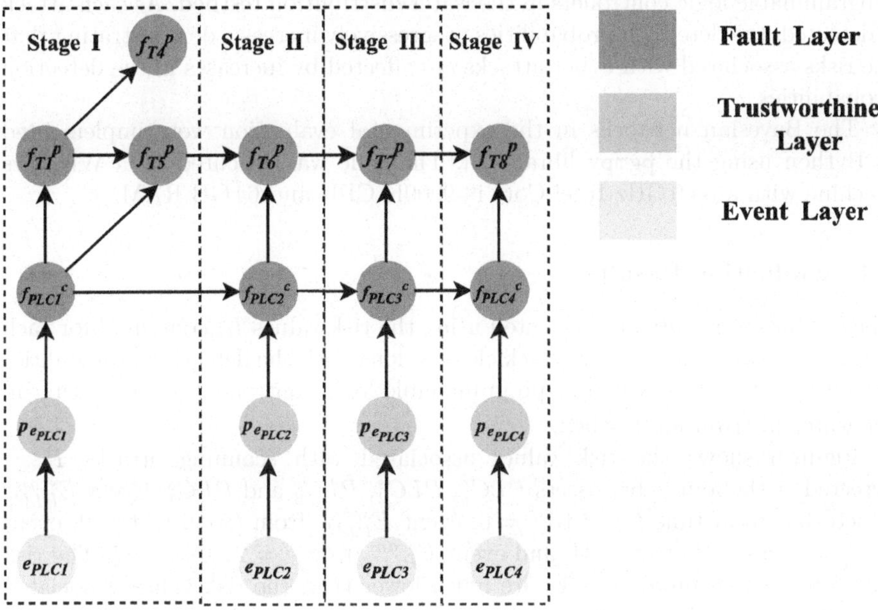


**Fig. 5.** Structure of Bayesian network $BN_i$ used in the case study.

After setting up the individual Bayesian networks, the final step is to determine the total number of networks in the Bayesian network module. As mentioned in Sect. 3.2, the set of Bayesian networks is determined based on the number of cyber attack classes detected by the intrusion detection system module. In the case study, it was assumed that three classes of cyber attacks are detectable by the intrusion detection system module: scanning attacks, man-in-the-middle (MitM) attacks and denial-of-service (DoS) attacks (Table 4). As a result, three Bayesian networks were employed in the case study to model the spread of the three classes of attacks over the water distribution testbed assets. Figure 5 shows the structure of Bayesian network $BN_i$ used in the case study.

### 4.3 Evaluation Setup

The effectiveness of the proposed risk assessment methodology was evaluated by implementing an attack scenario with a duration of 50 s, during which an attacker sequentially targets the cyber assets of the water distribution testbed.

In the scenario, an attacker gains access to the testbed network and scans for programmable logic controllers. Upon locating the devices, the attacker initiates two man-in-the-middle attacks directed at $PLC_1^r$ and $PLC_2^s$, and two denial-of-service attacks directed at $PLC_3^s$ and $PLC_4^s$. The detection probabilities for the attacks were determined in the case study using simulation experiments. However, the probabilities may also be derived using supervised/unsupervised machine learning models or deep learning models [8,9].

Table 5 shows the cyber attack detection probabilities over time for the four programmable logic controllers in the water distribution testbed. As each attack is detected, the detection probabilities progressively increase, demonstrating that the risks associated with cyber attacks are affected by increases in the detection probabilities.

The Bayesian networks in the experimental evaluation were implemented in Python using the `pgmpy` library [2]. The code was executed on a Windows machine with a 3.60 GHz Intel Core i9-9900K CPU and 64 GB RAM.

### 4.4 Evaluation Results

The evaluation results are presented using the risk values $R_i$ computed for each of the three detectable cyber attack classes along with the detection probabilities $P_{E_j^i}$ of the attacks on the four programmable logic controllers (cyber assets) in the water distribution testbed.

Figure 6 shows the risk values associated with scanning attacks $R_{scan}$ detected at the four cyber assets $PLC_1^r$, $PLC_2^s$, $PLC_3^s$ and $PLC_4^s$. Event $E_{PLC_1^r}^{scan}$ is detected from time $t = 3$ to $t = 6$, event $E_{PLC_2^s}^{scan}$ from $t = 6$ to $t = 9$, event $E_{PLC_3^s}^{scan}$ from $t = 20$ to $t = 24$, and event $E_{PLC_4^s}^{scan}$ from $t = 22$ to $t = 27$. The risk values for the scanning attacks are much lower than the risk values associated with the man-in-the-middle and denial-of-service attacks discussed below. This is expected because scanning attacks do not impair the cyber-physical process as the attacker is only attempting to discover the cyber devices that are active in the industrial control system network.

In this case, the risk values are strongly dependent on the detection probability values, number of detected attacks and cyber assets targeted by the attacks. Indeed, $R_{scan}$ suddenly increases at $t = 6$ and $t = 22$ when two scanning attacks are detected at the same time. Moreover, the risk value associated with $E_{PLC_1^r}^{scan}$ is much higher than that for $E_{PLC_4^s}^{scan}$ because $PLC_1^r$ is more critical than $PLC_4^s$ ($w_{PLC_1^r} > w_{PLC_4^s}$). Also, the risk values increase proportionally to the detection probabilities as seen in the time intervals $\Delta t_1 = [7, 9]$, $\Delta t_2 = [20, 21]$, $\Delta t_3 = [22, 24]$ and $\Delta t_4 = [25, 27]$.

**Table 5.** Cyber attack detection probabilities over time.

| Time | Scanning Attacks | | | | MitM Attacks | | | | DoS Attacks | | | |
|---|---|---|---|---|---|---|---|---|---|---|---|---|
| | $PLC_1^r$ | $PLC_2^s$ | $PLC_3^s$ | $PLC_4^s$ | $PLC_1^r$ | $PLC_2^s$ | $PLC_3^s$ | $PLC_4^s$ | $PLC_1^r$ | $PLC_2^s$ | $PLC_3^s$ | $PLC_4^s$ |
| 1 | 0 | 0 | 0 | 0 | 0 | 0 | 0 | 0 | 0 | 0 | 0 | 0 |
| 2 | 0 | 0 | 0 | 0 | 0 | 0 | 0 | 0 | 0 | 0 | 0 | 0 |
| 3 | **0.8** | 0 | 0 | 0 | 0 | 0 | 0 | 0 | 0 | 0 | 0 | 0 |
| 4 | **0.8** | 0 | 0 | 0 | 0 | 0 | 0 | 0 | 0 | 0 | 0 | 0 |
| 5 | **0.8** | 0 | 0 | 0 | 0 | 0 | 0 | 0 | 0 | 0 | 0 | 0 |
| 6 | **0.8** | 0 | 0 | **0.6** | 0 | 0 | 0 | 0 | 0 | 0 | 0 | 0 |
| 7 | 0 | 0 | 0 | **0.7** | 0 | 0 | 0 | 0 | 0 | 0 | 0 | 0 |
| 8 | 0 | 0 | 0 | **0.9** | 0 | 0 | 0 | 0 | 0 | 0 | 0 | 0 |
| 9 | 0 | 0 | 0 | **0.9** | 0 | 0 | 0 | 0 | **0.6** | 0 | 0 | 0 |
| 10 | 0 | 0 | 0 | 0 | 0 | 0 | 0 | 0 | **0.6** | 0 | 0 | 0 |
| 11 | 0 | 0 | 0 | 0 | 0 | 0 | 0 | 0 | **0.6** | 0 | 0 | 0 |
| 12 | 0 | 0 | 0 | 0 | 0 | 0 | 0 | **0.2** | **0.6** | 0 | 0 | 0 |
| 13 | 0 | 0 | 0 | 0 | 0 | 0 | 0 | **0.2** | **0.7** | 0 | 0 | 0 |
| 14 | 0 | 0 | 0 | 0 | 0 | 0 | 0 | **0.2** | **0.7** | 0 | 0 | 0 |
| 15 | 0 | 0 | 0 | 0 | 0 | 0 | 0 | **0.2** | **0.7** | 0 | 0 | 0 |
| 16 | 0 | 0 | 0 | 0 | 0 | 0 | 0 | **0.2** | **0.7** | 0 | 0 | 0 |
| 17 | 0 | 0 | 0 | 0 | 0 | 0 | 0 | **0.2** | **0.7** | 0 | 0 | 0 |
| 18 | 0 | 0 | 0 | 0 | 0 | 0 | 0 | **0.6** | **0.7** | 0 | 0 | 0 |
| 19 | 0 | 0 | 0 | 0 | 0 | 0 | 0 | **0.6** | **0.75** | 0 | 0 | 0 |
| 20 | 0 | 0 | **0.6** | 0 | 0 | 0 | 0 | **0.6** | **0.75** | 0 | 0 | 0 |
| 21 | 0 | 0 | **0.7** | 0 | 0 | 0 | 0 | **0.6** | **0.75** | 0 | 0 | 0 |
| 22 | 0 | **0.6** | **0.8** | 0 | 0 | 0 | 0 | **0.7** | **0.75** | 0 | 0 | 0 |
| 23 | 0 | **0.6** | **0.9** | 0 | 0 | 0 | 0 | **0.7** | **0.75** | 0 | 0 | 0 |
| 24 | 0 | **0.8** | **0.9** | 0 | 0 | 0 | 0 | **0.7** | **0.75** | 0 | 0 | 0 |
| 25 | 0 | **0.8** | 0 | 0 | 0 | 0 | 0 | **0.7** | 0 | 0 | 0 | 0 |
| 26 | 0 | **0.9** | 0 | 0 | 0 | 0 | 0 | **0.7** | 0 | 0 | 0 | 0 |
| 27 | 0 | **1.0** | 0 | 0 | 0 | 0 | 0 | **0.7** | 0 | 0 | **0.7** | 0 |
| 28 | 0 | 0 | 0 | 0 | 0 | 0 | 0 | **0.8** | 0 | 0 | **0.7** | 0 |
| 29 | 0 | 0 | 0 | 0 | 0 | 0 | 0 | **0.8** | 0 | 0 | **0.7** | 0 |
| 30 | 0 | 0 | 0 | 0 | 0 | 0 | 0 | **0.8** | 0 | 0 | **0.8** | 0 |
| 31 | 0 | 0 | 0 | 0 | 0 | 0 | 0 | **0.8** | 0 | 0 | **0.85** | 0 |
| 32 | 0 | 0 | 0 | 0 | 0 | 0 | 0 | **0.8** | 0 | 0 | **0.85** | 0 |
| 33 | 0 | 0 | 0 | 0 | 0 | **0.7** | 0 | **0.8** | 0 | 0 | **0.85** | 0 |
| 34 | 0 | 0 | 0 | 0 | 0 | **0.7** | 0 | **0.9** | 0 | 0 | **0.85** | 0 |
| 35 | 0 | 0 | 0 | 0 | 0 | **0.7** | 0 | **0.9** | 0 | 0 | **0.85** | 0 |
| 36 | 0 | 0 | 0 | 0 | 0 | **0.7** | 0 | **0.9** | 0 | 0 | **0.85** | 0 |
| 37 | 0 | 0 | 0 | 0 | 0 | **0.7** | 0 | **0.9** | 0 | 0 | **0.85** | 0 |
| 38 | 0 | 0 | 0 | 0 | 0 | **0.7** | 0 | **0.9** | 0 | 0 | **0.85** | 0 |
| 39 | 0 | 0 | 0 | 0 | 0 | **0.8** | 0 | **0.9** | 0 | 0 | **0.85** | 0 |
| 40 | 0 | 0 | 0 | 0 | 0 | **0.8** | 0 | **0.9** | 0 | 0 | **0.85** | 0 |
| 41 | 0 | 0 | 0 | 0 | 0 | **0.8** | 0 | **1** | 0 | 0 | **0.85** | 0 |
| 42 | 0 | 0 | 0 | 0 | 0 | **0.8** | 0 | **1** | 0 | 0 | **0.85** | 0 |
| 43 | 0 | 0 | 0 | 0 | 0 | **0.8** | 0 | **1** | 0 | 0 | **0.85** | 0 |
| 44 | 0 | 0 | 0 | 0 | 0 | **0.8** | 0 | **1** | 0 | 0 | **0.95** | 0 |
| 45 | 0 | 0 | 0 | 0 | 0 | **0.8** | 0 | **1** | 0 | 0 | **0.95** | 0 |
| 46 | 0 | 0 | 0 | 0 | 0 | **0.9** | 0 | **1** | 0 | 0 | **0.95** | 0 |
| 47 | 0 | 0 | 0 | 0 | 0 | **0.9** | 0 | **1** | 0 | 0 | **0.95** | 0 |
| 48 | 0 | 0 | 0 | 0 | 0 | **0.9** | 0 | **1** | 0 | 0 | **0.95** | 0 |
| 49 | 0 | 0 | 0 | 0 | 0 | **0.9** | 0 | **1** | 0 | 0 | **1** | 0 |
| 50 | 0 | 0 | 0 | 0 | 0 | **0.9** | 0 | **1** | 0 | 0 | **1** | 0 |

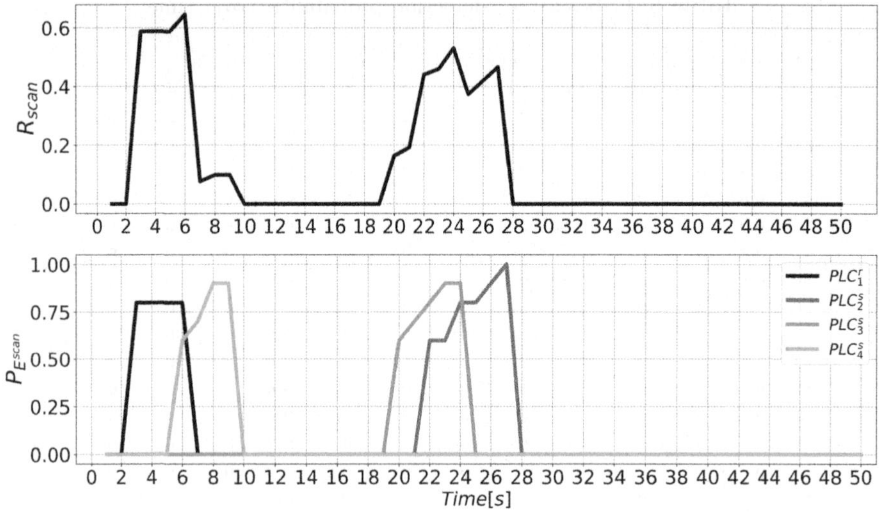


**Fig. 6.** Risk values associated with scanning attacks.

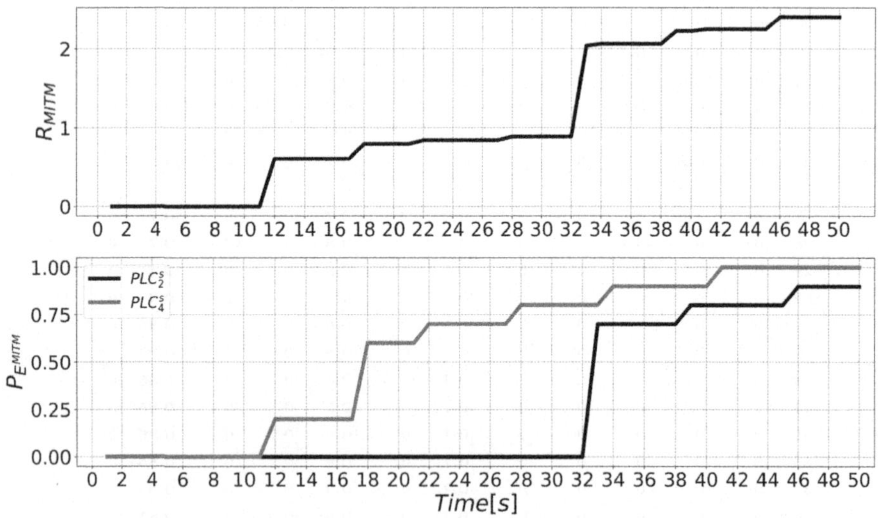


**Fig. 7.** Risk values associated with man-in-the-middle attacks.

Figure 7 shows the risk values associated with the man-in-the-middle attacks $R_{MitM}$ detected at the two cyber assets $PLC_2^s$ and $PLC_4^s$. Event $E_{PLC_2^s}^{MitM}$ is detected from time $t = 12$ to $t = 50$ and event $E_{PLC_4^s}^{MitM}$ from $t = 33$ to $t = 50$.

It is important to note that the risk values not only escalate in proportion to the attack detection probabilities, but they also increase with the number of cyber attacks detected at different cyber assets. This correlation is seen at time $t = 33$ when the risk value suddenly increases from $R_{MitM} = 0.9$ to $R_{MitM} = 2.1$. The increase is due to the detection of the second man-in-the-middle attack $E^{MitM}_{PLC^s_2}$, which occurs during event $E^{MitM}_{PLC^s_4}$. This arises because of the event and fault layers in the Bayesian network – the greater the number of events detected by the intrusion detection system module, the greater the possible failures of cyber and physical assets. The failures could be direct consequences of the detected attacks or they could result from cascading effects triggered by the impairment of other cyber and physical assets.

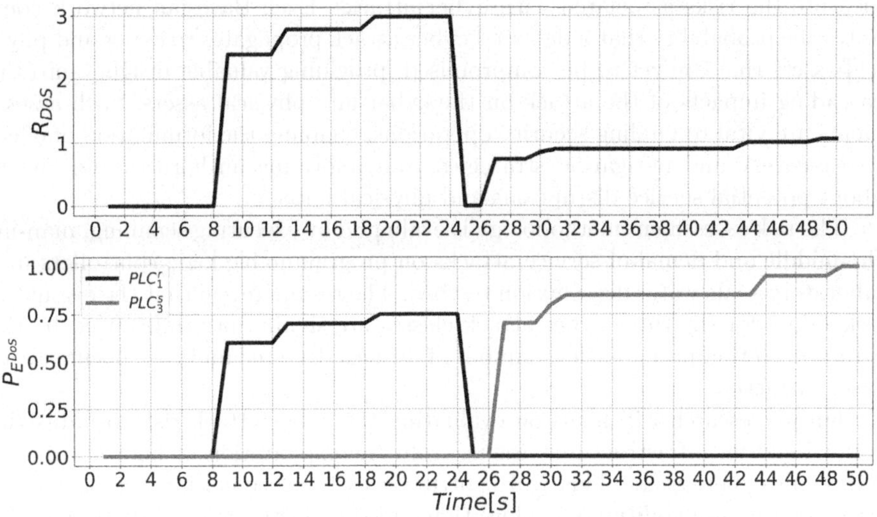


**Fig. 8.** Risk values associated with denial-of-service attacks.

Figure 8 shows the risk values associated with the denial-of-service attacks $R_{DoS}$ detected at the two cyber assets $PLC^r_1$ and $PLC^s_3$. Event $E^{DoS}_{PLC^r_1}$ is detected from time $t = 9$ to $t = 24$ and event $E^{DoS}_{PLC^s_3}$ from $t = 27$ to $t = 50$.

The risk values are significantly influenced by the detection probabilities associated with the two events as well as the cyber assets impacted by the attack. Notably, for events $E^{DoS}_{PLC^r_1}$ and $E^{DoS}_{PLC^s_3}$, the risk values increase proportionally to the detection probability values. This correlation is due to the trustworthiness layer in the Bayesian network that weights the detected events based on the detection likelihood provided by the intrusion detection system module – the greater the detection probability, the greater the risk associated with the specific attack. Furthermore, it is important to note that although the probability $P_{E^{DoS}_{PLC^s_3}}$ is higher than $P_{E^{DoS}_{PLC^r_1}}$, the risk value for $E^{DoS}_{PLC^r_1}$ is much higher than that for $E^{DoS}_{PLC^s_3}$. The difference stems from the different levels of criticality associated with the targeted cyber assets ($w_{PLC^r_1} = 0.80$ and $w_{PLC^s_3} = 0.40$). Indeed, $PLC^r_1$ is responsible for initiating the entire physical process by pumping water from tank $T_1^r$ to the other tanks. Therefore, a denial-of-service attack compromising $PLC_1^r$ poses a significantly higher risk to the entire water distribution process compared with a similar impairment of $PLC_3^s$ that controls fewer physical assets towards the end of the water distribution process.

## 5 Conclusions

The probabilistic risk assessment methodology described in this chapter is tailored to industrial control systems. It leverages multiple Bayesian networks to measure the risks associated with cyber attacks. Each Bayesian network computes the probability that a detected cyber attack propagates to cyber and physical assets that are yet to be compromised, providing valuable insights into the cascading impacts of the attack on the cyber and physical assets. Such assessments are vital to guiding security operations, enabling the formulation of effective recovery and mitigation strategies, and informing authorities and clients about potential service disruptions and physical impacts.

The risk assessment methodology is evaluated by executing scanning, man-in-the-middle and denial-of-service attacks on programmable logic controllers in a laboratory-scale water distribution testbed. The results reveal that the evaluated risk values for the three cyber attack classes are significantly influenced by the attack detection probabilities, number of attacks detected and the specific cyber assets attacked.

Future research will focus on evaluating the cyber attack risk to industrial control system infrastructures arising from the exploitation of known vulnerabilities in cyber assets. This will contribute to the formulation of risk indices based on the probabilities of exploitation and the severity scores associated with the common vulnerabilities and exposures (CVEs) identified for cyber assets in industrial control system infrastructures.

**Acknowledgement.** This research was funded by the Italian National Institute for Insurance Against Accidents at Work (INAIL) under Grant no. BRIC2021-ID03.

## References

1. Adaros-Boye, C., Kearney. P., Josephs, M.: Continuous risk management for Industrial IoT: a methodological view. In: Proceedings of the Fourteen International Conference on Risks and Security of Internet and Systems, pp. 34–49 (2020)
2. Ankan, A., Panda, A.: pgmpy: probabilistic graphical models using Python. In: Proceedings of the Fourteenth Python in Science Conference, pp. 6–11 (2015)
3. Barua, S., Gao, X., Pasman, H., Mannan, M.: Bayesian-network-based dynamic operational risk assessment. J. Loss Prev. Process Ind. **41**, 399–410 (2016)
4. Birnbaum, Z., Davis, M., Salman, S., Schaffter, J., Watkins, L., Yamajala, S., Paul, S.: Cyber-resilient SCADA systems via secure state restoration. In: ICCIP 2020. IAICT, vol. 596, pp. 183–207. Springer, Cham (2020). https://doi.org/10.1007/978-3-030-62840-6_9

5. Eckhart, M., Brenner, B., Ekelhart, A., Weippl, E.: Quantitative security risk assessment for industrial control systems: research opportunities and challenges. J. Internet Serv. Inf. Secur. **9**(3), 52–73 (2019)
6. De Felice, F., Baffo, I., Petrillo, A.: Critical infrastructures overview: past, present and future. Sustainability **14**(4), 2233 (2022)
7. Faramondi, L., Flammini, F., Guarino, S., Setola, R.: A hardware-in-the-loop water distribution testbed dataset for cyber-physical security testing. IEEE Access **9**, 122385–122396 (2021)
8. Faramondi, L., Flammini, F., Guarino, S., Setola, R.: A hybrid behavior- and Bayesian network-based framework for cyber-physical anomaly detection. Comput. Electr. Eng. **112**, 108998 (2023)
9. Faramondi, L., Flammini, F., Guarino, S., Setola, R.: Evaluating machine learning approaches for cyber and physical anomalies in SCADA systems. In: Proceedings of the Third IEEE International Conference on Cyber Security and Resilience, pp. 412–417 (2023)
10. Faramondi, L., Grassi, M., Guarino, S., Setola, R., Alcaraz, C.: Configuration vulnerability in Snort for Windows operating systems. In: Proceedings of the IEEE International Conference on Cyber Security and Resilience, pp. 82–89 (2022)
11. Faramondi, L., Guarino, S., Oliva, G., Setola, R.: A recovery model for a faulty networked system. IEEE Syst. J. **18**(1), 146–149 (2024)
12. Fioravanti, C., Guarino, S., Mazza, B., Nobili, M., Santucci, F., Ansaldi, S.: A risk assessment framework for critical infrastructure based on the analytic hierarchy process. IFAC PapersOnLine **55**(40), 277–282 (2022)
13. Guarino, S., Vitale, F., Flammini, F., Faramondi, L., Mazzocca, N., Setola, R.: A two-level fusion framework for cyber-physical anomaly detection. IEEE Trans. Ind. Cyber-Phys. Syst. **2**, 1–13 (2024)
14. Khoury, J., Nassar, M.: A hybrid game theory and reinforcement learning approach for cyber-physical systems security. In: Proceedings of the IEEE/IFIP Network Operations and Management Symposium (2020)
15. Lehto, M.: Cyber-attacks against critical infrastructure. In: Lehto, M., Neittaanmäki, P. (eds.) Cyber Security: Critical Infrastructure Protection, pp. 3–42. Springer, Cham (2022). https://doi.org/10.1007/978-3-030-91293-2_1
16. Liu, W., Song, Z.: Review of studies on the resilience of urban critical infrastructure networks. Reliab. Eng. Syst. Saf. **193**, 106617 (2020)
17. Lyu, X., Ding, Y., Yang, S.: Bayesian-network-based C2P risk assessment for cyber-physical systems. IEEE Access **8**, 88506–88517 (2020)
18. Munirathinam, S.: Industry 4.0: Industrial Internet of Things (IIOT). Adv. Comput. **117**(1), 129–164 (2020)
19. Peng, Y., Huang, K., Tu, W., Zhou, C.: A model-data integrated cyber security risk assessment method for industrial control systems. In: Proceedings of the Seventh IEEE Data Driven Control and Learning Systems Conference, pp. 344–349 (2018)
20. Qassim, Q., Jamil, N., Mahdi, M., Rahim, A.: Towards SCADA threat intelligence based on intrusion detection systems – a short review. In: Proceedings of the Eighth International Conference on Information Technology and Multimedia, pp. 144–149 (2020)
21. Setola, R., De Porcellinis, S., Sforna, M.: Critical infrastructure dependency assessment using the input-output inoperability model. Int. J. Crit. Infrastruct. Prot. **2**(4), 170–178 (2009)
22. Stouffer, K., Falco, J., Scarfone, K.: Guide to Industrial Control Systems (ICS) Security, NIST Special Publication 800-82 Revision 2, National Institute of Standards and Technology, Gaithersburg, Maryland (2015)

23. Xie, J., Sun, K., Lei, X.: Risk assessment method for power plant industrial control information security based on Bayesian attack graphs. J. Electr. Syst. **17**(4) (2021)
24. Zhang, Q., Zhou, C., Tian, Y., Xiong, N., Qin, Y., Hu, B.: A fuzzy probability Bayesian network approach for dynamic cybersecurity risk assessment in industrial control systems. IEEE Trans. Industr. Inf. **14**(6), 2497–2506 (2018)

# Automated Programmable Logic Controller Memory Forensics Using RGB Image Analysis and Deep Learning

Rima Asmar Awad[1(✉)], Michael Sprayberry[1], Irfan Ahmed[2], Michael Rogers[3], and Juan Lopez[1]

[1] Oak Ridge National Laboratory, Oak Ridge, TN, USA
awadrl@ornl.gov
[2] Virginia Commonwealth University, Richmond, VA, USA
[3] Tennessee Technological University, Cookeville, TN, USA

**Abstract.** The introduction of Industry 4.0 and Internet-based technologies has enhanced industrial control system operations but have inadvertently increased their vulnerabilities to cyber attacks. When an industrial control system is compromised, security analysts need to identify the root cause quickly to start the recovery process and develop mitigation strategies. Memory forensics is critical in the incident analysis process to ascertain what occurred. Approaches for analyzing the persistent memory in industrial control devices are limited and almost nonexistent for volatile memory.

This chapter proposes an automated methodology for programmable logic controller memory dump analysis using computer vision and deep learning techniques. The methodology converts the sequences of bytes in a programmable logic controller memory dump to red-green-blue pixels and employs a deep learning model that learns the underlying patterns and features of pre-labeled forensic artifacts in images and segments them into distinct regions. The trained model is employed to automatically segment new memory images and identify forensic artifacts. Evaluation of the methodology on a Schneider Electric Modicon M221 programmable logic controller under code injection and code modification attacks demonstrates its ability to detect attack artifacts in memory dumps.

**Keywords:** Industrial Control Systems · Memory Forensics · Image Analysis · Deep Learning

## 1 Introduction

Early industrial control systems that ran in isolation, unconnected from the Internet, were immune to network-based cyber attacks and did not need to implement security functions [1]. However, modern industrial control systems


Published by Springer Nature Switzerland AG 2025
J. Staggs and S. Shenoi (Eds.): ICCIP 2024, IFIP AICT 725, pp. 131–152, 2025.
https://doi.org/10.1007/978-3-031-81888-2_7

have evolved to communicate over local and wide area networks, exposing them to serious cyber threats [4]. Although attacks on industrial control systems date as far back as 1982 [17], dramatic increases in sophisticated targeted attacks are being reported. Stuxnet is recognized as the first cyber weapon to target critical infrastructure [10]. Duqu, Flame, Gauss and Wiper have followed Stuxnet; they are just a few examples of attacks targeting industrial control systems [16].

The increased cyber threats have drawn attention to securing industrial control systems and endpoint devices. When a system misbehaves or fails, it is essential to determine the root cause as quickly and reliably as possible. The cause can be a hardware failure, software bug or cyber attack, and the incident response depends on the correct diagnosis. Digital forensic techniques and tools are vital to understanding such incidents, instituting recovery plans and performing mitigations [4]. In general, forensic techniques and tools developed for information technology systems have been applied to industrial control systems [8]. However, the focus on information technology components leaves level 0 and 1 endpoint devices in industrial control systems without forensic support. Limited efforts have focused on analyzing the persistent memory of level 0 and 1 devices [4]. Moreover, as in the case of information technology systems, industrial control system incidents may not leave traces in persistent memory. Therefore, it is important to focus on the forensic acquisition and analysis of volatile memory of endpoint devices in industrial control systems [14].

Programmable logic controllers are standard endpoint devices in industrial control systems. Their lack of security mechanisms enables attacks to modify their firmware and control logic programs [1]. In a typical scenario, an attacker leverages a vulnerability to gain access to a target device and execute malicious code in volatile memory, leaving no traces in persistent storage. Programmable logic controller memory forensic analysis is crucial to collecting the artifacts and answering important questions about the incident. Although the memory analysis can be conducted manually [6], it is a tedious, time-consuming task that is prone to human error. Automating forensic artifact identification in a memory dump would significantly decrease the effort and time while enhancing accuracy.

This chapter describes an automated memory analysis methodology for programmable logic controllers that engages computer vision and deep learning techniques. A programmable logic controller memory dump is converted to red-green-blue (RGB) pixels and deep learning is used to create a model of pre-labeled forensic artifacts in the RGB image. The deep learning model is employed to automatically segment new memory images and identify forensic artifacts. The effectiveness of the automated analysis methodology is evaluated using code injection and code modification attacks from the literature [7,14,24] and validating the results against the results of manual analysis. An experimental evaluation demonstrates that the methodology effectively detects code injection and code modification attacks. Additionally, the visual results enhance the speed and accuracy of forensic analyses without the need for bytecode analysis.

## 2 Related Work

Memory acquisition is an important step in programmable logic controller memory forensics because it provides valuable information about the device configuration, state and operations that can be used to detect and respond to cyber attacks and other security incidents [5]. Partial memory acquisition is performed by connecting directly to the programmable logic controller or by extracting memory data from the programmable logic controller backup system [22]. After the memory data has been acquired, it is analyzed using various forensic tools and techniques. Very few works in the research literature describe full programmable logic controller memory acquisitions.

Wu and Nurse [23] investigated the possibility of using programmable logic controller debugging tools to acquire memory data. They employed the PLC Logger tool to communicate with a Siemens programmable logic controller and acquire data from memory addresses. However, the approach is limited to using a specific debugging tool on a Siemens programmable logic controller model.

Denton et al. [11] examined the proprietary General Electric GE-SRTP network protocol. They reverse engineered the protocol and analyzed it in relation to programmable logic controller requirements. Denton and colleagues subsequently developed a tool that communicates directly with a General Electric programmable logic controller and accesses its memory registers. They demonstrated that, by manipulating the protocol, they could change the logic of the program running on a programmable logic controller.

Findrik et al. [12] developed PLCBlockMon, a functional block for Siemens S7 controllers that implements a ladder-logic program for data logging and memory acquisition. However, because PLCBlockMon runs in device memory, it is vulnerable to memory attacks and additional verification is required.

Qasim et al. [19] extracted the control logic from captured network traffic of an attack instance by utilizing a built-in decompiler provided with programmable logic controller engineering software. Zubair et al. [26] proposed a framework for acquiring programmable logic controller memory remotely. Specifically, they appended a small amount of code to the control logic that would execute and read the memory contents from areas that are not authorized to be read via a network protocol. Zubair and colleagues also analyzed portions of the acquired memory, but their overall focus was on memory extraction, not memory analysis.

Rais et al. [20] acquired the memory of an Allen-Bradley Control Logix 1756 programmable logic controller via its JTAG interface and discussed the challenges and limitations of the approach that prevent it from being used for all programmable logic controller models. However, this work and others focus on identifying control logic attacks, firmware reverse engineering or intrusion detection. In contrast, the proposed methodology focuses on extracting forensic artifacts to identify the root causes and other details about anomalous behavior and attacks.

In subsequent work, Rais et al. [21] describe a differential-analysis-based framework that extracts forensic artifacts from programmable logic controller memory dumps. The extracted artifacts include programmable logic controller firmware, control logic, input and output pin states, and programmable logic controller operational parameters. However, the approach requires a programmable logic controller for profile generation. In contrast, the proposed methodology does not require a programmable logic controller to identify data structures in a memory dump, and it can be used on any device of the same model regardless of its project or operating environment.

Yoo et al. [25] proposed a technique for identifying control logic attacks on programmable logic controllers by creating and updating a local copy of the memory state using network communications. They employed a classification algorithm that uses 42 unique control logic features to identify malicious control logic injections and modifications.

The research literature in industrial control system forensics covers areas such as persistent network forensics and memory verification. However, very little research has focused on memory forensics of level 0–1 industrial control system devices such as programmable logic controllers. Because volatile memory dumps reflect the system states of programmable logic controllers, methodologies for acquiring and automatically analyzing memory images in a timely manner are needed to investigate abnormal system behavior caused by system failure or cyber attacks. Automating memory forensic analysis can speed up investigations and improve efficiency by automating time-consuming tasks such as data extraction and analysis. In addition, it reduces the risk of human error and ensures that investigations are consistent and accurate.

## 3 Proposed Methodology

Figure 1 provides an overview of the proposed automated programmable logic controller forensics methodology. After identifying the target device, the communications protocol function codes are used to obtain memory dumps. The manual analysis method described in [3,6] investigates the hardware and software components of a programmable logic controller to create its memory profile. The memory profile is employed as a reference for memory forensic analysis and forensic artifact identification. Forensic artifact identification is automated by converting the sequences of bytes in a memory dump to an image comprising RGB pixels and applying a trained deep learning model on the image.

Before training the deep learning model on RGB images of memory dumps, labels are assigned to the forensic artifacts identified during manual analysis. The model learns the underlying patterns and features in the images and automatically segments them into distinct regions. The trained deep learning model automatically segments new memory images and identifies forensic artifacts. After the trained model is validated, it can be used to analyze memory dumps. By integrating the model output in the memory analysis process, a forensic analyst can locate the memory regions of concern and the raw bytes in the regions are classified as belonging to one of the critical classes of forensic artifacts.

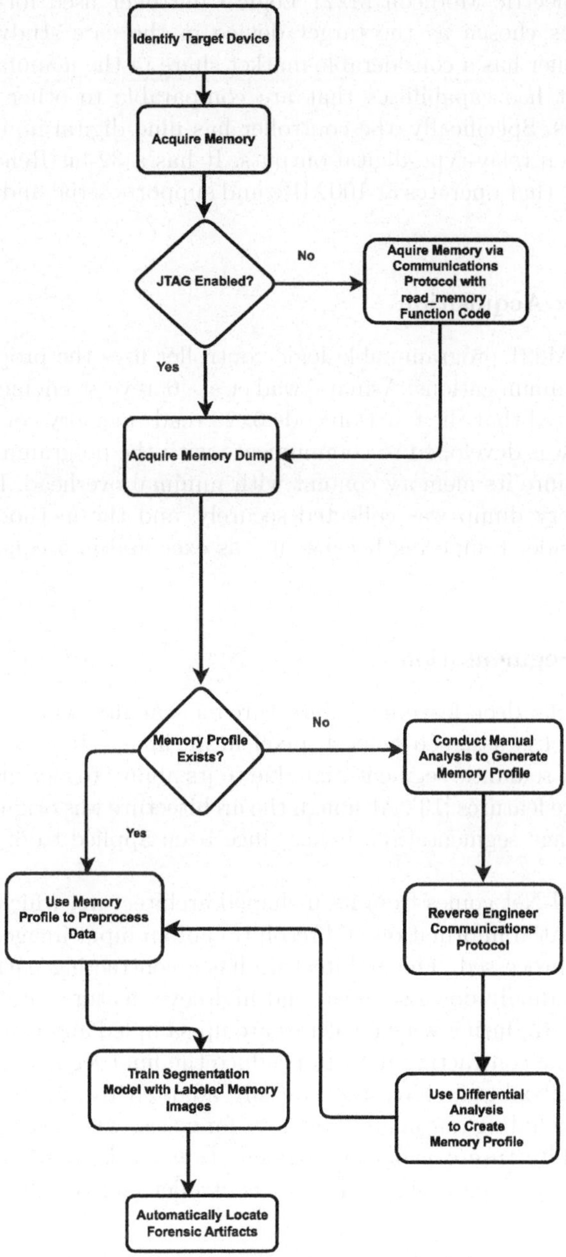


**Fig. 1.** Automated programmable logic controller forensics methodology.

### 3.1 Target Device

A Schneider Electric Modicon M221 Logic Controller used for basic machine automation was chosen as the target device in the case study. The general-purpose controller has a considerable market share in the manufacturing sector. Additionally, it has capabilities that are comparable to other programmable logic controllers. Specifically, the controller has nine digital inputs, two analog inputs and seven relay-type digital outputs. It has a 32-bit Renesas RX630221 microcontroller that operates at 100 MHz and supports serial and Ethernet communications.

### 3.2 Memory Acquisition

The Modicon M221 programmable logic controller uses the proprietary UMAS protocol for communications. Asmar Awad et al. [6] reverse engineered the protocol and discovered that the function code `0x28` reads memory content. A custom Python script was developed to communicate with the programmable logic controller and acquire its memory content with minimal overhead. It was assumed that the memory dump was collected securely, and the methodology was not subject to intruder tampering because it was executed in a controlled environment.

### 3.3 Image Segmentation

U-Net is a popular deep-learning architecture for semantic segmentation in which a semantic label is assigned to each pixel in an image. It is a highly effective architecture for semantic segmentation due to its ability to capture low-level and high-level image features [13]. Although the architecture was originally developed for medical image segmentation, it has since been applied to diverse computer vision tasks.

The name U-Net comes from its u-shaped architecture, which is designed to preserve the spatial information and resolution of an input image as features are extracted and processed. The architecture has a contracting path during which an image is gradually down-sampled and high-level features are extracted, and an expansive path during which features are up-sampled and combined with the features from the contracting path to produce the final segmentation mask [18].

The highly-flexible architecture is easily adapted to different datasets and applications, including automated memory forensics, where the output layer of the U-Net architecture can output segmentation masks that identify different regions of interest in programmable logic controller memory dumps.

**Data Collection and Preprocessing.** The U-Net model is trained by first assembling a dataset of memory dumps from the programmable logic controller under investigation and converting them to a format that can be processed by the deep learning model.

The memory dumps in the dataset used in the case study were collected by downloading various projects to the programmable logic controller and acquiring the memory after each project download while the device was running. Memory dumps corresponding to simulated attacks were obtained by replicating two attack scenarios. In the first attack scenario, code was injected and written to the data block [24]. In the second attack scenario, the original code was modified to create malicious code [14]. A total of 120 memory dumps of size 524 KB were collected.

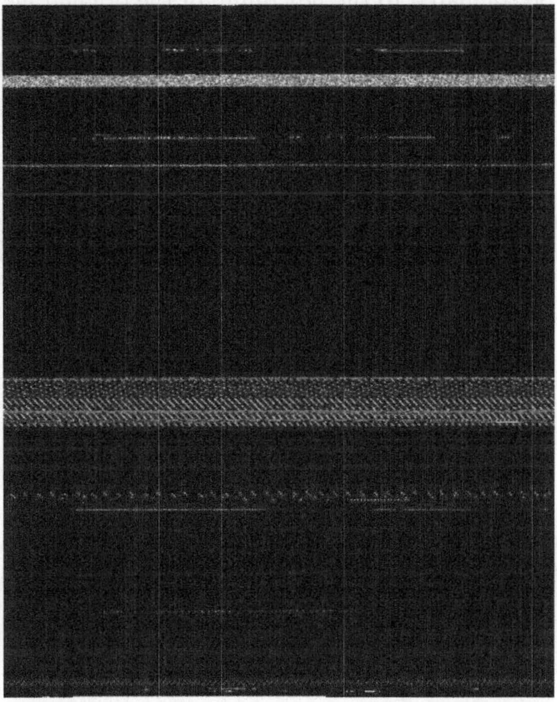

**Fig. 2.** RGB image of a raw memory dump.

The memory images cannot be ingested by a deep learning model in their raw formats. Therefore, the raw memory dump data must be preprocessed into a format that is amenable for training a deep learning model. Preprocessing the raw memory dumps involves the following steps:

- Each raw memory dump is converted to a 2D CMYK image of size 800 × 655, where each byte is plotted as a pixel in a heat map. Figure 2 shows an example of a raw memory dump converted to an image.
- Each CMYK image is resized to a fixed size of 256 × 256 and formatted to ensure that the images have three color channels (RGB). This step, which

employed the OpenCV Python library, is required to ensure that the U-NET deep learning model can learn from the data effectively.

- Areas of interest are annotated and a mask is created for each image. The mask, which defines the regions of interest in the memory dump, is created using an annotation tool or manually based on the programmable logic controller memory profile. Each mask has the same 256 × 256 size as the resized image. The CVAT annotation tool was employed to create the annotated images and output image masks. The tool was used to specify five forensic artifacts of interest. To ensure correct annotation, the image of the memory dump must be compared to the hex dump of the original memory dump.
- Each generated mask is segmented, i.e., assigned a class identifier, based on RGB color values to support U-Net model training. To train the U-Net model with the mask image, the images need to be segmented based on class identifiers (IDs). Performing RGB to class identifier segmentation requires a labeled data set comprising images and their corresponding segmentation maps. Each segmentation map assigns a unique class identifier to each pixel in the image based on the class to which the pixel belongs. For example, all the pixels belonging to the control logic class would be assigned the same class identifier and all the pixels belonging to the metadata class would be assigned a different class identifier. Figure 3 shows an example of an identifier-segmented mask.
- After the images and masks are created, the data is split into training and testing sets to ensure that the U-Net model can generalize well enough to classify new, unseen data. The data set of 120 images was split into 80% for the training set (96 images) and 20% for the testing set (24 images). To ensure that the learned model does not overfit a particular class, pre-assigned weights were assigned to each labeled class. Higher weights were assigned to classes with fewer pixels (such as the control logic class) and lower weights were assigned to classes with more pixels (such as the background class).

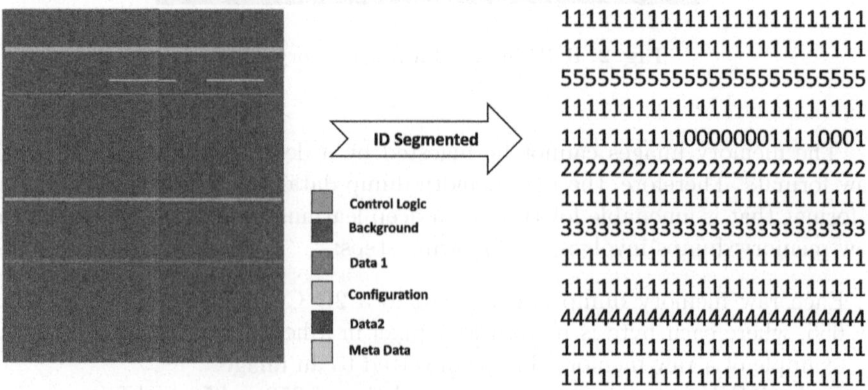


**Fig. 3.** Identifier-segmented mask.

At this point, the dataset can be used to train the U-Net model.

**U-Net Model Architecture and Training.** The U-Net model employed in this work has two encoding layers and two decoding layers. The model generates 121,062 trainable parameters. The model was compiled with Adam (adaptive moment estimation), the Tensorflow standard stochastic gradient descent optimizer, and a learning rate of 0.001. The Tensorflow *sparse_categorical_crossentropy* loss function was employed by the multi-class segmentation model with each output label assigned an integer value. The sparse categorical cross-entropy loss is computed as:

$$\text{Loss} = -\sum_{i=1}^{N} y_i \log(\hat{y}_i)$$

where $y_i$ is the ground truth label for the sample $i$ and $\hat{y}_i$ is the predicted probability of sample $i$ belonging to its correct class.

The U-Net architecture takes a (256, 256, 3) input vector and feeds it to two encoding layers and two decoding layers, each with the LeakyReLU activation function. The LeakyReLU activation function is defined as:

$$\text{leaky\_relu}(\mathbf{z}) = max(\beta * \mathbf{z}, \mathbf{z})$$

where $\mathbf{z}$ is the vector input to the activation function and $\beta$ is the slope of the negative part of the function, which is typically set to a small positive value such as 0.01.

The final output layer is activated with the softmax function that is often used in the final layer of a neural network classifier. The softmax function $\sigma$ is defined as:

$$\sigma(y_i) = \left( \frac{e^{y_i}}{\sum_{j=1}^{n} e^{y_j}} \right)$$

where $y_i$ is the vector of inputs to output layer and $j$ is the output unit index.

To account for the small dataset, the model was trained using batch sizes of 16 and 30 epochs. After compiling the model with the selected optimizer, loss function and class weights, the input images and their corresponding segmentation masks were used to train the model. Following training, the model performance yielded an accuracy metric of 0.98 and a loss metric of 0.067. However, the F1 score, intersection over union (IoU) score and confusion matrix did not reflect high accuracy. Because the dataset has imbalanced classes – some classes (e.g., background class) have significantly more pixels while others (e.g., control logic class) have significantly fewer pixels – the model yielded a high accuracy metric when in reality it has low accuracy. In fact, for the purpose at hand, the precision, recall and confusion matrix would better reflect model accuracy. Another reason for the observed results is the small dataset; segmentation models usually require very large datasets.

**Transfer Learning.** Transfer learning is useful when limited training data is available for a new task and when the new task is related to the original task on which the model was trained. When a pre-trained model is used as the starting point, a model can be trained more quickly and effectively because it has already learned general features appropriate for the new task. Backbone deep learning models are commonly used for transfer learning in semantic segmentation. The backbone models are trained on large-scale datasets such as ImageNet and have learned to extract useful features from images, enabling them to be used as a starting point for related tasks.

The weighted average ensemble technique was selected to enhance the results because it is relatively simple to implement and is easily parallelized for large datasets and models. To compute the weighted average of model predictions, the weights assigned to each model in the ensemble are typically determined based on their performance on a validation dataset. Models that perform better on the validation set are given higher weights in the ensemble. Alternatively, the weights can be determined based on model diversity, with more diverse models receiving higher weights.

## 4 Evaluation and Results

This section discusses the evaluation of the automated memory forensics methodology for programmable logic controllers along with the results obtained in cyber attack scenarios.

**Table 1.** Comparison of segmentation model results.

| Model | Accuracy | Recall | Precision | F1 Score | IoU Score |
|---|---|---|---|---|---|
| U-Net | 0.9822 | 0.5841 | 0.7390 | 0.6309 | 0.5255 |
| U-Net + ResNet34 | 0.9947 | 0.8614 | 0.9528 | 0.9123 | 0.8441 |
| U-Net + ResNet50 | 0.9916 | 0.8586 | 0.8861 | 0.8654 | 0.7700 |
| U-Net + ResNet18 | 0.9897 | 0.8874 | 0.8375 | 0.8564 | 0.7579 |
| U-Net + VGG16 | 0.9865 | 0.6678 | 0.8582 | 0.7122 | 0.5920 |
| U-Net + Inceptionv3 | 0.9843 | 0.7485 | 0.8459 | 0.7879 | 0.7080 |
| Ensemble Model | 0.9938 | 0.8965 | 0.9454 | 0.9167 | 0.8556 |

Table 1 shows the performance metrics for various trained models, including the ensemble model. As expected, the ensemble model yielded the best performance score. However, near-perfect prediction was not achieved because the training dataset was much smaller than those typically used to train deep learning models.

A confusion matrix provides a visual performance measure of the accuracy with which a model classifies image pixels. Figures 4 and 5 show the effects of

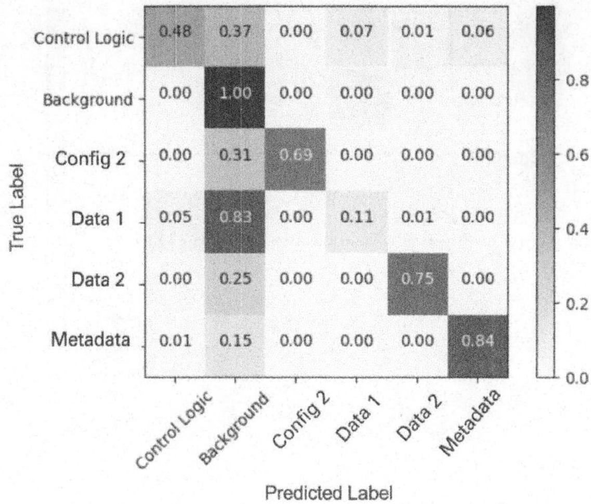


**Fig. 4.** Confusion matrix for the U-Net model.

transfer learning on classification accuracy. While the U-Net model in Fig. 4 does well in classifying background pixels, it does not do as well for the other classes. In contrast, improved accuracy is seen for most of the other classes with the weighted average ensemble model in Fig. 5.

**Test Data Predictions.** As mentioned earlier, the dataset was split into training (80%) and testing (20%) datasets. To evaluate the forensic artifact predictions, testing dataset images were input to the trained model, which outputted the masks. Figures 6, 7, 8, 9, 10 and 11 provide the predictions of the six classes for the testing dataset.

Code injection and code modification attacks were employed to evaluate the effectiveness of the manual and automated memory forensic analysis techniques.

**Code Injection Attack.** Code injection attacks usually leverage flaws in programmable logic controller hardware or software to cause undesired behavior that could result in catastrophic consequences as in the case of Stuxnet [10], TRITON and Black Energy [15]. The code injection attack employed in the evaluation leveraged the fact that programmable logic controllers do not enforce data execution prevention, enabling blocks other than the code block from being executed [24]. Specifically, the code injection attack involved writing malicious control logic in the data block and changing the address in the configuration block that points to the code block to the address of the malicious control logic. In fact, malicious control logic may be injected into any unused memory location. It may even overwrite the metadata block because overwriting the metadata does not interrupt programmable logic controller operation.

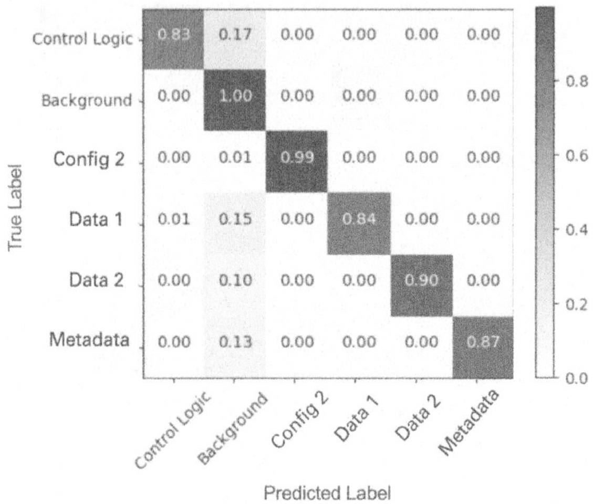


**Fig. 5.** Confusion matrix for the ensemble model.

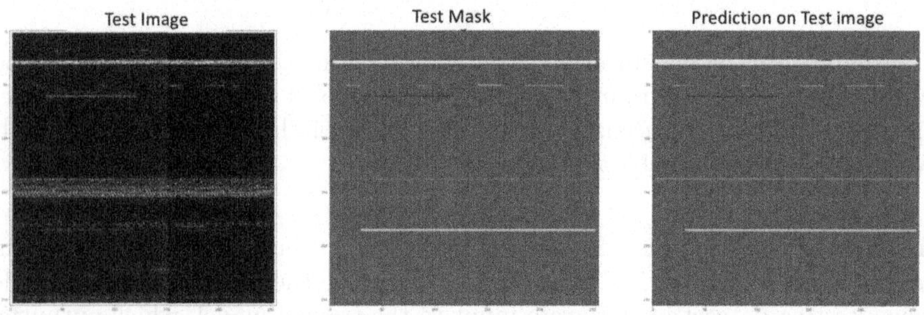


**Fig. 6.** Class 1 prediction with the testing dataset.

Before executing a code injection attack, a memory dump was acquired to obtain a baseline image for comparison. The baseline image was converted to pixels and the resulting image input to the trained ensemble model to classify image pixels into the forensic artifact classes. Figure 12 shows the baseline memory image and the model prediction.

Next, malicious code logic was injected into the data block and the memory dump was acquired. The memory image was converted to pixels and the trained ensemble model classified the image pixels into the forensic artifact classes. Figure 13 shows the code injection memory image and the model prediction. Comparison of the post-attack image in Fig. 13 against the baseline image in Fig. 12 shows extra pixels classified as code right below the data pixels. Since the approximate location of the injected code is known, the suspect memory block can be examined without analyzing the entire memory.

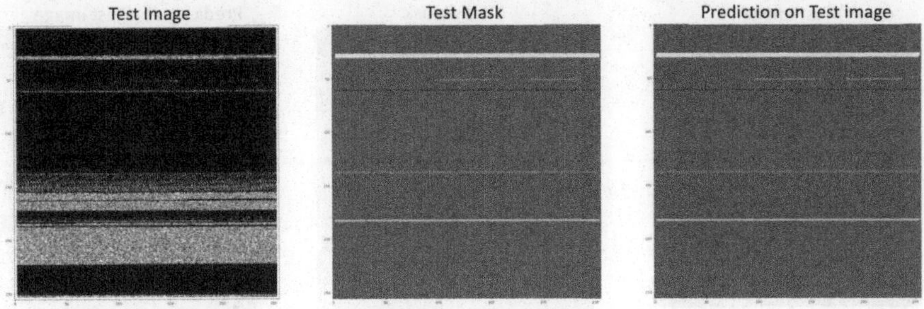


**Fig. 7.** Class 2 prediction with the testing dataset.

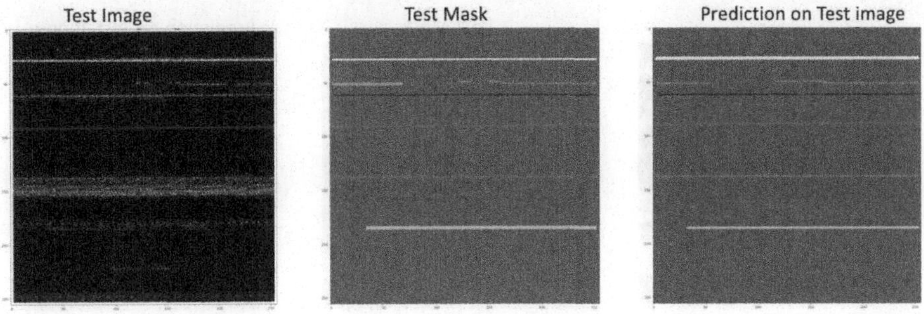


**Fig. 8.** Class 3 prediction with the testing dataset.

Code modification attacks manipulate code residing in the code block to change the programmable logic controller control logic. Biham et al. [9] developed a stealthy program that modifies execution code and source code in a Simatic S7 programmable logic controller. Alsabbagh and Langendorfer [2] decompiled code obtained from Simatic S7 programmable logic controller memory, injected malicious code and recompiled the code before inserting it into the controller. A similar approach was employed in this work to execute the code modification attack.

A baseline memory dump was acquired before executing a code modification attack. The baseline image was converted to pixels and the resulting image input to the trained ensemble model to classify image pixels into the forensic artifact classes. Figure 14 shows the baseline memory image and the model prediction.

Next, malicious code modification was executed, and the memory dump was acquired. The memory image was converted to pixels and the trained ensemble model classified the image pixels into the forensic artifact classes. Figure 15 shows the code modification memory image and the model prediction. Comparison of the post-attack image in Fig. 15 against the baseline image in Fig. 14 shows extra pixels classified as code.

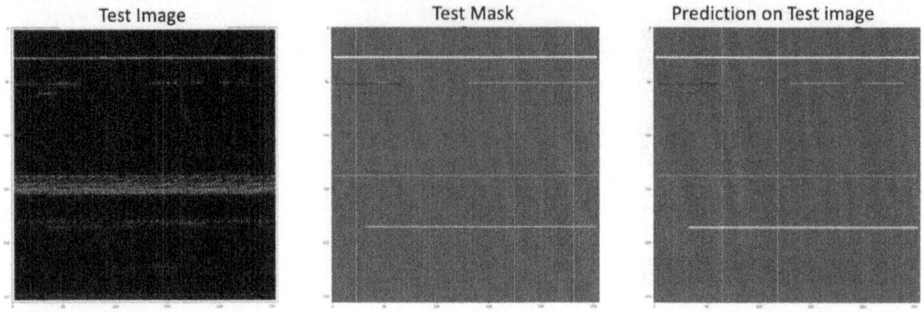


**Fig. 9.** Class 4 prediction with the testing dataset.

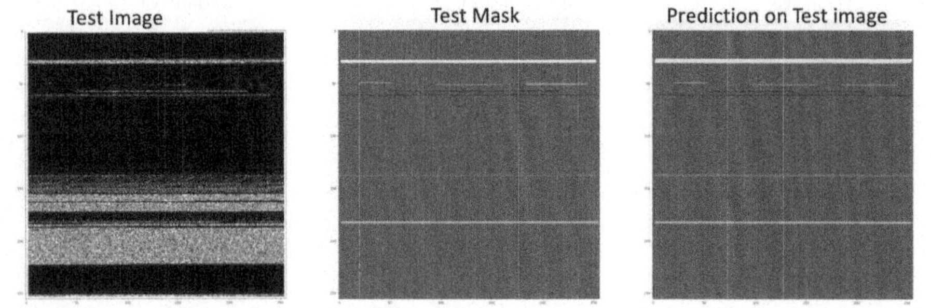


**Fig. 10.** Class 5 prediction with the testing dataset.

### 4.1 Validating Automated Analysis Results with Manual Analysis

The automated memory forensic analysis approach was validated by repeating the code injection and code modification attacks, conducting manual memory forensic analysis and comparing the results against the automated forensic analysis results.

Manual forensic analysis was conducted by reverse engineering the communications protocol and performing differential analysis to understand the memory layout and create a memory profile for the programmable logic controller. The memory profile provides a reference for the addresses of forensic artifacts.

The following forensic artifacts were identified via manual analysis:

- **Configuration Blocks:** Two blocks containing information about the other blocks in memory.
- **Metadata File:** ZIP file containing project metadata.
- **Control Logic:** Code for processing programmable logic controller inputs and producing outputs that determine controller behavior.
- **Input/Output Data Blocks:** Two blocks containing input and output values from the input/output modules.

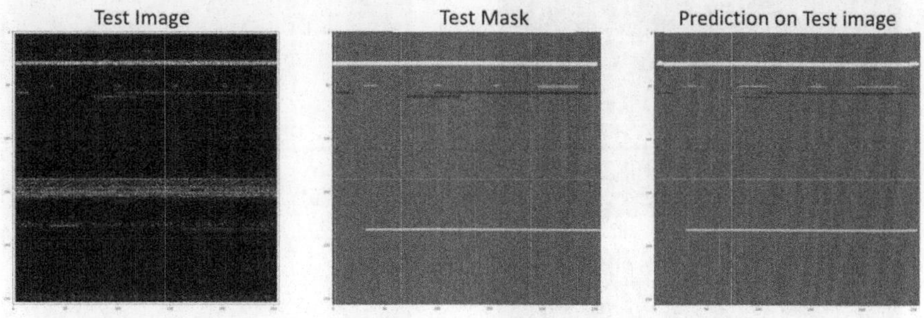


**Fig. 11.** Class 6 prediction with the testing dataset.

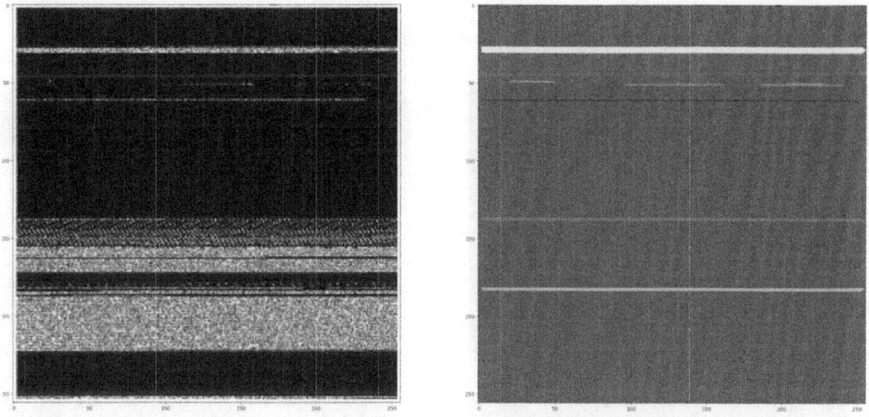

**Fig. 12.** Baseline memory image (left) and model prediction (right).

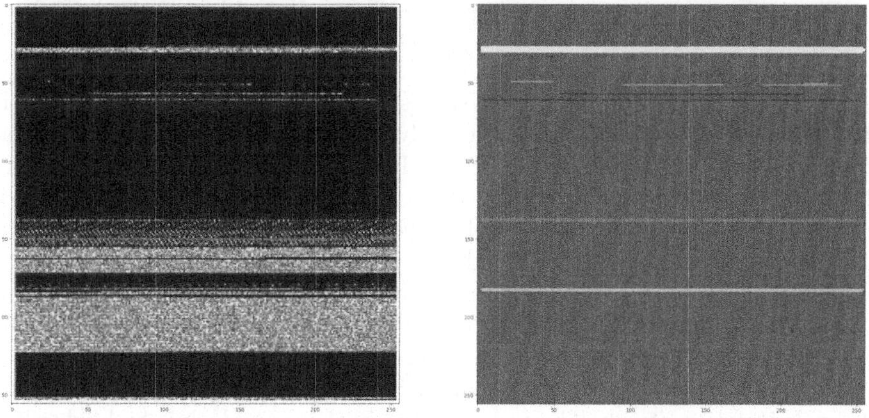

**Fig. 13.** Code injection memory image (left) and model prediction (right).

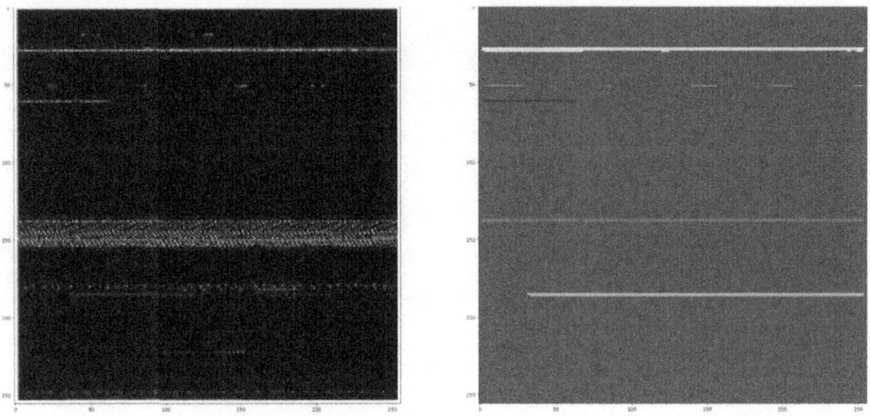

**Fig. 14.** Baseline memory image (left) and model prediction (right).

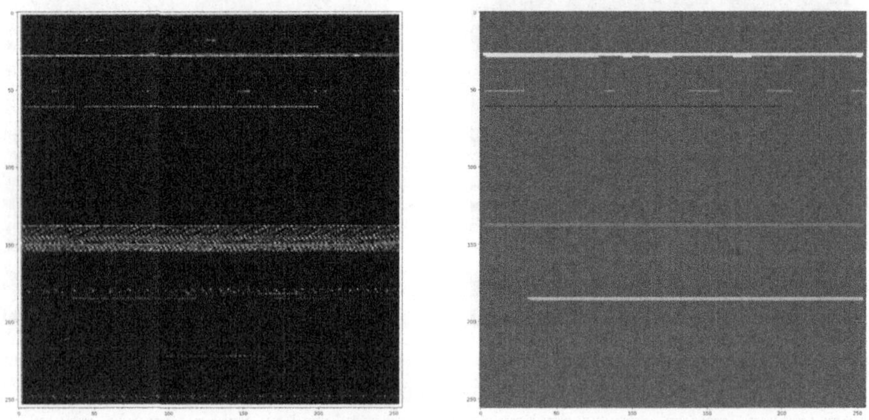

**Fig. 15.** Code modification memory image (left) and model prediction (right).

To validate the automated analysis results, manual analysis of the memory dump used for the automated forensic analysis was performed. The manual forensic analysis was performed by extracting the configuration block and comparing it against the configuration block of the baseline memory dump. The change in the control logic pointer value was observed. The new pointer value was used to acquire the injected code from its address in the data block.

Figure 16 compares the configuration blocks in the baseline memory dump and in the memory dump after the code injection attack. The changed pointer value in the configuration block is highlighted.

Figure 17 compares the baseline memory dump and the memory dump after the code injection attack. The code injected in the data block is highlighted.

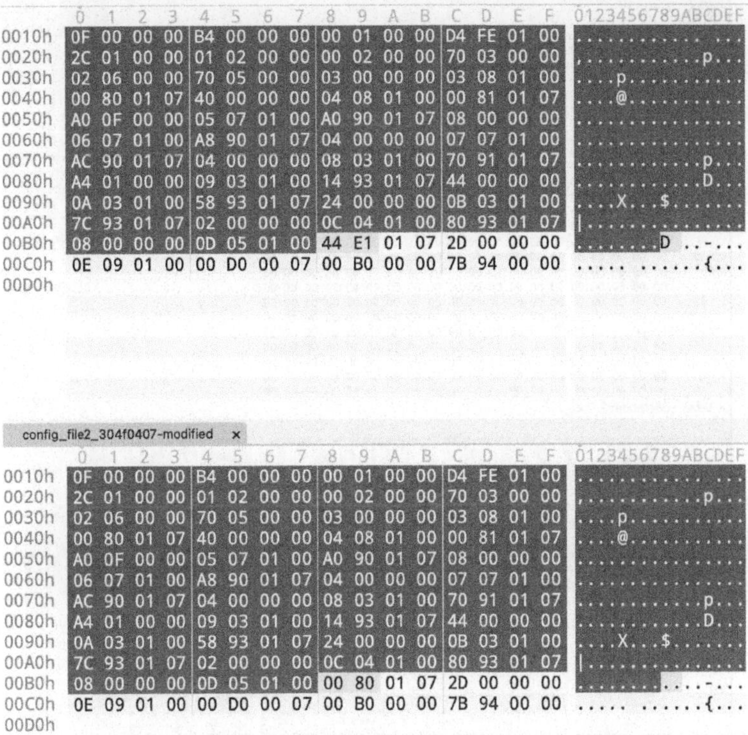


**Fig. 16.** Original and changed control logic pointer values.

**Code Modification Attack.** Manual forensic analysis to detect control logic manipulation attacks was performed to verify the automated memory analysis. This was accomplished by acquiring memory dumps before and after control logic manipulation and extracting the control logic block from the two dumps. The two extracted control logic blocks were compared and the differences were noted. Figure 18 shows that the instruction introduced via code logic manipulation is visible.

During the manual analysis it was discovered that examination of the contained configuration block located the pointer to the control logic. Consequently, the configuration block is an important forensic artifact that can be examined rapidly to check if the pointer to the code block has been modified or not in the event of anomalous behavior. This saves considerable time because it is necessary to focus on the configuration block instead of analyzing the entire memory dump. Thus, the attack scenario demonstrates that the initial investigation satisfies the two key forensics goals of correctness and speed.

However, because the manual analysis requires the configuration block to be examined during the search for pointers to the other blocks, dormant code injected in memory by an attacker without changing the pointer in the configu-

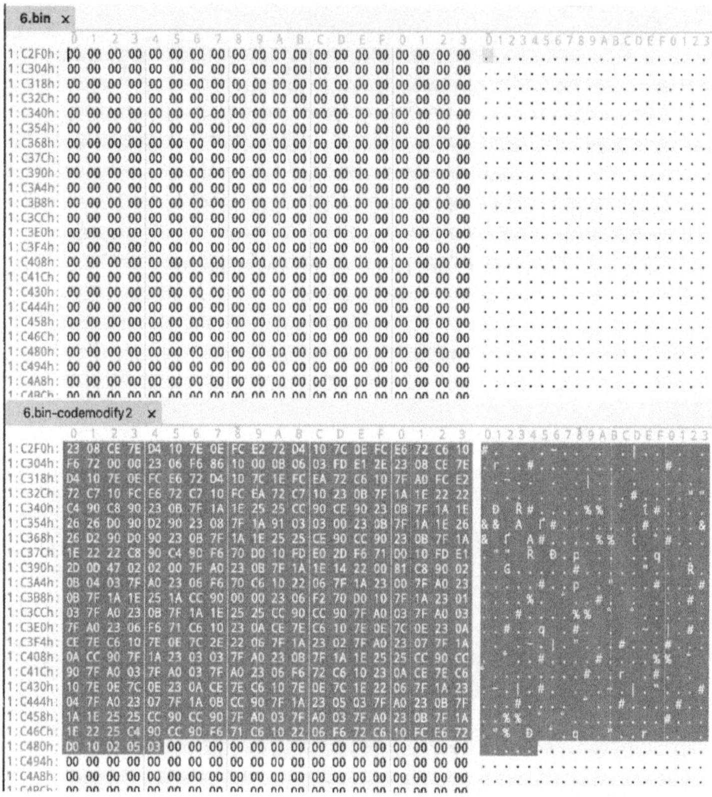


**Fig. 17.** Injected code found using the pointer in the configuration block.

ration block would be missed. The alternative is to analyze the entire memory dump manually, which would be very time consuming and prone to human error.

Table 2 summarizes the manual and automated memory analysis results. The evaluation results reveal that automated programmable logic controller memory analysis overcomes some of the limitations of manual analysis, namely, reduced analysis time and increased accuracy. This is because forensic artifacts are detected by a deep learning model that can be trained and fine-tuned until the desired accuracy is achieved. The deep learning model was trained to identify only five forensic artifacts. However, it is possible to train the model to identify other forensically-valuable artifacts in memory.

The automated memory analysis methodology can quickly present the system state during forensic analysis. However, the results are not sufficient for a forensic investigation. The solution is to integrate the methodology in the forensic investigation process to identify the forensic artifact that is the root cause of the anomalous behavior. The forensic analyst must then isolate the identified forensic artifact and analyze it manually.

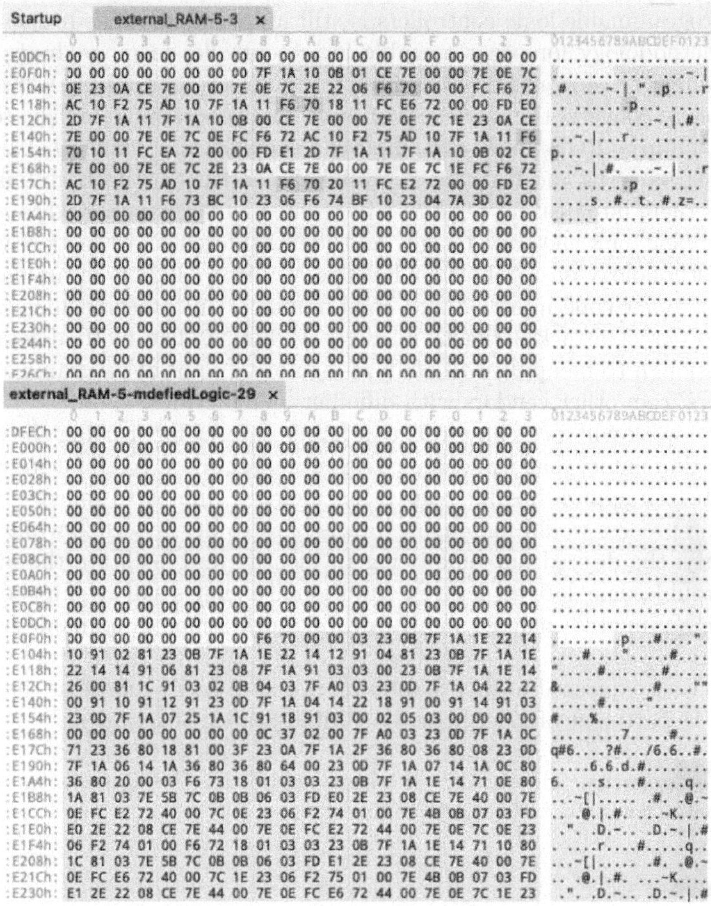


**Fig. 18.** Differences between the original and manipulated control logic.

**Table 2.** Comparison of manual and automated memory analysis.

| Criterion | Manual Analysis | Automated Analysis |
|---|---|---|
| Time | 4 to 8 h | 30 to 40 s |
| Accuracy | Human errors possible | 91% F1 score |
| Dormant Code | Likely to go undetected | Can be detected |
| Visualization | No visualization | Visualization of system state |

## 5 Conclusions

As industrial control systems are increasingly targeted by cyber attacks, memory forensic analyses of programmable logic controllers are vital to investigating attacks and implementing the appropriate mitigations. However, memory forensics of programmable logic controllers is still in its infancy. The proposed automated methodology for programmable logic controller memory dump analysis using computer vision and deep learning techniques is a promising solution. The methodology converts the sequences of bytes in a programmable logic controller memory dump to RGB pixels and employs a deep learning model that learns the underlying patterns and features of pre-labeled forensic artifacts in images and segments them into distinct regions. The trained model is employed to automatically segment new memory images and identify forensic artifacts. Evaluation of the methodology on a Schneider Electric Modicon M221 programmable logic controller under code injection and code modification attacks demonstrates its ability to detect attack artifacts in memory dumps. The methodology is also general enough to be applied to analyze memory dumps of programmable logic controllers from other vendors with different architectures.

Future work will focus on creating a larger dataset for training the semantic segmentation model that will enhance detection accuracy. Also, future work will explore better approaches for converting memory dumps to images. An ideal conversion process would map image pixels back to raw bytecode while preserving fidelity, the desired outcome being to identify and facilitate the identification of troublesome data structures. Additionally, efforts will attempt to develop a generic automated memory analysis framework for programmable logic controllers.

The views expressed in this chapter do not necessarily represent the views of the U.S. Department of Energy or the United States Government.

**Acknowledgement.** This research was supported by the U.S. Department of Energy under Contract no. DE-AC05-00OR22725.

## References

1. Ahmed, I., Obermeier, S., Naedele, M., Richard, G.: SCADA systems: challenges for forensic investigators. IEEE Comput. **45**(12), 44–51 (2012)
2. Alsabbagh, W., Langendorfer, P.: A control injection attack against S7 PLCs – manipulating the decompiled code. In: Proceedings of the Forty-Seventh Annual Conference of the IEEE Industrial Electronics Society (2021)
3. Asmar Awad, R.: Automated volatile memory forensics for programmable logic controllers, Ph.D. Dissertation, Department of Computer Science and Engineering, Tennessee Technological University, Cookville, Tennessee (2023)
4. Asmar Awad, R., Beztchi, S., Smith, J., Lyles, B., Prowell, S.: Tools, techniques and methodologies: a survey of digital forensics for SCADA systems. In: Proceedings of the Fourth Annual Industrial Control System Security Workshop (2018)
5. Asmar Awad, R., Lopez, J., Rogers, M.: Volatile memory extraction based approach for level 0-1 CPS forensics. In: Proceedings of the IEEE International Symposium on Technologies for Homeland Security (2019)
6. Asmar Awad, R., Rais, M., Rogers, M., Ahmed, I., Paquit, V.: Towards a generic memory forensic framework for programmable logic controllers. Forensic Sci. Int. Digit. Invest. **44**, 301513 (2023)

7. Ayub, A., Yoo, H., Ahmed, I.: Empirical study of PLC authentication protocols in industrial control systems. In: Proceedings of the IEEE Security and Privacy Workshops, pp. 383–397 (2021)
8. Azzam, M., Pasquale, L., Provan, G., Nuseibeh, B.: Forensic readiness of industrial control systems under stealthy attacks. Comput. Secur. **125**, 103010 (2023)
9. Biham, E., Bitan, S., Carmel, A., Dankner, A., Malin, U., Wool, A.: Rogue7: Rogue engineering station attacks on S7 Simatic PLCs. In: Presented at Black Hat USA (2019)
10. Chen, T., Abu-Nimeh, S.: Lessons from Stuxnet. IEEE Comput. **44**(4), 91–93 (2011)
11. Denton, G., Karpisek, F., Breitinger, F., Baggili, I.: Leveraging the SRTP protocol for over-the-network memory acquisition of a GE Fanuc Series 90-30. Digit. Invest. **22**(S), S26–S38 (2017)
12. Findrik, M., Smith, P., Quill, K., Kieran, M.: PLCBlockMon: data logging and extraction on PLCs for cyber intrusion detection. In: Proceedings of the Fifth International Symposium on ICS and SCADA Cyber Security Research, pp. 102–111 (2018)
13. Gu, X., Li, S., Ren, S., Zheng, H., Fan, C., Xu, H.: Adaptive enhanced Swin transformer with U-Net for remote sensing image segmentation. Comput. Electr. Eng. **102**, 108223 (2022)
14. Kalle, S., Ameen, N., Yoo, H., Ahmed, I.: CLIK on PLCs! Attacking control logic with decompilation and virtual PLC. In: Proceedings of the Workshop on Binary Analysis Research (2019)
15. Kumar, R., Kela, R., Singh, S., Trujillo-Rasua, R.: APT attacks on industrial control systems: a tale of three incidents. Int. J. Crit. Infrastruct. Protect. **37**, 100521 (2022)
16. Manoj, K.: Cyber Security in Industrial Automation. Notion Press, Chennai, India (2020)
17. Miller, B., Rowe, D.: A survey of SCADA and critical infrastructure incidents. In: Proceedings of the First Annual Conference on Research in Information Technology, pp. 51–56 (2012)
18. Petit, O., Thome, N., Rambour, C., Themyr, L., Collins, T., Soler, L.: U-Net transformer: self and cross attention for medical image segmentation. In: Lian, C., Cao, X., Rekik, I., Xu, X., Yan, P. (eds.) MLMI 2021. LNCS, vol. 12966, pp. 267–276. Springer, Cham (2021). https://doi.org/10.1007/978-3-030-87589-3_28
19. Qasim, S., Smith, J., Ahmed, I.: Control logic forensics framework using a built-in decompiler of engineering software in industrial control systems. Forensic Sci. Int. Digit. Invest. **33**(S), 301013 (2020)
20. Rais, M., Asmar Awad, R., Lopez, J., Ahmed, I.: JTAG-based PLC memory acquisition framework for industrial control systems. Forensic Sci. Int. Digit. Invest. **37**(S), 301196 (2021)
21. Rais, M., Asmar Awad, R., Lopez, J., Ahmed, J.: Memory forensic analysis of a programmable logic controller in industrial control systems. Forensic Sci. Int. Digit. Invest. **40**(S), 301339 (2022)
22. Rajput, P., Maniatakos, M.: Towards non-intrusive malware detection for industrial control systems. In: Proceedings of the Design, Automation and Test in Europe Conference and Exhibition, pp. 1703–1706 (2021)
23. Wu, T., Nurse, J.: Exploring the use of PLC debugging tools for digital forensic investigations on SCADA systems. J. Digit. Forensics Secur. Law **10**(4), 79–96 (2015)

24. Yoo, H., Ahmed, I.: Control logic injection attacks on industrial control systems. In: Dhillon, G., Karlsson, F., Hedström, K., Zúquete, A. (eds.) SEC 2019. IAICT, vol. 562, pp. 33–48. Springer, Cham (2019). https://doi.org/10.1007/978-3-030-22312-0_3
25. Yoo, H., Kalle, S., Smith, J., Ahmed, I.: Overshadow PLC to detect remote control-logic injection attacks. In: Perdisci, R., Maurice, C., Giacinto, G., Almgren, M. (eds.) DIMVA 2019. LNCS, vol. 11543, pp. 109–132. Springer, Cham (2019). https://doi.org/10.1007/978-3-030-22038-9_6
26. Zubair, N., Ayub, A., Yoo, H., Ahmed, I.: PEM: remote forensic acquisition of PLC memory in industrial control systems. Forensic Sci. Int. Digit. Invest. **40**(S), 301336 (2022)

# Infrastructure Modeling

# A Fail-Safe Challenge-Response Mechanism for User Equipment to Detect Rogue IMSI/SUPI Catchers

James Wright(✉) and Stephen Wolthusen

Norwegian University of Science and Technology, Gjøvik, Norway
james.g.wright@ntnu.no

**Abstract.** This chapter formalizes the security promise of channel tranquility, where an agent will not transmit messages unless it can verify that the communications channel has not been manipulated by an adversary. In the 5G standard, user equipment presumes that no manipulation can occur in the wireless channel with a radio node. However, analysis of international mobile subscriber identity/subscription permanent identifier catchers has revealed that an adversary denies service to all the legitimate radio nodes in an administrative area to exploit user equipment vulnerabilities. To limit the adversary's ability to compromise the 5G authentication and confidentiality promises, channel tranquility imposes an upper bound on the number of messages that the adversary can transmit.

This work presents a verified challenge-response mechanism that detects channel tranquility violations and responds to prevent the adversary from compromising authentication and confidentiality. An applied pi calculus model of a 5G registration procedure augmented with the challenge-response mechanism is presented. The mechanism builds a layer of defense in depth into the 5G registration procedure by incorporating an independent, redundant cryptographic system that must be undermined before other security promises can be attacked. Channel tranquility enables user equipment to quickly establish if a radio node has access to the public key infrastructure of the 5G control network. Specifically, user equipment can deduce whether an international mobile subscriber identity/subscription permanent identifier catcher has been deployed in an administrative area and then deny the adversary the ability to exploit any vulnerabilities. The challenge-response mechanism is verified using a secrecy proof that demonstrates that the adversary cannot learn the semantics of the challenge and response semantics if at least one legitimate session between user equipment and a radio node has been completed.

**Keywords:** 5G Security · Rogue IPSI/SUPI Catchers · Denial of Service · Defense in Depth · Applied Pi Calculus

## 1 Introduction

The 5G standard [7] presumes that the wireless channel between user equipment $UE$ and a radio node $gNB$ has not been manipulated by an adversary.


Published by Springer Nature Switzerland AG 2025
J. Staggs and S. Shenoi (Eds.): ICCIP 2024, IFIP AICT 725, pp. 155–178, 2025.
https://doi.org/10.1007/978-3-031-81888-2_8

However, rogue radio nodes – specifically, international mobile subscriber identity (IMSI) and subscription permanent identifier (SUPI) catchers – can exploit this assumption to compromise the confidentiality of user equipment semantics. Specifically, an adversary can launch denial-of-service attacks on all the legitimate radio nodes in an administrative area to force the targeted user equipment to connect with the adversary's rogue radio node (IMSI/SUPI catcher) [17]. The rogue radio node simulates the communications models of a legitimate radio node and control network and proceeds to exploit user equipment vulnerabilities. The manipulation of the wireless channel to force user equipment to connect to the rogue node violates the "channel tranquility" security promise. The 5G standard does not mitigate this attack vector on user equipment.

This chapter formalizes the security promise of channel tranquility that enables user equipment to deduce if a wireless communications channel has been manipulated via the absence of particular communications model semantics. A fail-safe mechanism is incorporated that the adversary must overcome before it can attack the key security promises of authentication and confidentiality. In particular, the mechanism adds an authentication burden to a rogue radio node beyond the current condition of merely broadcasting the strongest signal in an administrative area. Verifying that the adversary has not manipulated the wireless communications channel limits the opportunity for an adversary to attack the 5G security promises even if it has found a vulnerability in the mutual key generation procedure, because the adversary would have limited time and limited semantics to achieve its goal. This is in contrast to the current guaranteed success of an adversary that denies service to all legitimate radio nodes in an administrative area and forces all user equipment to connect to the rogue radio node.

The proposed solution maintains the channel tranquility promises by adding a challenge-response mechanism in the 5G registration procedure that enables user equipment to detect a rogue node in an administrative area. The mechanism is contingent on user equipment having at least one successful registration procedure with a legitimate radio node and begins upon the establishment of the first encrypted session channel. The first legitimate access and management function $AMF$ generates challenge tokens, a nonce and a key, and passes it to user equipment via the encrypted channel of the first session, along with the globally unique temporary id (GUTI) of the user equipment. When the user equipment moves into a new administrative area, the mechanism leverages the security context transfer between the old $AMF$ and new $AMF$, which occurs behind the public key infrastructure trust barrier. The old $AMF$ passes the encrypted response semantics to the new $AMF$, which forwards them to the user equipment. If the user equipment can decrypt the message and match it to the semantics it received in the previous session, the registration procedure will continue. The encryption scheme of the challenge-response mechanism is independent of the encryption scheme used by the remainder of the 5G registration procedure that establishes the authentication and confidentiality promises. This enables the user equipment to quickly deduce if the radio node to which it is connecting has access to the public key infrastructure of the control network. The mechanism is similar to the post-compromise security model of Cohn-Gordan et al. [4], which shows that the forward secrecy promise can be maintained as long as at least one legitimate session has been completed.

The challenge-response mechanism greatly restricts the number of messages that an adversary can transmit to compromise the other 5G security promises because the user equipment terminates the registration procedure immediately if the radio node cannot prove it has access to the radio node/control network public key infrastructure. This drastically restricts the adversary's ability to exploit any vulnerabilities it may have discovered against the 5G promises of authentication and confidentiality. The mechanism is designed to preserve the 5G security promises even in situations where availability has been compromised, implying that the mechanism is fail-safe rather than fail-operational. The mechanism is still dependent on the 5G network operator ejecting the adversary from the administrative area and restoring connectivity [21].

An applied pi calculus process algebra is employed to model the 5G registration procedure and challenge-response mechanism because it can encapsulate multiple interleaving communications models across distributed agents. The channel tranquility promise is constructed using various secrecy proofs that ensure that the adversary cannot learn challenge-response mechanism content as long as at least one legitimate registration procedure has occurred and that the mechanism has the ratcheting and link-failure sensitivity properties.

## 2 Related Work

This section presents an overview of the literature pertaining to denial-of-service attacks on wireless networks and their countermeasures, denial-of-service attacks on cellular networks, and how rogue IMSI/SUPI catchers utilize denial-of-service attacks to exploit user equipment vulnerabilities. This is done to demonstrate how an adversary can compromise channel tranquility to force user equipment to connect to a rogue radio node. These capabilities are employed in a subsequent section to direct the design of the adversary model and challenge-response mechanism.

Several taxonomies have been proposed for classifying adversarial denial-of-service attacks on wireless networks. Lichtman et al. [14] have categorized adversaries based on their ability to correlate their actions with the targeted signal, their knowledge of the targeted communications protocol and the ability to spoof legitimate actors. Pelechrini et al. [18] classify adversaries based on the ratio of the power to the number of packets broadcasted to saturate channels. Grover et al. [9] classify adversaries by attack vector complexity. Consistent across all these taxonomies are four kinds of denial-of-service strategies. One is random, bursting out noise at random intervals. The second is reactive, launching denial-of-service only when the targeted signal appears. The third is deceptive, overwhelming the network while pretending to be a legitimate user. The fourth is constant jamming that continuously fills the network with noise.

The countermeasures in all the taxonomies are focused on reacting to an attack mostly at the physical layer and occasionally at the link layer. The principal means for detecting denial-of-service attacks is to look for anomalies in the legitimate wireless signal strength or look for "greedy behavior" [18] by radio nodes in the link layer. The primary method for responding to wireless denial-of-service attacks is to change the frequency or channel to a pre-shared alternative [10,20]. None of these countermeasures are implemented at the protocol level.

Research has also analyzed denial-of-service attacks on cellular networks. Lichtman et al. [16] computed the signal to power ratio an adversary would need to jam specific signals in the 4G registration procedure; they showed that the adversary would have the same success targeting physical downlink and uplink shared channels as it would with ubiquitous signal saturation. In subsequent work, Lichtman et al. [15] identified other parts of the 5G registration procedure that were still vulnerable to denial-of-service attacks and suggested that a timestamp be encoded in the signal synchronization procedure to prevent malicious actions. Jover [12] theorized how an adversary could jam 4G networks by exploiting vulnerabilities in the communications protocols and standard infrastructure deployments instead of attempting to deny signals.

Park et al. [17] have conducted the most recent public analysis of rogue IMSI/SUPI catcher capabilities of devices sold to governments. They found that nearly all the rogue devices as of 2019 could jam legitimate radio nodes and connect to the targeted user equipment. However, they did not comment on how the rogue devices would deny legitimate signals.

After a rogue IMSI/SUPI catcher connects to user equipment it either records the temporary identifier of the user equipment and releases it, or it exploits vulnerabilities to further compromise the 5G promises of authentication and confidentiality. The rogue devices may also utilize downgrade attacks [22] or simulate legitimate radio nodes [11] to increase the likelihood of undermining the security promises. After user equipment is compromised, a rogue device can intercept the permanent identifier and track the user equipment, and potentially eavesdrop on communications if the control network can be compromised.

Park et al. [17] also provide a taxonomy of IMSI/SUPI catcher detection schemes. All the schemes detect rogue devices based on the artifacts they leave after the opportunity to attack user equipment in an administrative area. Responses to detection alerts are left to the network operator.

The review of related work demonstrates that the countermeasures to denial-of-service attacks in cellular networks are all reactive in nature. This means that the countermeasures can be executed only after the adversary has had the opportunity to exploit vulnerabilities. The literature does not discuss measures that prevent the adversary from manipulating the communications channel to force a connection.

# 3 Adversary Model and Challenge-Response Mechanism

This section provides qualitative descriptions of the adversary model and the challenge-response mechanism used to detect attempts to undermine channel tranquility. However, the section first describes the 5G registration procedure, which is expanded to cover the communications models in the control network that were omitted in previous work [21]. The additions are necessary to model the challenge-response mechanism operations.

## 3.1 5G Device Registration Procedure

Figure 1 shows the 5G standalone device registration procedure [6]. The procedure involves three participants across multiple communications models, culminating in more than one hundred steps. This work focuses on modeling the procedure up to the establishment of an encrypted communications channel between user equipment $UE$ and a radio node $gNB$ represented by Step 22 in the figure. Steps 8, 12 through 16, and 20 are outside the scope of this work because they do not contribute to encrypted channel creation.

The first stage is to establish radio communications between user equipment $UE$ and a radio node $gNB$ in an administrative area that constantly broadcasts a synchronization signal. The user equipment $UE$ chooses the strongest signal in the administrative area and begins the radio resource control $RRC$ procedure to establish a dedicated channel between the devices. The user equipment $UE$ messages the selected radio node $gNB$ and begins a timer to complete the handshake. During this time, the radio node $gNB$ sends the frequency of a direct communications channel and requests a temporary identifier from user equipment $UE$. After switching to the new channel, the radio node $gNB$ sets up the signal radio bearer $SRB_1$ message and sends it to user equipment $UE$ in an $RRCSetup$ message. The final message sent by the radio node $gNB$ requests an identifier from user equipment $UE$. This is usually the GUTI of the user equipment that was generated and sent to it by the access and management function $AMF$ of the previous session behind the public key infrastructure trust barrier. However, if it is the first session for user equipment $UE$, the identifier is its temporary IMSI (TIMSI).

Following this, the radio node $gNB$ informs the new $AMF$ that user equipment $UE$ wishes to connect to its administrative area. If user equipment $UE$ has sent a GUTI, then the new $AMF$ initiates a security context transfer with the $AMF$ of the previous administrative area that returns the subscriber permanent identifier SUPI of user equipment $UE$.

After the transfer is complete, the new $AMF$ performs an identity request with user equipment $UE$ in a non-access stratum ($NAS$) identity procedure. The $AMF$ sends a key $K_{NAS}$, which is derived from the SUPI of user equipment $UE$ and then requests the subscriber concealed identifier SUCI of user equipment $UE$. The $AMF$ sends the SUCI to the authentication server function $AUSF$, which returns the SUPI. If a security context transfer has occurred, the $AMF$ compares the SUPI received from the old $AMF$ with the one sent by the $AUSF$.

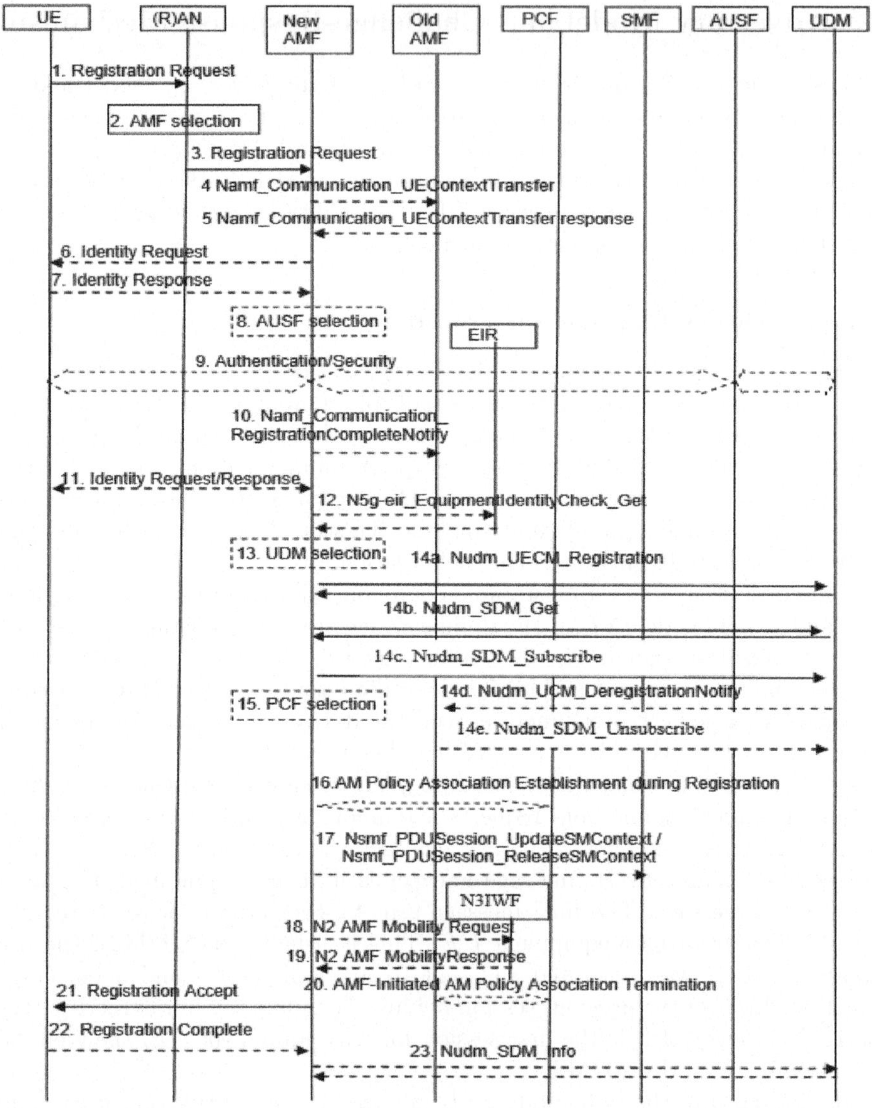


**Fig. 1.** 5G device registration procedure [6].

At this point, the control network $CN$ performs a series of checks to see if user equipment $UE$ is a legitimate network subscriber. These checks are outside the scope of this work.

After the checks, the new $AMF$ performs a non-access stratum (NAS) authentication request with user equipment $UE$. The $AMF$ uses the established secure channel from the identity request semantics and the two entities send each other their pre-shared keys $K_{AC1}$ and $K_{AC2}$ for validation. The $AMF$

then requests the information it needs to select an appropriate cypher suite for the encrypted channel session. The new $AMF$ generates the session key $K_{gNB}$ and passes the information to radio node $gNB$, which begins the security procedure $SP$ that establishes the encrypted channel session. After this is done, the new $AMF$ sends a new GUTI for user equipment $UE$.

### 3.2 Adversary Model

The adversary model brings together research on the most recent IMSI/SUPI catcher capabilities that are leveraged to compromise the 5G promises of authentication and confidentiality. The adversary model does not have to simulate specific types of jamming like those described in the related work section. Instead, the model just needs to undermine the promise of availability.

As a result, the adversary drops all the packets between the radio node $gNB$ and user equipment $UE$. In fact, it is trivial for a Dolev-Yao adversary [5] to manipulate the channel to drop all the radio node $gNB$ messages it intercepts. However, for the adversary to compromise the authentication and/or confidentiality promises it is necessary to defeat the cryptography used by user equipment $UE$ and radio node $gNB$, while not being able to intercept the communications between the radio node $gNB$ and control network $CN$.

This situation can be modeled by stating that the adversary only has access to the wireless communications channel, so the security of the public key infrastructure of the control network $CN$ remains intact. It also means that the adversary needs cryptanalytic capabilities that would be an extension to the Dolev-Yao model. The model encapsulates this situation by the adversary knowing the NAS identity and session keys after the initial registration. As mentioned above, at least one complete registration is required for the challenge-response mechanism to work. This is ensured by restricting the adversary to conducting passive reconnaissance during the first registration so that the keys in the first session are not known. The adversary's objective is to leverage only the keys it knows and learns to read the messages in the encrypted channel session.

### 3.3 Challenge-Response Mechanism

The challenge-response mechanism is designed to enable user equipment $UE$ to detect if an adversary is attempting to force a connection by denying connections to legitimate radio nodes $gNB$ using an otherwise reliable channel. The user equipment achieves this by challenging a radio node $gNB$ before proceeding with the registration procedure to prove that it has access to the public key infrastructure of the control network $CN$. With access to the infrastructure, the radio node communicates with the access and management function $AMF$ of the previous administrative area located behind the trust barrier of the public key infrastructure. If the adversary fails the challenge then, even if the radio node is the only active node in the administrative area due to the denial-of-service attacks, the adversary can only use the radio resource control $RRC$ semantics to circumvent the authentication and confidentiality promises. This is the only communications model that completes before the user equipment $UE$ drops the registration procedure, so it serves as a fail-safe mechanism to maintain the authentication and confidentiality promises.

The challenge-response model begins after the first complete registration procedure has occurred between user equipment $UE$ and a legitimate radio node $gNB$. During the first session the access and management function $AMF$ generates two identity tokens, a nonce and an encryption key along with the GUTI. The $AMF$ passes one of the identity tokens, the nonce, and the key to the radio node $gNB$ so they can be transmitted to user equipment $UE$ via the first established encrypted channel.

When user equipment $UE$ enters a new administrative area and connects with a new radio node $gNB$, the first action performed after a dedicated channel has been established through the radio resource control $RRC$ is to pass the GUTI from the previous session. A security context transfer begins between the old $AMF$ and new $AMF$ behind the trust barrier of the public key infrastructure. In this transfer the new $AMF$ passes one of its identity tokens to the old $AMF$. The old $AMF$ encrypts the nonce, the identity token it has already passed to user equipment $UE$ and the token it received in the context transfer with the generated key it gave user equipment $UE$. Upon completion, the old $AMF$ returns this encrypted message with the GUTI. The new $AMF$ transmits the encrypted message along with a cleartext copy of the token it used in the context transfer to user equipment $UE$. If the nonce, identity token passed during the last session or copy of the token sent with the encrypted message (which is also inside the message) do not match, user equipment $UE$ terminates the registration procedure.

## 4 Formal Challenge-Response Mechanism

This section presents the formal applied pi calculus models of the 5G registration procedure, adversary model and 5G registration procedure augmented with the challenge-response mechanism.

### 4.1 Applied Pi Calculus

This section does not describe the pi-calculus or the applied pi calculus. Interested readers are referred to Sangiorgi and Walker [19] and Abadi et al. [1] for thorough treatments of the pi-calculus and applied pi calculus, respectively.

The applied pi calculus is an abstraction that represents the evolution of terms across concurrent processes in a distributed system. The calculus comprises terms, names, variables and functions:

$$\begin{array}{ll} L, M, N ::= & \text{Terms} \\ a, b, c... & \text{Names} \\ \text{x, y, z...} & \text{Variables} \\ f(M_1, ..., M_n) & \text{Functions} \end{array}$$

The terms comprise infinite numbers of names and variables, or a finite number of functions. The names are variables themselves or represent communications channels. The functions are primarily used to represent encryption operations.

The following applied pi calculus operations are employed in this work:

$$P ::= P.Q \mid x < y > .P \mid x(z).P \mid \nu z\ z.P \mid P|P' \mid$$
$$P + P' \mid [x = y].xP \mid P! \mid \{P/x\} \mid \emptyset$$

where $P$ is a process or the underlying state machine of a device. The operations are defined as follows:

- **P.Q** : Sequential processes can occur.
- **< x > y.P** : The process $P$ sends the name or variable $y$ along channel $x$.
- **x(z).P** : The process $P$ receives the name or variable $z$ from channel $x$. Any subsequent names or variables $z$ in the process are replaced by the input $y/z$.
- $\nu$**z z.P** : A restriction of the name or variable $z$, where sending or receiving along $z$ can only occur if the involved processes already know that $z$ exists. This operation is used to make an explicit restriction of a name or variable or to represent the generation of a fresh name or variable. Multiple names and variables are expressed using a single $\nu$. Each is separated by a comma.
- **P|P′** : The composition of processes $P$ and $P'$ represents two processes that can occur concurrently.
- **P + P′** : The summation of processes $P$ and $P'$ represents the selection of one of the two processes.
- **[x = y].xP** : The matching of names $x$ and $y$ represents an if-then statement in the distributed system.
- **P!** : The replication of process $P$ generates infinite copies of the process.
- **{P/x}** : The substitution process replaces all instances of process $P$ with the name or variable $x$.
- $\emptyset$ : The null process has no further process transitions.

The processes can evolve by communications with other intra-agent processes or with the environment (processes external to the one being analyzed). The functions used in a model have an associated equational theory that defines how they are treated in process reductions and equivalence proofs. This work uses the symmetric encryption equational theory defined by Abadi et al. [1]:

$$sdec(senc(x; y); y) = y$$

### 4.2 5G Registration Procedure Model

Figure 2 shows a representation of the communications channels of the $5G$ registration procedure. Each arrow corresponds to a communications channel, which is represented by a name. The registration procedure occurs when user equipment

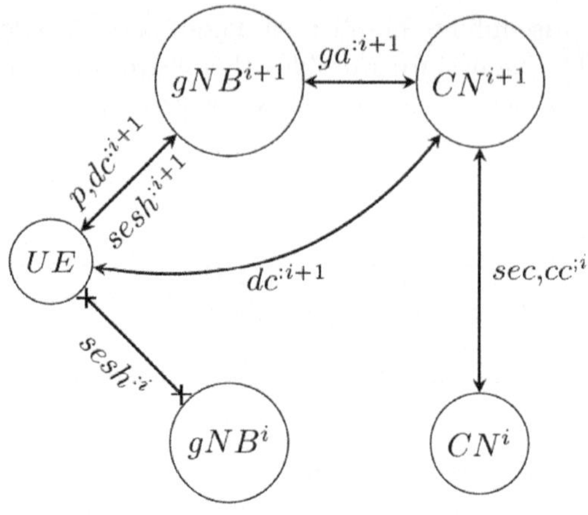


**Fig. 2.** 5G registration procedure communications channels.

$UE$ has disconnected from radio node $gNB^i$ and has moved into the administrative area of radio node $gNB^{i+1}$. The disconnection is represented by the arrow marked with x symbols.

The model only encapsulates the semantics involved in establishing an encrypted channel. It excludes the semantics for deciding if user equipment $UE$ is a valid resource consumer.

The structure of the names and variables in this model is expressed as:

$$v_a^{sd;i}$$

where $s$ is the source process of the name/variable, $d$ is the destination, $i$ is the session iteration index and $a$ is additional semantic information. If there is only the index after ; then it is specific session iteration of a name/variable generated in the process. This is used to encapsulate the mutual key generation process. However, the derivation of keys [7] from the semantics is beyond the scope of this model.

In the following equation, process $C$ represents user equipment $UE$ and process $S$ represents the intra-agent communications between a radio node $gNB$ and the control network $CN$ behind the public key infrastructure trust barrier. Upon initialization, the process generates $UE$'s authentication key (which is invariant over the iterations) and the inter-$AMF$ channel:

$$P \triangleq \nu \text{ sec, ausf, SUPI K}_{AC2}(C|S)$$

where sec is the inter-$AMF$ channel and ausf is the name that connects with the authentication server function $AUSF$.

The process $C$ representing user equipment $UE$ is expressed as:

$$C \triangleq \nu \; iua, \; iub \, UE!$$

where $iua$ and $iub$ are inter-session communications channels in user equipment $UE$ that pass the GUTI between registration sessions.

The $S$ intra-agent communications process generates a fresh $gNB/CN$ pair with an inter-process wired channel for each iteration of the registration procedure:

$$S \triangleq (\nu\ ga^i\ gNB^i|CN^i)!$$

where $ga^i$ is a fresh wired channel used by the new $gNB$ and $CN$ to communicate.

The process flows of $UE$ and $gNB$ are:

$$UE^i \triangleq (SSG_u^i.RRC_u^i.NASI_u^i.NASA_u^i.SP_u^i)|G_u^i \tag{1}$$

$$gNB^i \triangleq \nu\ ignb^i\ (SSG_g^i.RRC_g^i.NGAPI_g^i.NGAPR_g^i.SP_g^i)|G_g^i \tag{2}$$

The control network $CN$ process flow depends on whether it receives a GUTI or TIMSI from the radio node $gNB$. If it does not receive a GUTI, it is the initial session and the control network $CN$ skips the context transfer:

$$\begin{aligned} CN^i \triangleq \nu\ cc^{;i}\ G_c^i|(NGAPI_c^i.([\mathrm{id}_t^{gc;i} = GUTI^{;i}]AMFCQ^i + \emptyset) \\ .NASI_c^i.AUSF_c^i.NASA_c^i.NAGAPR_c^i)|AMFCR^i \end{aligned} \tag{3}$$

The order of $UE$, $gNB$ and $CN$ in Eqs. 1–3 above is the order that is used throughout this chapter.

The radio node $gNB$ always broadcasts its synchronization signal. This is represented by the semantics of $UE$'s home network, which includes the mobile country code MCC, mobile network code MNC and its public key PK [6], from which $UE$ formulates its SUPI and subscription concealed identifier SUCI for the registration:

$$SSG_u^i \triangleq \nu\ \mathrm{SUCI}^{;i}\ p(\mathrm{mc}^{gu}, \mathrm{mn}^{gu}, \mathrm{pk}^{gu})$$

$$SSG_g^i \triangleq \nu\ \mathrm{MCC},\ \mathrm{MNC},\ \mathrm{PK}\ p < \mathrm{MCC}, \mathrm{MNC}, \mathrm{PK} >$$

$UE$ begins the initial radio resource control $RRC$ procedure with the radio node $gNB$. If it is the first time, the TIMSI is sent; otherwise, the GUTI from the previous session is sent. In return, the radio node $gNB$ initializes a dedicated channel and sends its $\mathrm{SRB}_1$ message, which contains its MAC address.

The process flow of the radio resource control $RRC$ procedure is given by:

$$\begin{aligned} RRC_u^i \triangleq p < \mathrm{init} > .p(dc^{gu;i}).([\mathrm{g}^{uu;i-1} = \cancel{\mathrm{GUTI}^{;i-1}}]dc^{gu;i} < \mathrm{TIMSI}^{;i} > \\ + iub(\mathrm{g}^{uu;i-1}).dc^{gu;i} < \mathrm{g}^{uu;i-1} >).dc^{gu;i}(\mathrm{s}^{gu;i}).dc^{gu;i} < \mathrm{rfin} > \end{aligned}$$

$$RRC_g^i \triangleq \nu\ dc^{;i}\ p(\mathrm{i}).p < dc^{;i} > .dc^{;i}(\mathrm{id}_t^{ug;i}).dc^{;i} < \mathrm{SRB}_1 > .dc^{;i}(\mathrm{rf})$$

The radio node $gNB$ passes the initialized dedicated channel and the $UE$'s GUTI or TIMSI to the control network $CN$ using the next generation application protocol $NGAPI$:

$$NGAPI_g^i \triangleq ga^{;i} < dc^{;i}, \mathrm{id}_t^{ug;i} > + \, ga^{;i} < dc^{;i} >$$
$$NAGPI_c^i \triangleq ga^{;i}(dc^{gc;i}, \mathrm{id}_t^{gc;i})ga^{;i}(dc^{gc;i})$$

If $UE$ uses the GUTI as its identifier, the control network $CN$ performs a security context transfer between the old $CN$'s access and mobility management function $AMFCR$ and the new function $AMFCQ$. The old $AMF$ does an inter-session context transfer and receives the GUTI along channel $cc$ and, if it passes the integrity check, returns the $UE$'s SUPI. After this, the old CN process terminates.

$$AMFCQ^i \triangleq sec < \mathrm{id}_t^{gc;i} > .sec(\mathrm{id}_p^{oc}) \tag{4}$$

$$AMFCR^i \triangleq cc^i(\mathrm{g}^{cc;i}).sec(\mathrm{id}_t^{nc;i+1}).[\mathrm{id}_t^{nc;i+1} = \mathrm{g}^{cc;i}]sec < \mathrm{SUPI} > \tag{5}$$

The control network $CN$ requests the $UE$'s SUCI over the dedicated channel using a non-access stratum identity NASI as a key, represented by the variable $\mathrm{K}_{NAS}^{c;i}$, derived from the $UE$'s SUPI to encrypt the channel:

$$NASI_u^i \triangleq \nu \, \mathrm{K}_{NAS}^{u;i} \, dc^{gu;i}(senc(\mathrm{sr}; \mathrm{k}_{NAS}^{cu;i}))$$
$$.sdec(senc(\mathrm{sr}; \mathrm{k}_{NAS}^{cu;i}); \mathrm{K}_{NAS}^{u;i}).dc^{gu;i} < senc(\mathrm{SUCI}^{;i}; \mathrm{K}_{NAS}^{u;i}) >$$
$$NASI_c^i \triangleq \nu \, \mathrm{K}_{NAS}^{c;i} \, dc^{gc;i} < senc(\mathrm{Suci-Request}; \mathrm{K}_{NAS}^{c;i}) >$$
$$.dc^{gc;i}(senc(\mathrm{id}_t^{uc;i}; \mathrm{k}_{NAS}^{uc;i})).sdec(senc(\mathrm{id}_t^{uc;i}; \mathrm{k}_{NAS}^{uc;i}); \mathrm{K}_{NAS}^{c;i})$$

The non-access stratum $NAS$ confirms the inter-session identity of $UE$ with the larger control network $CN$ with an authentication server function $AUSF$ request:

$$AUSF_c^i \triangleq ausf < \mathrm{id}_t^{cc;i} > .ausf(\mathrm{id}^{cc}).([\mathrm{id}^{cc} = \mathrm{id}_p^{oc}] + \emptyset)$$
$$ausf(\mathrm{sc}^{;i}).ausf < \mathrm{SUPI} >$$

The access and management function $AMF$ of the new session sends the SUCI it received during the $NASI$ process to the $AUSF$ server. The server returns $UE$'s SUPI. If it is not the initial session, $AMF$ compares $AUSF$'s SUPI with the one it received during the security context transfer.

The non-access stratum $NAS$ authentication procedure begins with the control network $CN$ sending the pre-shared authentication key $\mathrm{K}_{AC1}$. If $UE$ validates the key, it responds with the pre-shared authentication key $\mathrm{K}_{AC2}$. Then, $CN$ selects the $NAS$ security mode and $UE$ confirms the selection in the $NASA$ process:

$$
\begin{aligned}
NASA_u^i \triangleq\; & dc^{gu;i}(senc(\mathrm{K}_L^{cu;i};\mathrm{k}_{NAS}^{cu;i})).sdec(senc(\mathrm{K}_L^{cu;i};\mathrm{k}_{NAS}^{cu;i});\mathrm{K}_{NAS}^{u;i}) \\
& .[\mathrm{K}_L^{cu;i} = \mathrm{K}_{AC1}]dc^{gu;i} < senc(\mathrm{K}_{AC2};\mathrm{K}_{NAS}^{u;i}) > \\
& .dc^{gu;i}(senc(\mathrm{ns}^{cu;i};\mathrm{k}_{NAS}^{cu;i})).sdec(senc(\mathrm{ns}^{cu;i};\mathrm{k}_{NAS}^{cu;i});\mathrm{K}_{NAS}^{u;i}) \\
& .dc^{gu;i} < senc(\mathrm{NAS-fin};\mathrm{K}_{NAS}^{u;i}) > \\
NASA_c^i \triangleq\; & \nu\, \mathrm{NAS-Sel}^{;i}\; dc^{gc;i} < senc(\mathrm{K}_{AC1}^{;i};\mathrm{K}_{NAS}^{c;i}) > \\
& .dc^{gc;i}(senc(\mathrm{K}_L^{uc;i};\mathrm{k}_{NAS}^{uc;i})).sdec(senc(\mathrm{K}_L^{uc;i};\mathrm{k}_{NAS}^{uc;i});\mathrm{K}_{NAS}^{c;i}) \\
& .[\mathrm{K}_L^{uc;i} = K_{AC2}]dc^{gc;i} < senc(\mathrm{NAS-Sel}^{;i};\mathrm{K}_{NAS}^{c;i}) > \\
& .dc^{gc;i}(senc(\mathrm{nf};\mathrm{k}_{NAS}^{uc;i})).sdec(senc(\mathrm{nf};\mathrm{k}_{NAS}^{uc;i});\mathrm{K}_{NAS}^{c;i})
\end{aligned}
$$

The control network $CN$ generates the session key $\mathrm{K}_{gNB}^{;i}$ and passes it and the $NAS$ key to the radio node $gNB$ via the NG application protocol $NGAPR$:

$$
\begin{aligned}
NGAPR_g^i &\triangleq ga^{;i}(\mathrm{a},\mathrm{k}_{NAS}^{cg;i},\mathrm{k}_{gNB}^{cg;i}). \\
NGAPR_c^i &\triangleq \nu\, \mathrm{K}_{gNB}^{;i}\; ga^{;i} < \mathrm{ack},\mathrm{K}_{NAS}^{c;i},\mathrm{K}_{gNB}^{;i} >
\end{aligned}
$$

The radio node $gNB$ generates the session channel $sesh^{;i}$ and sends it along with the session key to $UE$ using the $SP$ process. $UE$ confirms and then begins communicating via the encrypted channel:

$$
\begin{aligned}
SP_u^i \triangleq\; & dc^{gu;i}(senc(\mathrm{k}_{gNB}^{gu;i},se^{gu;i};\ \mathrm{k}_{NAS}^{cu;i})) \\
& .sdec(senc(\mathrm{k}_{gNB}^{gu;i},se^{gu;i};\ \mathrm{k}_{NAS}^{cu;i});\mathrm{K}_{NAS}^{u;i}) \\
& .dc^{gu;i} < senc(\mathrm{sfin};\mathrm{K}_{NAS}^{u;i}) > \\
& .(se^{gu;i} < senc(\mathrm{M};\mathrm{k}_{gNB}^{gu;i}) > |iua < \mathrm{k}_{gNB}^{gu;i},se^{gu;i} >) \\
SP_g^i \triangleq\; & \nu\, sesh^{;i}\; dc^{;i} < senc(\mathrm{k}_s^{cg;i}gNB,sesh^{;i};\mathrm{k}_{NAS}^{u;i}) > \\
& .dc^{;i}(senc(\mathrm{sf};\mathrm{k}_{NAS}^{u;i})).sdec(senc(\mathrm{sf};\mathrm{k}_{NAS}^{u;i});\mathrm{k}_{NAS}^{cu;i}) \\
& .(sesh^{;i}(senc(M;\mathrm{k}_{gNB}^{cg;i}))|ignb^i < \mathrm{k}_{gNB}^{cg;i},sesh^{;i} >)
\end{aligned}
$$

The control network $CN$ generates $UE$'s new GUTI and sends it through the encrypted channel for $UE$ to use as its identifier in the next registration [7]. This is modeled by the $G$ processes:

$$
\begin{aligned}
G_u^i \triangleq\; & iua(\mathrm{k}_s^{uu;i},se^{uu;i}).se^{uu;i}(senc(\mathrm{g}^{gu;i};\mathrm{k}_s^{uu;i})) \\
& .sdec(senc(\mathrm{g}^{gu;i};\mathrm{k}_s^{uu;i});\mathrm{k}_s^{uu;i}).iub(\mathrm{g}^{gu;i}) \\
G_g^i \triangleq\; & (ignb^i(\mathrm{k}_s^{gg;i},se^{gg;i})|ga^{;i}(\mathrm{g}^{cg;i})).se^{gg;i} < senc(\mathrm{g}^{cg;i};\mathrm{k}_s^{gg;i}) > \\
G_c^i \triangleq\; & \nu\, \mathrm{GUTI}^i\; (ga^{;i} < \mathrm{GUTI}^i > |\ cc^{;i} < \mathrm{GUTI}^i >)
\end{aligned}
$$

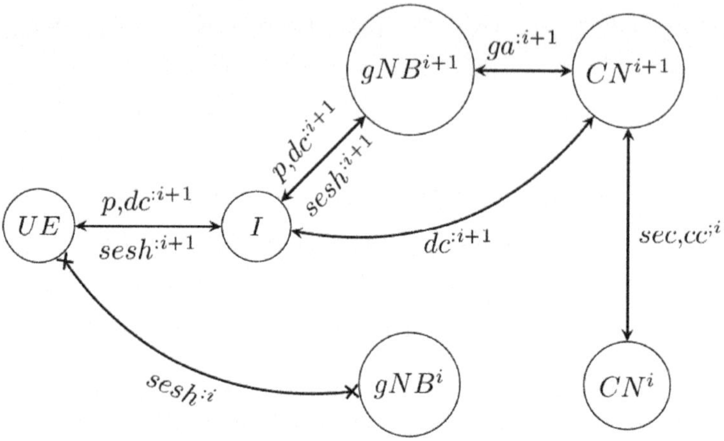


**Fig. 3.** 5G registration procedure communications channels (modified).

### 4.3 Adversary Model

The objective of the adversary is to prevent user equipment $UE$ from ever connecting to a legitimate radio node $gNB$ so that the adversary can exploit $UE$ vulnerabilities. Figure 3 shows a modified representation of the communications channels of the 5G registration procedure with the interception point of the adversary's $I$ process when the adversary is situated in the registration procedure of a new administrative area. The adversary only has access to the names, $p$, $dc^{;i>1}$ and $sesh^{;i>1}$, corresponding to the $UE/gNB$ wireless communications channel. This is because the adversary does not have access behind the trust barrier of the public key infrastructure that secures $gNB/CN$ communications.

It is assumed that the adversary can drop, modify or encrypt all the messages between user equipment $UE$ and radio node $gNB$. This is expressed by the substitution operation $\{M/x\}$, the generation of null processes $\emptyset$ and the generation of a fresh key $\nu\ K_I$ [5].

In addition to the denial-of-service capability, the adversary is able to simulate $gNB/CN$ messages in the registration process [21] using the operations in Sect. 4.1 and has found vulnerabilities in the 5G authentication procedure that enables $UE$'s privacy to be violated. Examples of the vulnerabilities are discussed by Jover [13].

However, certain restrictions are imposed on the adversary model. The adversary may conduct passive reconnaissance during $UE$'s entire session, but it is not allowed to act until after the first complete registration. This simulates a scenario where $UE$ has already completed a full registration procedure in a different administrative area. The ability of the adversary to break the encryption after the first session is represented by the adversary knowing the keys $\mathrm{K}_{NAS}^{;\forall i>1}$ and $\mathrm{K}_{gNB}^{;\forall i>1}$. It is also assumed that the challenge-response mechanism uses encryption independent of the authentication scheme that has not been compromised

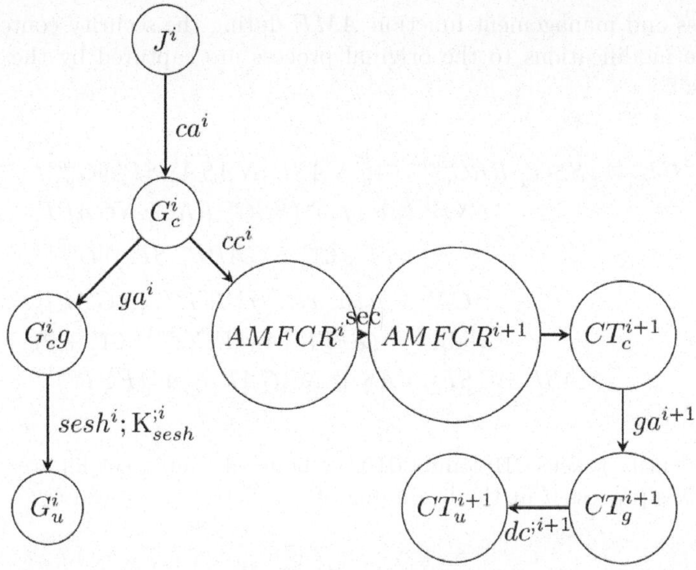


**Fig. 4.** Semantic flow of variables in the challenge-response mechanism.

by the adversary. Also, the adversary has not compromised $gNB/CN$ wired communications and, therefore, cannot read their messages.

The applied pi calculus model of the semantic knowledge and abilities of the adversary process $I$ is given by:

$$I \triangleq \nu\, K_I\, P \mid (A|B) | \;\nu\, n\, n.A \mid p < x > \; \mid p(x) \mid P! \mid \\ sdec(x;k) \mid senc(x;k) \mid \{M/x\} \mid \emptyset\, |\mathrm{K}_{NAS}^{;\forall i>1}|\mathrm{K}_{gNB}^{;\forall i>1}| \\ p|dc^{;\forall i}|sesh^{;\forall i} \tag{6}$$

### 4.4 Challenge-Response Mechanism Model

This section presents the formal challenge-response mechanism model. The modifications and additional processes added to the registration procedure are denoted using the font `ABCabc` in the equations and the superscript $^{\mathtt{mod}}$.

Figure 4 shows the semantic flow of variables through the processes of the challenge-response mechanism. The labeled arrows represent inter-process names. Note that the challenge-response mechanism has two parts, The left branch expresses the challenge semantics flow and the right branch expresses the response semantics flow.

The left branch models the transmission of the challenge semantics and key to user equipment $UE$ via the initial and subsequent encrypted channels $sesh^{;i}$. The right branch models the transmission of the encrypted semantics to the new access and management function $AMF$ during the security context transfer. These modifications to the original process are captured by the following equations:

$$
\begin{aligned}
UE^i \triangleq (SSG_u^i.RRC_u^{\mathtt{mod}\ i}.\mathtt{CT}_\mathtt{u}^\mathtt{i}.NASI_u^i.NASA_u^i.SP_u^i)|G_u^{\mathtt{mod}\ i} \\
gNB^i \triangleq \nu\ ignb^i\ (SSG_g^i.RRC_g^i.NGAPI_g^i \\
.(\mathtt{CT}_\mathtt{g}^\mathtt{i}|NGAPR_g^i.SP_g))|G_g^{\mathtt{mod}\ i} \\
CN^i \triangleq \nu\ ca^i\ cb^i,\ cc^i\ \mathtt{J}|G_c^{\mathtt{mod}\ i}|NGAPI_c^i \\
.([\mathrm{id}_t^{gc;i} = \cancel{GUTI}^i]AMFCQ^{\mathtt{mod}\ i}.\mathtt{CT}_\mathtt{c}^\mathtt{i} + \emptyset) \\
.NASI_c^i.AUSF_c^i.NASA_c^i.NAGAPR_c^i|AMFCR^{\mathtt{mod}\ i}
\end{aligned}
$$

Two identity tokens $\mathtt{CID}^{;i}$ and $\mathtt{COID}^{;i}$, a nonce $\mathtt{N}^{;i}$ and a key $\mathtt{K}_J^{;i}$ are generated by the $CN$'s process $J$ at the beginning of a registration procedure:

$$
J \triangleq \nu\ \mathtt{CID}^{;\mathtt{i}},\ \mathtt{N}^{;\mathtt{i}},\ \mathtt{K}_\mathtt{J}^{;\mathtt{i}},\ \mathtt{COID}^{;\mathtt{i}}\ \mathtt{ca}^\mathtt{i} < \mathtt{CID}^{;\mathtt{i}}, \mathtt{N}^{;\mathtt{i}}, \mathtt{K}_\mathtt{J}^{;\mathtt{i}} > |\mathtt{cb}^\mathtt{i} < \mathtt{COID}^{;\mathtt{i}} > \tag{7}
$$

Note that one identity token is passed to the old $AMF$ during the security context transfer process via channel $cb^{;i}$. The other semantics are passed to the GUTI generation process of the current session via channel $ca^{;i}$.

One of the identity tokens, the nonce and key are passed through the same path of processes as the freshly-generated GUTI, after a successful registration has been completed. These modifications to the GUTI generation process, which represent the completion of the challenge branch of the challenge-response mechanism, are described in the following equations:

$$
\begin{aligned}
G_u^{\mathtt{mod}\ i} \triangleq iua(\mathrm{k}_s^{uu;i}, se^{uu;i}) \\
.se^{uu;i}(senc(\mathrm{g}^{gu;i}, \mathtt{cid}_\mathtt{o}^{\mathtt{gu;i}}, \mathtt{n}_\mathtt{o}^{\mathtt{gu;i}}, \mathtt{k}_\mathtt{j}^{\mathtt{gu;i}}; \mathrm{k}_s^{uu;i})) \\
.sdec(senc(\mathrm{g}^{gu;i}, \mathtt{cid}_\mathtt{o}^{\mathtt{gu;i}}, \mathtt{n}_\mathtt{o}^{\mathtt{gu;i}}, \mathtt{k}_\mathtt{j}^{\mathtt{gu;i}}; \mathrm{k}_s^{uu;i}); \mathrm{k}_s^{uu;i}) \\
.iub(\mathrm{g}^{gu;i}, \mathtt{cid}_\mathtt{o}^{\mathtt{gu;i}}, \mathtt{n}_\mathtt{o}^{\mathtt{gu;i}}, \mathtt{k}_\mathtt{j}^{\mathtt{gu;i}})
\end{aligned}
$$

$$
\begin{aligned}
G_g^{\mathtt{mod}\ i} \triangleq (ignb^i(\mathrm{k}_s^{gg;i}, se^{gg;i})|ga^{;i}(\mathrm{g}^{cg;i}, \mathtt{cid}_\mathtt{o}^{\mathtt{cg;i}}, \mathtt{n}_\mathtt{o}^{\mathtt{cg;i}}, \mathtt{k}_\mathtt{j}^{\mathtt{cg;i}})) \\
.se^{gg;i} < senc(\mathrm{g}^{cg;i}, \mathtt{cid}_\mathtt{o}^{\mathtt{cg;i}}, \mathtt{n}_\mathtt{o}^{\mathtt{cg;i}}, \mathtt{k}_\mathtt{j}^{\mathtt{cg;i}}; \mathrm{k}_s^{gg;i}) >
\end{aligned} \tag{8}
$$

$$
\begin{aligned}
G_c^{\mathtt{mod}\ i} \triangleq \nu\ \mathrm{GUTI}^i\ \mathtt{ca}^\mathtt{i}(\mathtt{cid}^{\mathtt{cc;i}}, \mathtt{n}^{\mathtt{cc;i}}, \mathtt{k}_\mathtt{j}^{\mathtt{cc;i}}) \\
.(ga^{;i} < \mathrm{GUTI}^i, \mathtt{cid}^{\mathtt{cc;i}}, \mathtt{n}^{\mathtt{cc;i}}, \mathtt{k}_\mathtt{j}^{\mathtt{cc;i}} > \\
|cc^{;i} < \mathrm{GUTI}^i, \mathtt{cid}^{\mathtt{cc;i}}, \mathtt{n}^{\mathtt{cc;i}}, \mathtt{k}_\mathtt{j}^{\mathtt{cc;i}} >)
\end{aligned}
$$

The response part of the challenge-response mechanism begins when user equipment $UE$ moves into a new administrative area. After user equipment

$UE$ has completed the radio resource control $RRC$ process, the new access and management function $AMF$ requests a security context transfer with the old $AMF$. The new $AMF$ then sends one of the identity tokens $\mathtt{COID}^{;i}$, which it generated concurrently at the beginning of the session. The following equation specifies the process flow of the new $AMF$ process:

$$\begin{aligned} AMFCQ^{\mathtt{mod}\ i} &\triangleq \mathtt{cb}^{\mathtt{i}}(\mathtt{cod}_{\mathtt{o}}^{\mathtt{cc;i}}). \\ &sec < \mathrm{id}_t^{gc;i}, \mathtt{cod}^{\mathtt{cc;i}} > \\ .sec(\mathrm{id}_p^{oc;i}, &senc(\mathtt{cid}_{\mathtt{i}}^{\mathtt{oc;i}}, \mathtt{cid}_{\mathtt{i}}^{\mathtt{oc;i-1}}, \mathtt{n}_{\mathtt{i}}^{\mathtt{oc;i-1}}; \mathtt{k}_{\mathtt{j}}^{\mathtt{oc;i-1}})) \end{aligned}$$

The old $AMF$ encrypts the previous challenge-response mechanism semantics along with the new $AMF$'s identity token that it received. It proceeds to return the encrypted message along with the security context:

$$\begin{aligned} AMFCR^{\mathtt{mod}\ i} &\triangleq cc^{i}(\mathrm{g}^{cc;i}, \mathtt{cid}_{\mathtt{i}}^{\mathtt{cc;i}}, \mathtt{n}_{\mathtt{i}}^{\mathtt{cc;i}}, \mathtt{k}_{\mathtt{j}}^{\mathtt{cc;i}}) \\ &.sec(\mathrm{id}_t^{nc;i+1}\mathtt{cod}_{\mathtt{i}}^{\mathtt{nc;i+1}}).[\mathrm{id}_t^{nc;i+1} = \mathrm{g}^{cc;i}] \\ sec < \mathrm{SUPI}^{;i}, &senc(\mathtt{cod}_{\mathtt{i}}^{\mathtt{nc;i+1}}, \mathtt{cid}_{\mathtt{i}}^{\mathtt{cc;i}}, \mathtt{n}_{\mathtt{i}}^{\mathtt{cc;i}}; \mathtt{k}_{\mathtt{j}}^{\mathtt{cc;i}}) > \end{aligned}$$

The new $AMF$ sends the encrypted message along with a copy of the identity token it used in the context transfer to radio node $gNB$, which proceeds to forward it to user equipment $UE$ that has entered its administrative area. Upon receipt, user equipment $UE$ decrypts the message using $\mathtt{K}_J^{;i}$ and compares it the unencrypted identity token, and the token and nonce it received from the last session with the contents of the decrypted message. If the contents do not match or the message is not received, user equipment $UE$ terminates the session and restarts a session with a new radio resource control $RRC_u^{mod\ i}$ process as a fail-safe to protect the confidentiality of its semantics. This check, which occurs in all but the initial session, is represented as $[sei = \mathrm{noinit}]$. If user equipment $UE$ is able to decrypt the message and match the two identity tokens and the nonce, it continues with the registration procedure.

The $RRC$ process is modified to receive the challenge semantics from the previous session of the process via the name $iub$. Also, it sends a message to the $\mathrm{CT}_u^i$ process using the name $gs$ to inform it if it is first session or not:

$$\begin{aligned} \mathtt{CT}_{\mathtt{u}}^{\mathtt{i}} &\triangleq \mathtt{gs}^{\mathtt{uu;i}}(\mathtt{sei}).[\mathtt{sei} = \mathtt{noinit}](\mathtt{dc}^{\mathtt{gu;i}}(\emptyset).\mathrm{RRC}_{\mathtt{u}}^{\mathtt{mod}\ \mathtt{i}} + \\ &(\mathtt{dc}^{\mathtt{gu;i}}(\mathtt{cod}_{\mathtt{o}}^{\mathtt{gu;i}}, senc(\mathtt{cod}_{\mathtt{i}}^{\mathtt{gu;i}}, \mathtt{cid}_{\mathtt{i}}^{\mathtt{gu;i-1}}, \mathtt{n}_{\mathtt{i}}^{\mathtt{gu;i-1}}; \mathtt{k}_{\mathtt{j}}^{\mathtt{gu;i-1}})) \\ &.sdec(senc(\mathtt{cod}_{\mathtt{i}}^{\mathtt{gu;i}}, \mathtt{cid}_{\mathtt{i}}^{\mathtt{gu;i-1}}, \mathtt{n}_{\mathtt{i}}^{\mathtt{gu;i-1}}; \mathtt{k}_{\mathtt{j}}^{\mathtt{gu;i-1}}); \mathtt{k}_{\mathtt{j}}^{\mathtt{uu;i-1}}) \\ .[\mathtt{cod}_{\mathtt{o}}^{\mathtt{gu;i}} &\neq \mathtt{cod}_{\mathtt{i}}^{\mathtt{gu;i}}]\mathrm{RRC}_{\mathtt{u}}^{\mathtt{mod}\ \mathtt{i}} + ([\mathtt{cid}_{\mathtt{o}}^{\mathtt{uu;i-1}} \neq \mathtt{cid}_{\mathtt{i}}^{\mathtt{gu;i-1}}]\mathrm{RRC}_{\mathtt{u}}^{\mathtt{mod}\ \mathtt{i}} \\ &+[\mathtt{n}_{\mathtt{o}}^{\mathtt{uu;i-1}} \neq \mathtt{n}_{\mathtt{i}}^{\mathtt{gu;i-1}}]\mathrm{RRC}_{\mathtt{u}}^{\mathtt{mod}\ \mathtt{i}})))+\emptyset \qquad (9) \\ \mathtt{CT}_{\mathtt{g}}^{\mathtt{i}} &\triangleq \mathtt{ga}^{\mathtt{;i}}(\mathtt{cod}_{\mathtt{o}}^{\mathtt{cg;i}}, senc(\mathtt{cod}_{\mathtt{i}}^{\mathtt{cg;i}}, \mathtt{cid}_{\mathtt{i}}^{\mathtt{cg;i-1}}, \mathtt{n}_{\mathtt{i}}^{\mathtt{cg;i-1}}; \mathtt{k}_{\mathtt{j}}^{\mathtt{cg;i-1}})) \\ &.\mathtt{dc}^{\mathtt{;i}} < \mathtt{cod}_{\mathtt{o}}^{\mathtt{cg;i}}, senc(\mathtt{cod}_{\mathtt{i}}^{\mathtt{cg;i}}, \mathtt{cid}_{\mathtt{i}}^{\mathtt{cg;i-1}}, \mathtt{n}_{\mathtt{i}}^{\mathtt{cg;i-1}}; \mathtt{k}_{\mathtt{j}}^{\mathtt{cg;i-1}}) > \\ \mathtt{CT}_{\mathtt{c}}^{\mathtt{i}} &\triangleq \mathtt{ga}^{\mathtt{i}} < \mathtt{cod}_{\mathtt{o}}^{\mathtt{cc;i}}, senc(\mathtt{cod}_{\mathtt{i}}^{\mathtt{oc;i}}, \mathtt{cid}_{\mathtt{i}}^{\mathtt{oc;i-1}}, \mathtt{n}_{\mathtt{i}}^{\mathtt{oc;i-1}}; \mathtt{k}_{\mathtt{j}}^{\mathtt{oc;i-1}}) > \end{aligned}$$

The process flow of the modified radio resource control $RRC$ is given by:

$$\begin{aligned} RRC_u^{\mathtt{mod}\ i} &\triangleq p < \text{int} > .p(dc^{gu;i}) \\ .([\mathrm{g}^{uu;i-1} = \cancel{\mathrm{GUTI}^{;i-1}}](dc^{gu;i} &< \text{TIMSI}; i > |\mathtt{gs}^{\mathtt{uu;i}} < \mathtt{init} >) \\ +iub(\mathrm{g}^{uu;i-1}, \mathtt{cid}_{\mathtt{o}}^{\mathtt{uu;i-1}}, \mathtt{n}_{\mathtt{o}}^{\mathtt{uu;i-1}}, \mathtt{k}_{\mathtt{j}}^{\mathtt{uu;i-1}}).(dc^{gu;i} &< \mathrm{g}^{uu;i-1} > | \\ |\mathtt{gs}^{\mathtt{uu;i}} < \mathtt{noinit} >)).dc^{gu;i}(\mathrm{s}^{gu;i}).dc^{gu;i} &< \text{rfin} > \end{aligned}$$

## 5 Channel Tranquility Security Promise

This section constructs the promise of channel tranquility using a secrecy proof and the formal properties of the challenge-response mechanism. The first secrecy proof shows that an adversary never learns the challenge-response mechanism semantics needed to convince user equipment $UE$ that it has access behind the trust barrier of the radio node/control network ($gNB/CN$) public key infrastructure as long as at least one legitimate registration procedure has taken place. The subsequent proofs verify that the challenge-response mechanism has the ratcheting [2] and link failure sensitivity [8] properties that prevent the adversary from circumventing the channel tranquility promise. These properties are proven in the context of the adversary attacking the challenge-response mechanism directly.

### 5.1 Secrecy of Challenge-Response Mechanism Semantics

This section presents the proof that it is impossible for the adversary to learn the challenge-response mechanism semantics if at least one registration procedure has occurred between user equipment $UE$ and a legitimate radio node $gNB$.

As stated in Sect. 4.3, the model assumes that the adversary has not compromised the public key infrastructure, and thus cannot intercept communications between radio node $gNB$ and control network $CN$ because the adversary only knows the names $p$, $dc^{;i}$ and $sesh^{;i}$.

**Theorem 1.** *The adversary will never learn the terms* $\mathrm{CID}^{;i}$, $\mathrm{N}^{;i}$, $\mathrm{K}_J^{;i}$ *in process* $P!|I$ *after a legitimate registration procedure has occurred* ($i > 1$)

**Proof.** *Proof by contradiction. The adversary has not compromised the* $gNB/CN$ *public key infrastructure so the adversary can only see communications between radio node* $gNB$ *and user equipment* $UE$*. Each replication process of process* $J_c^i$ *leads to the generation of a fresh nonce, key and two challenge-response mechanism identity tokens. The adversary can only learn variables that are transmitted as cleartext or for which it has keys during each iteration of process* $J_c^i$ *shown in Fig. 4 and given by:*

$$J_c^i.G_c^i.((G_g^i.G_u^i)|(AMFCR^i.AMFCQ^{i+1}.CT_c^{i+i}.CT_g^{i+i}.CT_u^{i+i}))|I$$

*Variable exposure is shown by the reduction of the equations to the processes $G^i_c g$ and $CT^{i+1}_g$. Due to the restrictions on the adversary, it cannot read the messages transmitted in session $i = 1$. The reduction process of the above equation is trivial given the rules in [1, 19]. Therefore, the proof analyzes the two cases in which the variables* $\mathrm{CID}^{;i}$, $\mathrm{N}^{;i}$, $\mathrm{K}^{;i}_J$ *are transmitted between radio node $gNB^i$ and user equipment $UE$.* □

**Case 1.** *The transmission occurs between the processes $G^i_g.G^i_u$ after the initial ($i = 1$) channel $sesh^{;i}$. In the initial case, the adversary cannot read the messages. The subsequent instantiations of the $sesh^{;i}$ channel are dependent on the new access and management function $AMF$ having completed the security context transfer and sending the encrypted challenge-response mechanism message (discussed in Case 2). Being able to learn the encrypted message would require the adversary to have access to either of the names, sec or $ga^{;i}$, but they are behind the public key infrastructure. Therefore, according to the challenge-response mechanism proposal, subsequent $sesh^{;i}$ channels will not be generated for the adversary to intercept and decrypt messages.*

**Case 2.** *The transmission occurs between the processes $CT^{i+i}_g.CT^{i+i}_u$ over the channel $dc^{;i}$. Radio node $gNB$ sends message $dc^{;i+1} < \mathrm{cod}^{cg;i+1}_o$, $senc(\mathrm{cod}^{cg;i+1}_i$, $\mathrm{cid}^{cg;i}_i$ , $\mathrm{n}^{cg;i}_i; \mathrm{k}^{cg;i}_j) >$ whose terms are encrypted by $\mathrm{K}^{;i}_j$. The adversary cannot read the targeted terms, because, as discussed in Case 1, it cannot obtain the key*

**Proof.** *In Cases 1 and 2, all the terms are encrypted and the adversary cannot learn the key $\mathrm{K}^{;i}_j$ because it is encrypted by $\mathrm{K}^{;i}_{sesh}$ when transmitted to user equipment $UE$, and the adversary cannot deduce this key. In neither case can the adversary learn the terms. This is a contradiction.* □

**Corollary 1.** *In the message $< \mathrm{cod}^{cg;i+1}_o, senc(\mathrm{cod}^{cg;i+1}_i, \mathrm{cid}^{cg;i}_i, \mathrm{n}^{cg;i}_i ; \mathrm{k}^{cg;i}_j) >$, the adversary is still able to manipulate the variable $\mathrm{cod}^{cg;i+1}_o$. If the adversary does alter the variable it will not match $\mathrm{cod}^{cg;i+1}_i$ inside the message passed to user equipment $UE$ and $UE$ immediately terminates the registration procedure, maintaining the channel tranquility promise.*

### 5.2 Attacks on the Challenge Semantics

This section presents two proofs that demonstrate that the adversary is unable to attack the challenge portion of the challenge-response mechanism. The first proof demonstrates that the GUTI and the challenge semantics are coupled in an atomic manner. The second proof demonstrates that the adversary cannot force user equipment $UE$ to accept an initial registration session if $UE$ has already transmitted a GUTI. The two proofs collectively prove the ratcheting property of the challenge-response mechanism.

**Proposition 1.** *It is impossible for the adversary to break the atomicity of the $se^{gg;i} < senc(\mathrm{g}^{cg;i}, \mathrm{cid}^{cg;i}_o, \mathrm{n}^{cg;i}_o, \mathrm{k}^{cg;i}_j; \mathrm{k}^{gg;i}_s) >$ message in Eq. 8.*

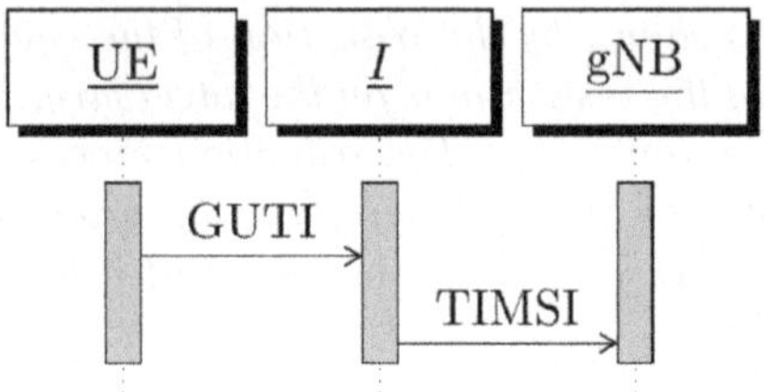


**Fig. 5.** Man-in-the-middle attack to force an initial registration session.

**Proof.** *Proof by contradiction. Assume that the name* $sesh^{;i}$ *denotes a reliable communications channel and the radio node* $gNB$ *and control network* $CN$ *processes do not experience faults. Then, there is only one process that transmits the GUTI and challenge-response mechanism semantics. This is specified in Eq. 8. In order for the adversary to break the atomicity of the message, it would have to send malicious variables to radio node* $gNB$ *through the name* $ga^{;i}$*. As specified in Sect. 4.3, the adversary does not know this name. This is a contradiction.* □

**Proposition 2.** *It is impossible for the adversary to force user equipment* $UE$ *into an initial registration session with radio source* $gNB$*.*

**Proof.** *Because the adversary resides in a man-in-the-middle position it is possible for the adversary to swap the GUTI for a TIMSI. Figure 5 shows this scenario where the adversary wishes to launch a man-in-the-middle attack to force an initial registration session to circumvent the challenge-response mechanism. However, if user equipment* $UE$ *does not receive the* $se^{gg;i} < senc(\mathrm{g}^{cg;i}, \mathrm{cid}_o^{cg;i}, \mathrm{n}_o^{cg;i}, \mathrm{k}_j^{cg;i}\ ; \mathrm{k}_s^{gg;i}) >$ *message from radio node* $gNB$ *due to the adversary's swap, the* $UE$ *will immediately terminate the session. This is due to the matching process* $[sei = \mathrm{noinit}]$ *in Eq. 9* □

**Theorem 2.** *The challenge-response mechanism satisfies the ratcheting property*

**Proof.** *Proposition 1 demonstrates an attempt by the adversary to circumvent the channel tranquility promise. However, user equipment* $UE$ *must receive the response mechanism after the initial session or it will terminate the registration procedure. It is impossible for the adversary to deprecate the challenge-response mechanism to the initial registration.* □

### 5.3 Attacks on the Response Semantics

This section describes an attack on the challenge-response mechanism response semantics that can only lead to a channel tranquility violation. The reason is that the response semantics is deliberately made to be sensitive to link failure. The sensitivity to link failure comes from the response semantics and communications

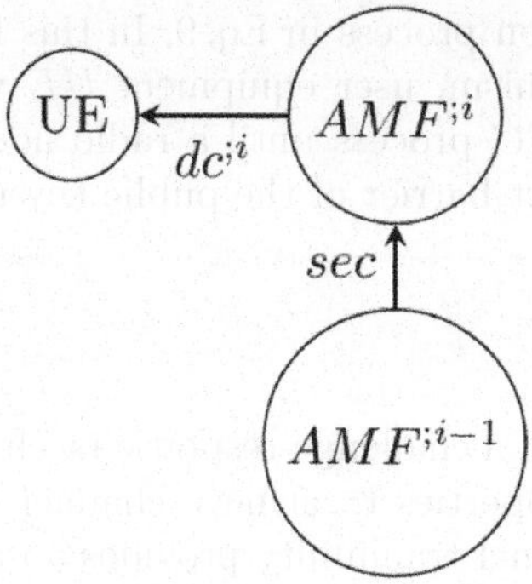


**Fig. 6.** Single link channel between the old $AMF$ and $UE$.

channels being reducible to the classic "two generals problem" formulated by Gray [8].

The two generals problem describes a synchronous distributed system in which two processes are attempting to reach a terminating agreement. In the case of the challenge-response mechanism, the two processes trying to reach terminating agreement are the old access and management function $AMF$ and user equipment $UE$ via the new $AMF$.

Figure 6 shows the single link communications channel between the old $AMF$ and user equipment $UE$. The link consists of the names $dc^{;i}$ and $sec$ and the new $AMF$ process. The two parties are attempting to agree on the semantic content of the encrypted response message $dc^{;i} < \mathrm{cod}_o^{cg;i}, senc(\mathrm{cod}_i^{cg;i}, \mathrm{cid}_i^{cg;i-1}, \mathrm{n}_i^{cg;i-1}, \mathrm{k}_j^{cg;i-1}) >$. Gray's proof states that if there is a single communications link – in this scenario, the concatenation of the names $dc^{;i}$ and $sec$ and the process $AMF^{;i}$ – between the distributed processes, and if the link fails, then it is impossible to reach a terminating agreement.

**Theorem 3.** *During the response phase of the challenge-response mechanism, it is impossible for the old* $AMF$ *and user equipment* $UE$ *to reach consensus if the adversary drops all the packets in the name* $dc^{;i}$.

**Proof.** *The proof follows directly from the two generals problem impossibility result [8].* □

**Corollary 2.** *Another potential single link failure exists in the response mechanism between the old and new* $AMF$*s during the security context transfer as shown in Eqs. 4 and 5. If the link fails, user equipment* $UE$ *would be unable to tell between a violation of the channel tranquility promise and an error in the security context transfer. In both cases, user equipment* $UE$ *would be fail-safe and terminate the registration procedure until the link is restored.*

Theorem 3 proves that the response semantics are purposely sensitive to link failure. If the adversary attacks the name $dc^{;i}$, user equipment $UE$ immediately terminates the registration procedure. This is explicitly represented in the first term of the summation process in Eq. 9. In this formal construction of the challenge-response mechanism, user equipment $UE$ would keep restarting the radio resource control $RRC$ process until a radio node $gNB$ can prove that it has access behind the trust barrier of the public key infrastructure.

## 6 Conclusions

This chapter has described a challenge-response mechanism with ratcheting and link failure sensitivity properties to achieve channel tranquility in the 5G registration procedure. Channel tranquility provides an additional layer of defense to the 5G registration procedure promises of authentication and confidentiality. The additional layer reduces the impacts of zero day vulnerabilities that could be discovered in implementations of 5G-AKA [7] because the adversary has to undermine channel tranquility before it can attack the other promises.

The challenge-response mechanism introduces a redundant and independent cryptographic system that enables user equipment to quickly authenticate a radio node with which it is registering by verifying that the radio node has access to the public key infrastructure of the control network and the previous radio node it was registered with. Conversely, the mechanism imposes further restrictions on an adversary operating in an administrative area because the registration procedure is made more sensitive to interference – any attempt by the adversary to force a user equipment connection will terminate the registration procedure.

The challenge-response mechanism requires the access and management function of a session to generate a challenge semantics along with the user equipment GUTI at the beginning of a session, and to distribute them to the user equipment after a legitimate encrypted channel has been established. A copy of the semantics is encrypted and passed to the new access and management function during the registration procedure in the next administrative area. The new access and management function transmits the encrypted semantics to the user equipment after the radio resource control process has completed. The user equipment continues the registration procedure only if the semantics have not been modified. The challenge-response mechanism is contingent on at least one legitimate registration with a radio node having been completed previously by the user equipment.

The specification of the challenge-response mechanism using the applied pi calculus has enabled its formal verification. The challenge-response mechanism may not be the most efficient at enforcing channel tranquility, but the methodology demonstrates it is possible to formally model and verify communications models that have layers of security promises that must be compromised in a strict sequence.

Future work will attempt to verify that the challenge-response mechanism is not susceptible to replay attacks. This will be accomplished by encoding models of the challenge-response mechanism and cryptanalytic adversary into an automated solver such as ProVerif [3].

**Acknowledgement.** This research was funded by the Norwegian Research Council SFI-NORCICS Grant no. 310105.

## References

1. Abadi, M., Blanchet, B., Fournet, C.: The applied pi calculus: mobile values, new names, and secure communication. J. ACM **65**(1), 1–41 (2018). https://doi.org/10.1145/3127586
2. Alwen, J., Coretti, S., Dodis, Y.: The double ratchet: security notions, proofs, and modularization for the signal protocol. In: Ishai, Y., Rijmen, V. (eds.) EUROCRYPT 2019. LNCS, vol. 11476, pp. 129–158. Springer, Cham (2019). https://doi.org/10.1007/978-3-030-17653-2_5
3. Blanchet, B.: Automatic verification of security protocols in the symbolic model: the verifier ProVerif. In: Aldini, A., Lopez, J., Martinelli, F. (eds.) FOSAD 2012-2013. LNCS, vol. 8604, pp. 54–87. Springer, Cham (2014). https://doi.org/10.1007/978-3-319-10082-1_3
4. Cohn-Gordon, K., Cremers, C., Garratt, L.: On post-compromise security. In: Proceedings of the Twenty-Ninth IEEE Computer Security Foundations Symposium, pp. 164–178 (2016)
5. Dolev, D., Yao, A.: On the security of public key protocols. IEEE Trans. Inf. Theor. **29**(2), 198–208 (1983)
6. European Telecommunications Standards Institute, 5G; Procedures for the 5G System, ETSI Technical Specification 23.502, version 15.2.0, release 15, Sophia Antipolis, France (2018)
7. European Telecommunications Standards Institute, 5G; Security Architecture and Procedures for 5G System, ETSI Technical Specification 33.501, version 16.3.0, release 16, Sophia Antipolis, France (2019)
8. Gray, J.N.: Notes on data base operating systems. In: Bayer, R., Graham, R.M., Seegmüller, G. (eds.) Operating Systems. LNCS, vol. 60, pp. 393–481. Springer, Heidelberg (1978). https://doi.org/10.1007/3-540-08755-9_9
9. Grover, K., Lim, A., Yang, Q.: Jamming and anti-jamming techniques in wireless networks: a survey. Int. J. Ad Hoc Ubiquit. Comput. **17**(4), 197–215 (2014)
10. Hamamreh, J., Furqan, H., Arslan, H.: Classifications and applications of physical layer security techniques for confidentiality: a comprehensive survey. IEEE Commun. Surv. Tut. **21**(2), 1773–1828 (2019)
11. Holtrup, G., Lacube, W., David, D., Mermoud, A., Bovet, G., Lenders, V.: 5G system security analysis. arXiv arXiv:2108.08700v2 (2021)
12. Jover, R.: Security attacks against the availability of LTE mobility networks: overview and research directions. In: Proceedings of the Sixteenth International Symposium on Wireless Personal Multimedia Communications (2013)
13. Jover, R.: The current state of affairs in 5G security and the main remaining security challenges. arXiv arXiv:1904.08394v2 (2019)
14. Lichtman, M., et al.: A communications jamming taxonomy. IEEE Secur. Priv. **14**(1), 47–54 (2016)
15. Lichtman, M., Rao, R., Marojevic, V., Reed, J., Jover, R.: 5G NR jamming, spoofing and sniffing: threat assessment and mitigation. In: Proceedings of the IEEE International Conference on Communications Workshops (2018)

16. Lichtman, M., Reed, J., Clancy, T., Norton, M.: Vulnerability of LTE to hostile interference. In: Proceedings of the IEEE Global Conference on Signal and Information Processing, pp. 285–288 (2013)
17. Park, S., Shaik, A., Borgaonkar, R., Seifert, J.: Anatomy of commercial IMSI catchers and detectors. In: Proceedings of the Eighteenth ACM Workshop on Privacy in the Electronic Society, pp. 74–86 (2019)
18. Pelechrinis, K., Iliofotou, M., Krishnamurthy, S.: Denial of service attacks in wireless networks: the case of jammers. IEEE Commun. Surv. Tut. **13**(2), 245–257 (2011)
19. Sangiorgi, D., Walker, D.: The Pi-Calculus: A Theory of Mobile Processes. Cambridge University Press, Cambridge, United Kingdom (2003)
20. Shiu, Y., Chang, S., Wu, H., Huang, S., Chen, H.: Physical layer security in wireless networks: a tutorial. IEEE Wirel. Commun. **18**(2), 66–74 (2011)
21. Wright, J., Wolthusen, S.: A contextual integrity property to impede privacy violations in 5G networks. In: Staggs, J., Shenoi, S. (eds.) Critical Infrastructure Protection XVII: 17th IFIP WG 11.10 International Conference, ICCIP 2023, Arlington, VA, USA, March 13–14, 2023, Revised Selected Papers, pp. 115–139. Springer, Cham (2024). https://doi.org/10.1007/978-3-031-49585-4_6
22. Yocam, E., Gawanmeh, A., Alomari, A., Mansoor, W.: 5G mobile networks: reviewing security control correctness for mischievous activity. SN Appl. Sci. **4**(11), 304 (2022)

# Improved Distribution Network Topology Generation with Hierarchical Information Overlay

Nataša Gajić[1(✉)] and Stephen Wolthusen[2]

[1] Norwegian University of Science and Technology, Trondheim, Norway
natasa.gajic@ntnu.no
[2] Norwegian University of Science and Technology, Gjøvik, Norway

**Abstract.** Topological models of critical infrastructures such as power distribution networks (grids) enable the determination and validation of properties ranging from feasibility to susceptibility to attacks contingent on the placement of adversaries. Future distribution networks will require large numbers of sensors and actuators to be positioned efficiently. While it is possible to employ the same structures for power networks as information and control networks, this excessive constraint can reduce the robustness of power networks to attacks.

This chapter extends previous work by incorporating a separate information layer that allows the incorporation of multiple hierarchical layers. The information layer facilitates the discovery of topological structures in which information and control aspects may still be retained, at least partially, in the presence of partial compromise of a power network structure by exploiting the limited redundancy in the information overlay hierarchy. The extended model also expresses the propagation of the effects of adversarial influence.

**Keywords:** Topology Generation · Distribution Network · Communications and Control Network · Multilayered Graph · Supervisory Control and Data Acquisition System

## 1 Introduction

Graph models of critical infrastructure networks have been studied extensively, but not all infrastructures have been given similar consideration; in fact, attention has been quite uneven even in individual sectors. While considerable attention has been paid to power networks (grids), most of the work has focused on power transmission networks instead of power distribution networks.

Power distribution networks are expected to play an out-sized role in the ongoing energy transition because several demands are being levied ranging from the need to accommodate bi-directional power flows from distributed generation and storage systems to substantially larger power demands due to the transitioning towards electric vehicles and greater reliance on domestic energy usage.


Published by Springer Nature Switzerland AG 2025
J. Staggs and S. Shenoi (Eds.): ICCIP 2024, IFIP AICT 725, pp. 179–190, 2025.
https://doi.org/10.1007/978-3-031-81888-2_9

These demands will require substantial upgrades to power distribution networks, especially with regard to how they have been instrumented. Future power distribution networks will need to have substantially more intelligence and integrated sensors and actuators along with their interconnections. However, existing models and model generators for studying distribution networks do not incorporate the added instrumentation, which limits the ability to study how the networks would behave in the presence of adversaries that can compromise portions of the information and communications networks interconnecting power system components.

The imbalance is seen in the study of attacks on distribution networks. Considerable attention has focused on attacks against measurements and sensing in power transmission networks [12]. However, the diverse attack surfaces of entities connected to power distribution networks highlighted by work on modeling the intelligence levels of smart homes [11] as well as studies of smart neighborhoods [16] and smart cities [10,18] indicate considerable gaps in understanding the influence of structure and topology on the overall robustness and efficiency of distribution networks.

Surprisingly, the modeling of power distribution networks has remained relatively static in that models mostly focus on power network aspects while largely ignoring measurement and control and assuming tacitly that the topologies are identical. An example is recent work by Shi et al. [15] describing a "transformer distribution-box meter-box meter" model for low voltage topology generation of distribution grids derived from an analysis of power outages in low voltage networks. Chen et al. [3] have reviewed topology models of distributed feeder automation that incorporate international standards (IEC 61970 and IEC 61968). Ali et al. [1] have also focused on distributed feeders, but their work involves synthetic networks and does not consider international standards. Pisano et al. [14] describe synthetic distribution grid topology models for areas of Italy. Their approach uses different types of available data (e.g., geographical, geological and electrical) to constrain the generated topology models.

Previous work by the authors of this chapter [5] describes a flexible and adaptable topology generator that is mainly used for distribution networks. Depending on inputs such as the number of nodes and branching factor, the generator produces a graph model that can be used in multiple domains. The graph model comprises three layers – distribution network layer, information overlay layer and interconnecting layer. The distribution network layer models the geometry of the physical network that includes lines and substations. The information overlay layer models smart network components in geometrical (topological) terms as well as proximal smart components that provide communications functionality such as radio stations, cellular base stations and Internet servers. The interconnecting layer resides between and connects the distribution network layer and information overlay layer. In theory, it mostly consists of edges that connect physical components of the distribution network to smart components of the network. However, the model has the flexibility to accommodate additional nodes, for example, if processing is to be modeled explicitly. Discussions with network operators reveal that topology generation can be generalized efficiently by having the information overlay layer become multilayered and hierarchical to enable explicit specifications of information flows as well as interconnection structures at the logical and physical levels.

Several observations justify the approach. First, not every node in the information layer has the same importance and it is important to explicit allow redundant information flows and processing paths. Second, not every node in the information layer has the same processing power; this requires vertex annotations to accommodate the appropriate labeling. Third, while the information layer is inherently hierarchical because control is centralized, the internal structure of the information processing and transmission layer must exhibit a certain degree of flexibility. Finally, the information layer is partially independent of the underlying physical structure; therefore, it is necessary to capture constraints such as physical proximity to constrains feasible instances.

The proposed approach enables the exploration and explicit construction of a multilayer network for monitoring and controlling distribution networks. The multilayer network incorporates insights from the theory of multilayer networks and the requirements imposed by supervisory control and data acquisition (SCADA) networks as well as by distribution networks. In particular, the approach extends the basic three-layer model of a distribution network to a multilayer network in which the monitoring and control flow topologies can be modeled by sets of constraints. Various hierarchical layers may represent explicit components (as in other SCADA architectures) and can be assigned processing and decision-making powers. However, the principal objective is to facilitate the expression of possible information and control flows and their susceptibility to adversarial influence. The model allows the study of efficient increases in local and global densities of intermediate graph structures, resulting in optimal resilience to adversarial influence. It enables distribution network designers to decide on necessary and sufficient levels of (local) redundancy and provides an understanding of the ability to maintain distribution network control during partial compromises while minimizing the required redundant interconnections.

## 2 Related Work

Multilayer network theory [2], which is tightly connected to graph theory, has been applied in several scientific domains such as social networks, transportation networks, infrastructures, banking and international markets, molecular networks and neurological networks. Like any graph, a multilayer network can be directed or undirected and can have weighted edges. However, a multilayer network can also have edges that are active only at certain times [6] or be intergrouped into a network of networks [4].

Earlier works [13,17] have identified graph models in which nodes are explicitly assigned different roles with different levels of importance, some of them considered as "central nodes." Figure 1 compares visual representations of a supervisory control and data acquisition system, neural network and multilayer

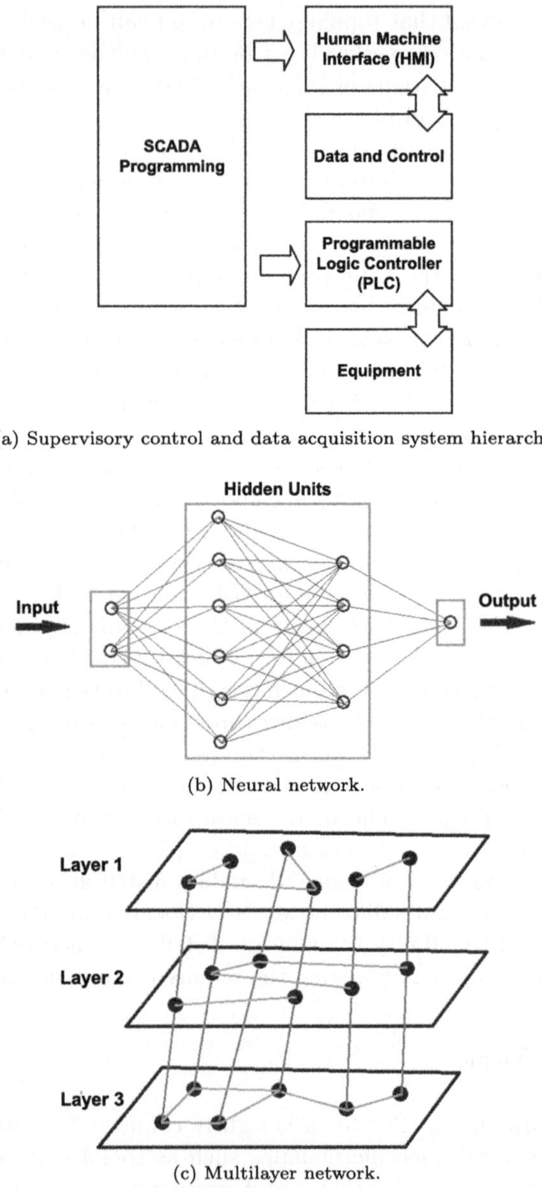


(a) Supervisory control and data acquisition system hierarchy.

(b) Neural network.

(c) Multilayer network.

**Fig. 1.** Comparison of visual representations.

network. A neural network is structured in a hierarchical manner whereas a multilayer network often allows lateral interconnection as well.

Multilayer networks have been employed to model hybrid electrical and optical networks [19] as well as agent interactions in host-pathogen systems where

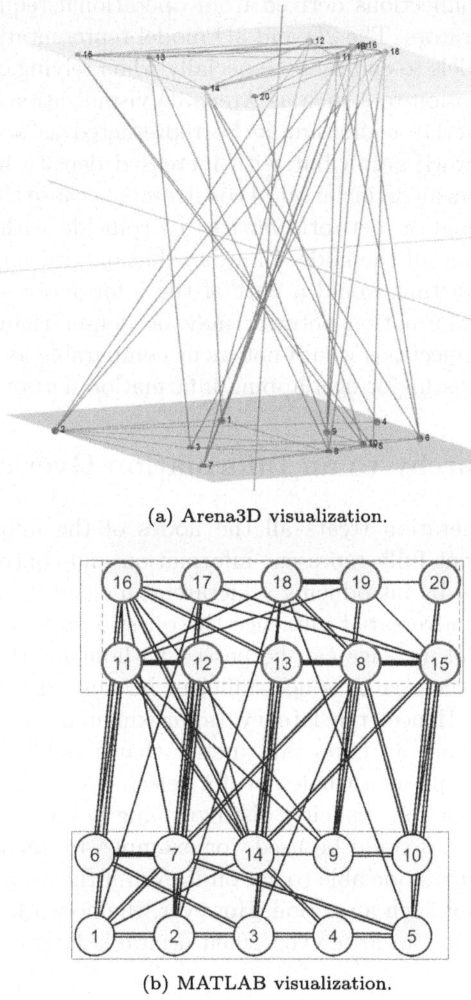


(a) Arena3D visualization.

(b) MATLAB visualization.

**Fig. 2.** Visualizations of a 20-node network.

different layers are defined as multiple types of transmission-relevant interactions [7]. Interested readers are referred to [8] for a discussion of variations on multilayer networks and their applications in various domains, including critical infrastructure networks.

## 3 Multilayer Model

This section briefly reviews a baseline multilayer model described in [5]. Figure 2 shows two visualizations of multilayer model instances with the parameter choices for the interconnections derived from operational requirements of distribution network operators. The 2D and 3D model representations are effective at communicating models to end users, especially when relying on 3D renderings provided by a visualization tool such as Arena3D visualization tool [9].

An information overlay could simply be represented as a duplicate of the underlying power network graph but with increased density by adding edges. However, this represents an artificial set of constraints because there is no explicit requirement for information network vertices to coincide with power network vertices. This is because all the nodes in a distribution grid must have a smart component inside them that would a part of the information overlay and vice versa. However, the information network may be denser than the underlying graph because interconnections would not incur comparable levels of cost while easily incorporating existing or overlapping information network nodes.

## 4 Adding Hierarchy to an Information Overlay

Baseline topology generation treats all the nodes of the information overlay as equal, which does not fully represent information and control flows. Several advantages are realized by introducing a hierarchical element.

In the presence of adversarial influence the question arises whether a given measurement or control message can be passed without interference. However, the mere existence of such paths is not sufficient because distribution networks are sensitive to time. Hence, the latency (approximated by path lengths) of alternative paths becomes an important metric that should guarantee a given construction for the graph as a whole and for selected sub-graphs. This can be further refined in a model by explicitly distinguishing between different types of vertices. Vertex categories could be used, for example, to determine whether a measurement can reach a node able to act on it even if the node would not ordinarily be responsible for such an action. However, the network structure ensure that no duplicate action can arise even when desirable lateral interconnections are in place.

Topology generation incorporates constraints imposed on the construction of the distribution network and information overlay hierarchy. Of course, since it is more important to be able to replicate existing structures, the distribution network requires parameters that can be tuned separately. The constraint mechanism can then construct local hierarchies that also allow the use of alternative paths while guaranteeing that the path lengths are bounded by an approximation of the acceptable latency deemed appropriate by network designers.

## 5 Proposed Approach

Hierarchy delegation can be approached in several ways. Figure 1 shows three possible approaches that are partially realized as options during topology generation. The approaches range from replicating a conventional supervisory control and data acquisition system hierarchy shown in Fig. 1(a) to a neural network

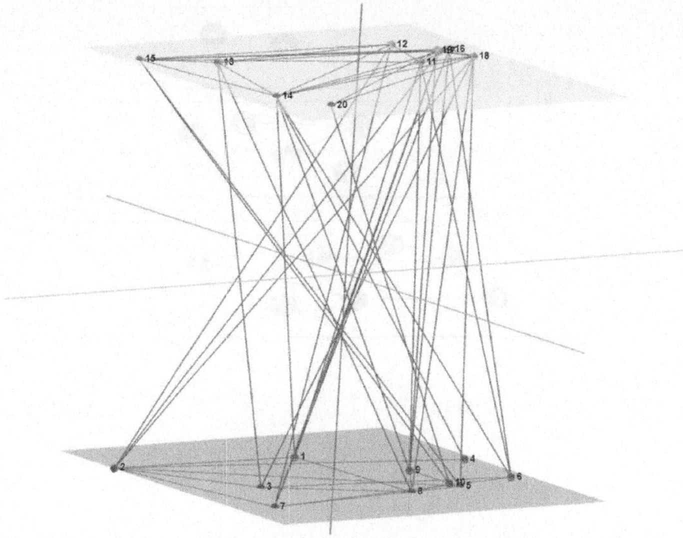


**Fig. 3.** Original model without a hierarchy in its information overlay.

using a strict layered-network approach shown in Fig. 1(b) to a pure multilayer network shown in Fig. 1(c).

However, the key requirement is, starting with the original model of the power network element of a distribution network without any hierarchy in its overlay, to faithfully create a new model with a hierarchy in its information overlay. Figure 3 shows the original model without any hierarchy in its information overlay. The bottom layer is the distribution network and the top layer in the information overlay. The interconnecting layer residing between the distribution network layer and information overlay layer connects the two layers.

Figure 4 shows visualizations of the original model (bottom) and the new model (top) with a strict set hierarchy in its information overlay. The three floating graphs in Fig. 4(top) demonstrate that there can be multiple layers in the information overlay instead of a single layer. Also, in addition to demonstrating that there can be many layers in the information overlay, the floating graphs convey that there would generally be progressively fewer nodes in subsequent layers.

## 6 Algorithms

The research described in [5] is leveraged to specify algorithms for constructing a network graph for an information overlay. Algorithm 1 in [5] creates a distribution network with the appropriate parameters and constraints. The algorithm is specified as a function *MakeADistributionGrid(n, pNode, pTree, branchingFactor)* where $n$ is the required size of the distribution network, *pNode* is the probability that a new node added to the graph remains a node, *pTree* is the

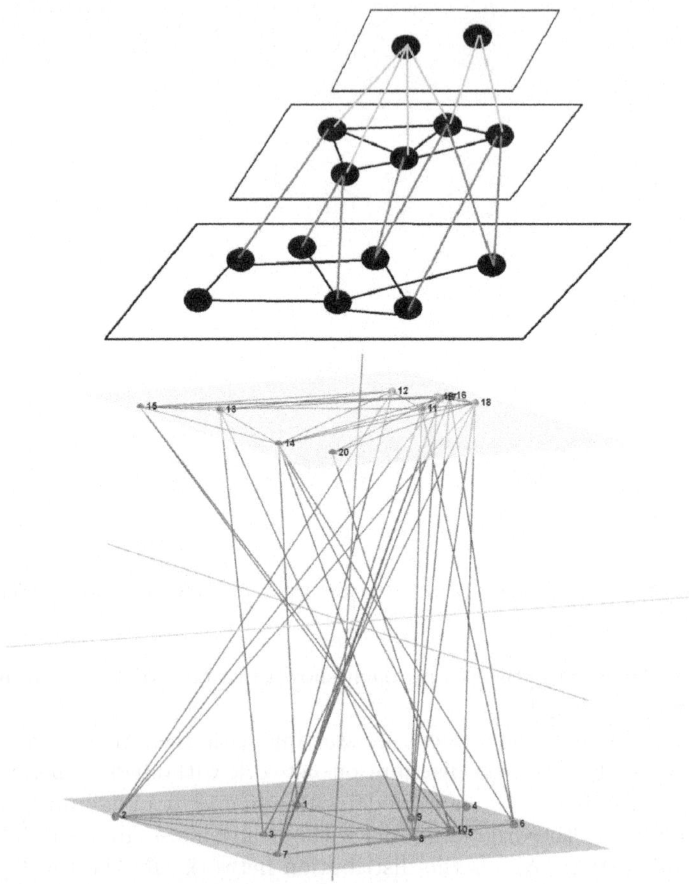

**Fig. 4.** New model with a strict set hierarchy in its information overlay.

probability that the network turns into a more complex tree-like structure, and *branchingFactor* is the graph branching factor. The algorithm has been shown to produce a connected distribution network graph.

After a distribution network with the desired properties is created, the next step is to generate the dependent layer structures. Algorithm 2 in [5] creates a mirrored information overlay. The algorithm is specified as a function `MakeInformationNetwork`*(DG, n, pNodeLimit, pConLimit pE, pELimit)* where *DG* is the distribution network graph produced by Algorithm 1, $n$ is the graph size, *pNodeLimit* is the probability limit at which the algorithm should stop creating nodes, *pConLimit* is the probability limit at which the algorithm should stop creating edges, *pErase* is the starting probability to erase edges and *pEraseLimit* is the probability limit at which the algorithm should stop erasing edges. The algorithm initially creates a mirrored copy of the distribution grid network model

**Algorithm 1:** Hierarchical expansion of information overlay.

```
Input: IN, nIN, pHierarchy, pLimit, highest
Output: Hierarchical information network
MakeHierarchyforIN(IN, nIN, pHierarchy, pLimit, highest) {
G ← ∅
n ← 0
G2temp ← IN
while n <= nIn do
    nstay ← pdfforHierarchy(sizeof(G2temp) − 1, pLimit)
    k ← 0
    G1temp ← ∅
    while k ≤ nstay do
        G1temp ← assignNode(sizeof(G2temp))
        G2temp ← update(G2temp, G1temp)
        k = k + 1
    end
    G ← G; G1temp
    n ← n + 1
    if sizeof(G2temp) ≤ highest then
        break
    end
end
G ← MakeHierarchicalConnections(G, pHierarchy, pLimit)
HIN ← G
return HIN
}
```

that is the basis of the information overlay and then, using the given probabilities, changes the edges of some nodes.

Algorithm 1 above specifies the steps involved in the refinement and hierarchical expansion of the information overlay. The algorithm creates new layers and simultaneously leaves a subset of nodes in the lowest layer. The process is repeated until there are no more nodes to assign to a layer or until the algorithm has reached the maximum number of nodes desired in the highest layer.

The inputs to Algorithm 1 are an information overlay graph *IN*, its size *nIN*, the probability *pHierarchy* of choosing a connection for a node in a higher level of hierarchy over a connection to the node on the same layer and *pLimit*, the limit for decreasing probability when creating a probability density function. The variable *highest* specifies the maximum number nodes desired in the highest layer of the hierarchy. Function *pdfforHierarchy*$(n, probability)$ creates the probability density function that determines the number of nodes that remain in the current level of hierarchy. Function *assignNode*$(n)$ selects a random node from a given number of nodes and adds it to another graph. Function *update*$(G, G1)$ updates a graph by removing portions of graph *G1* that exist in graph *G*.

Algorithm 2 above creates new connections based on a preferential allocation to different levels of hierarchy to the connections at the same level.

**Algorithm 2:** Connection hierarchy among nodes at different levels.

**Input**: $IN, pHierarchy, pLimit$
**Output**: $HIN$
$MakeHierarchicalConnections(G, sizeof(G))$ {
$Gtemp \leftarrow IN(end)$
$Grest = \leftarrow IN$
$Grest \leftarrow update(IN, Gtemp)$
$lvl = 1$
**while** $lvl \leq size(IN, 1)$ **do**
  $n \leftarrow 1$
  **while** $n \leq size(Gtemp, 2)$ **do**
    **while** $p1 > pLimit$ **do**
      $MakeInformationNetwork(G, sizeof(G))$
    **end**
  **end**
**end**
$HIN \leftarrow Gtemp$
**return** $HIN$
}

The inputs to Algorithm 2 are an information overlay graph $G$, the probability *pHierarchy* of choosing a connection for a node in a higher level of hierarchy over a connection to the node in the same layer and *pLimit*, the limit for decreasing probability when creating a probability density function. Function *update*($G$, *G1*) updates a graph by removing portions of graph *G1* that exist in graph $G$. Function *sizeof*($G$) returns size of an input graph.

Note that the validation argument for the underlying distribution network graph described in [5] remains because the construction described above does not modify the topology of a graph layer.

The benefit of the construction is that it permits the study of several parameters that are currently not found in distribution networks but are expected to be important in the future to accommodate functional and security requirements. The most straightforward of these parameters is an increase in the number of measurements on current systems (and ultimately control actions, e.g., for voltage stabilization), but more important is the need to aggregate and respond to network changes. While it is possible to construct a strict hierarchical network given the generation model, it is anticipated that having distributed and partially local control for robustness, performance and resilience would be desirable. Therefore, the algorithms are constructed so that the placements of intermediate executive nodes and the densities of layers can be configured appropriately and in a modular manner while satisfying functional constraints.

The overall network is constructed by joining the constituent graphs. This is accomplished using Algorithm 3 in [5]. The algorithm is specified as a function *MakeAdaptiveLayer(DG, n, IN, neighborhoodFactor)* where *DG* is a distribution network graph produced by Algorithm 1 in [5], $n$ is its size, *IN* is the newly constructed information network graph with hierarchy and *neighborhoodFactor* defines the node neighborhood. The model also accommodates additional labels for vertices. An example is a label that denotes that the integrity of a node is suspect (i.e., it may be controlled by an adversary).

## 7 Conclusions

Future critical infrastructures, including power distribution networks, will need to be resilient and adapt to unforeseen situations, including attacks, and remain functional even if parts of the networks are compromised. Topological structures that enable resilience while requiring only moderate overhead over baseline systems with limited redundancy to deliberate attacks are the subject of active study.

This work has focused on incorporating existing graph structures as constraints to support structures with increased resilience. Specifically, topology generation that produces three-layered graph models with a base layer, top information overlay layer and single interconnecting layer connecting the two layers has been extended to multilayer models that incorporate multiple constraints in optimizing resilient, but parsimonious extensions, that may include localized redundancy and control. The explicit construction of multilayer networks also distinguishes between information and control messages originating in close proximity and helps establish paths that conform to latency requirements.

Future research will engage the graph structures of distribution networks to prove resilience properties in the presence of limited adversaries. This will be facilitated by constraints imposed by the underlying power distribution network, where bounds can be placed on the extent to which information and control are required to be exerted over bounded sub-graphs. This would enable distributed system operators to provide bounded estimates of the levels of service offered by the overall network as well as the maximal impacts on the operational network during adversarial interactions.

## References


1. Ali, M., Prakash, K., Macana, C., Raza, M., Bashir, A., Pota, H.: Modeling synthetic power distribution networks and datasets with industrial validation. J. Ind. Inf. Integr. **31**, 100407 (2023)
2. Bianconi, G.: Multilayer Networks: Structure and Function. Oxford University Press, Oxford, United Kingdom (2018)
3. Chen, R., Lu, J., Liu, M., Ying, J., Chen, Y., Yue, Y.: Distribution network topology model generation method for distributed feeder automation. In: Proceedings of the IEEE Innovative Smart Grid Technologies - Asia, pp. 1057–1062 (2019)
4. D'Agostino, G., Scala, A. (eds.): Networks of Networks: The Last Frontier of Complexity. Springer, Cham, Switzerland (2014)
5. Gajić, N., Wolthusen, S.D.B.: Adaptable smart distribution grid topology generation for enhanced resilience. In: Pickl, S., Hämmerli, B., Mattila, P., Sevillano, A. (eds.) Critical Information Infrastructures Security: 18th International Conference,

CRITIS 2023, Helsinki Region, Finland, September 13–15, 2023, Revised Selected Papers, pp. 100–119. Springer, Cham (2024). https://doi.org/10.1007/978-3-031-62139-0_6
6. Holme, P., Saramaki, J.: Temporal networks. Phys. Rep. **519**(3), 97–125 (2012)
7. Kinsley, A., Rossi, G., Silk, M., VanderWaal, K.: Multilayer and multiplex networks: an introduction to their use in veterinary epidemiology. Front. Vet. Sci. **7**, 596 (2020)
8. Kivela, M., Arenas, A., Barthelemy, M., Gleeson, J., Moreno, Y., Porter, M.: Multilayer networks. J. Complex Netw. **2**(3), 203–271 (2014)
9. Kokoli, M., et al.: Arena3Dweb: interactive 3D visualization of multilayered networks supporting multiple directional information channels, clustering analysis and application integration. NAR Genomics Bioinform. **5**(2) (2023)
10. Kurniawan, B., Supangkat, S., Lumban Gaol, F., Ranti, B.: Framework for developing smart city models in Indonesian cities (based on the Garuda Smart City Framework). In: Proceedings of the International Conference on ICT for Smart Society (2022)
11. Liu, J., Wang, M., Wang, X.: Research on a general model of intelligence levels for smart homes. In: Proceedings of the Seventh International Conference on Computer and Communications Systems, pp. 123–129 (2022)
12. Liu, Y., Ning, P., Reiter, M.: False data injection attacks against state estimation in electric power grids. ACM Trans. Inf. Syst. Secur. **14**(1), 13 (2011)
13. Newman, M.: Networks. Oxford University Press, Oxford, United Kingdom (2018)
14. Pisano, G., et al.: Synthetic models of distribution networks based on open data and georeferenced information. Energies **12**(23), 4500 (2019)
15. Shi, Z., Liang, Y., Wang, X., Li, S.; Research on low voltage distribution network topology generation method based on "transformer distribution-box meter-box meter" model. In: Proceedings of the Third International Conference on Computer Vision, Image and Deep Learning and International Conference on Computer Engineering and Applications (2022)
16. Thakre, K., Goswami, B.: Designing neighborhood area networks of smart grid using software defined networks. In: Proceedings of the Fourth International Conference on Electrical, Computer and Communication Technologies (2021)
17. Wasserman, S., Faust, K.: Social Network Analysis: Methods and Applications. Cambridge University Press, Cambridge, United Kingdom (1994)
18. Yang, J., Kwon, Y., Kim, D.: Regional smart city development focus: The South Korean National Strategic Smart City Program. IEEE Access **9**, 7193–7210 (2021)
19. Zhang, J., et al.: Dynamic virtual network embedding over multilayer optical networks. J. Opt. Commun. Netw. **7**(9), 918–927 (2015)

# Author Index





Published by Springer Nature Switzerland AG 2025
J. Staggs and S. Shenoi (Eds.): ICCIP 2024, IFIP AICT 725, p. 191, 2025.
https://doi.org/10.1007/978-3-031-81888-2

The manufacturer's authorised representative in the EU is Springer Nature Customer Service Centre GmbH, Europaplatz 3, 69115 Heidelberg, Germany. If you have any concerns regarding our products, please contact ProductSafety@springernature.com

Printed and bound by CPI Group (UK) Ltd, Croydon, CR0 4YY
30/09/2026
02225558-0003